The First Sexual Revolution

The American Social Experience

S E R I E S

General Editor:
JAMES KIRBY MARTIN

Editors:
PAULA S. FASS, STEVEN H. MINTZ, CARL PRINCE,
JAMES W. REED & PETER N. STEARNS

The First Sexual Revolution

The Emergence of Male Heterosexuality in Modern America

KEVIN WHITE

NEW YORK UNIVERSITY PRESS
New York and London

NEW YORK UNIVERSITY PRESS
New York and London

Copyright © 1993 by New York University

Library of Congress Cataloging-in-Publication Data
White, Kevin, 1959–
    The first sexual revolution : male heterosexuality in Modern
America / Kevin White.
        p.   cm.   — (American social experience series : 27)
    Includes bibliographical references and index.
    ISBN 0-8147-9256-1 (cl) — ISBN 0-8147-9258-8 (pbk)
    1. Men—United States—Sexual behavior—History—20th century.
    2. Men—United States—History—20th century.   3. Men—United
States—Social conditions.   I. Title.   II. Series.
    HQ28.W47   1992
305.31'0973'0904—dc20   92-26868
                        CIP

New York University Press books are printed on acid-free paper,
and their binding materials are chosen for strength and durability.

Manufactured in the United States of America

c   10   9   8   7   6   5   4   3   2   1
p   10   9   8   7   6   5   4   3   2   1

To Sharon McMannus; and Rick Edgar

Contents

Acknowledgments

In the course of the transatlantic adventure that has given me such pleasure, if not a little aggravation, over the last ten years, I have, as usually happens, incurred many debts. The oldest and greatest must be to Leila Rupp, who was a model adviser. John Burnham has inspired me with his conception of American history and culture, as he has so many others before me—and, hopefully, others after me. Early in my career, Laurel Richardson taught me everything there is to know about gender. The manuscript has benefited from readings by James Reed and Christina Simmons.

Few authors can have been as fortunate in the support of their friends. Randolf Reder, Mark Uric, and Wes Thompson were there when I needed them, though I didn't deserve them, and still don't. This book owes as much to the moral vision and graffiti of Paul Huffman as it does to Gramsci. The other transients and hoboes of our little "gang" on Lane Avenue in Columbus, Ohio, deserve a mention: James "Jemima Puddleduck" Dye, Jimmy Quinn, Jeff Lambert, Steve Kessler, and the hobo. These were indeed "the Days of Our Lives." The members of the "circle" formed part of a genuine graduate student intellectual community: Stuart Hobbs,

Larry Greenfield, and Dave Staley—and also Gary Tremper and Catherine Dentan. Appreciation is due to Francille Coulson, Bela Bajnok, and Adam Goldberger. Thanks also to Julia Courtney, David Barry, Martin Blaney, and Nigel Sharman in England—and to my parents, Colin and Mary White, for financial assistance at more than one key point.

Further, I extend gratitude to my editor at NYU Press, Niko Pfund. In addition, I extend thanks to the following individuals and institutions for permission to publish from papers in their ownership: the Schlesinger Library, Radcliffe College; Committee of Fourteen, Records, Rare Books, and Manuscript Division, The New York Public Library, Astor, Lenox, and Tilden Foundations; University of Chicago Regenstein Library; California Historical Society, San Francisco; Bureau of Social Hygiene Archives, Rockefeller Archive Center, North Tarrytown, New York; Oral History Research Office, Columbia University Special Collections; E. Haldeman-Julius Collection, Pittsburgh State University, Kansas Special Collections; Haldeman-Julius Family Papers, Special Collections, The University Library, University of Illinois at Chicago; Michael Clark; and David Middleton. Material from the Marie Stopes Papers is cited by courtesy of the Wellcome Trustees, Contemporary Archive Centre, the Wellcome Institute for the History of Medicine, London.

Above all else, however, it has been the unfailing commitment of Sharon McMannus and Rick Edgar to seeing me through this project that most helped bring it to final fruition. In appreciation, this book is dedicated to them.

CHAPTER ONE

Introduction

The "Flapper" has long been one of the major figures of the American popular imagination. H. L. Mencken's memorable term referred to the "New Woman" of the "Revolution in Manners and Morals" of the first decades of the twentieth century.[1] The "flapper," according to numerous historians, in imitation of men, smoked, drank, swore, freely petted and dated, was obsessed by the new psychology of Freud (if only as misinterpreted by his American popularizers), and, when she married, built her relationship according to the strictures of companionate marriage. Reading these writers, one is reminded of F. Scott Fitzgerald's conception of the "flapper" as "lovely and expensive and about nineteen."[2] She is a stereotype.

In recent years a number of women's historians, aware of the inadequacy of descriptions of the "flapper," have begun to address the question of what the reality was behind the stereotype. The "flapper" has become the New Woman, the focal point of the feminist reinterpretation of the "revolution in morals." She appears in recent literature, but as the "Charity Girl," the "Mannish Lesbian," and the "Androgyne," to name but three of her guises.[3] Understandably, her apparent difference from the Victorian stereotype of "passionlessness" and the "Cult of True Womanhood" has inspired much interest recently. But her boyfriend has received less attention.[4]

The pace of revolutionary change that had affected the social relations between the sexes in these years was the product of a number of factors. By 1920, over 50 percent of Americans lived in cities. Here a mass production economy that focused on consumption replaced an earlier entrepreneurial society of small businessmen and farmers with a "new middle class" of bureaucrats and managers that in its growing leisure time embraced an ethic of therapeutic release and pleasure.[5] The Victorian values of hard work, rugged individualism, and thriftiness that had held sway among the middle classes, albeit ever more precariously, until the second decade of the twentieth century became less influential: a heterosocial leisure world that was geared towards youth and vitality emerged as amusements grew up in the cities to cater to the demands of young people. These were the changes that produced a New Woman, and, one might speculate, could have produced a "New Man."

For indeed the question of men's part in this revolution in morals is an important, yet neglected, one. How were men affected when the bourgeois sexual system of Victorian America, which gave men the alternatives of either purity or use of prostitutes before marriage, crumbled? Who, then, was the New Man to accompany the New Woman?

Steadily a picture is emerging of both men and women's position in the Victorian system of morality that was dominant among the middle class of American society up to around 1912. As the United States industrialized, the old Victorian Protestant bourgeoisie presided over an expanding economy where the chances of class mobility were greater than in the twentieth century.[6] Victorians valued self-reliance, sobriety, self-sacrifice, thriftiness, and rugged individualism. They believed that gratification could be delayed: they therefore railed at self-indulgence, leisure, effeteness, and the exotic. Temperance and self-control marked the lives of the best people.[7] Such qualities were those appropriate for a production-oriented economy. Gratification could be delayed because of the genuine possibility of material rewards down the line if thrift were practiced in the present.

In this context, nineteenth-century Americans produced their own distinct construction of masculinity. Above all else, nineteenth-century American men were expected to acquire "character." This involved the attainment of two interlocking ideals: the "Masculine Achiever" and the "Christian Gentleman."[8] The "Self-Made Man" or Masculine Achiever was the dominant ideal on the road to this goal. Historian Irvin Wyllie has described this American ideal:

> The legendary hero of America is the self-made man. He has been active in every field from politics to the arts, but nowhere has he been more active, or more acclaimed, than in business. To most Americans he is the office boy who has become the Head of a great concern making millions in the process. He represents our most cherished conceptions of success, and particularly our belief that any man can achieve a fortune through the practice of frugality and sobriety.[9]

Yet this ideal of the Masculine Achiever demanded decisiveness and effort. A man must not rely on anyone else.[10] The breadwinner and provider must not cry. He must control and suppress his emotions. He must be tough and disciplined, autonomous and independent. One man who sounds almost like Horatio Alger or Benjamin Franklin, inspirers of this ideal, resolved "that he would improve his time so that he could spend every hour to an advantage, either in acquiring wealth, or arising to some honorable station in life."[11] By accomplishing as much, men acquired the respect of their peers but, more importantly, they satisfied an "inner-directed" and religious compulsion to do what they believed to be right and moral.[12]

Men of "character" were also expected to be Christian Gentlemen. Such men must be good citizens who practiced De Tocqueville's famous concept of "self-interest rightly understood."[13] The Christian Gentleman must temper the excesses of the Masculine Achiever that might develop from a too-obsessive devotion to the cause of manna. For the concept emphasized generosity and empathy as the basis for action.[14] Nevertheless, being a Christian Gentleman did not entail any fundamental rejection of the Masculine Achiever role, but rather involved a reaction to the excesses of the marketplace that must be tempered.[15] Rather, in all its aspects, this ideal entailed, too, above all, the development of "character," that is, the cultivation of "honor, reputation and integrity." For "character" involved not merely a personal, but a public ideal. As such, the man of "character" was indeed the central figure of Victorian culture.[16]

Above all, the attainment of "character" involved the cultivation of "morals." Men of character controlled their primitive urges. They followed a single standard of purity for themselves as well as for women. Victorian marriage manuals lauded the advantages of celibacy. Indeed, men were to be very "athletes of continence."[17] Procreation was the only justification for sexual intercourse, which was often described as an "unfortunate necessity."[18] Nineteenth-century writers warned that men not "spend" their semen for fear that they should lose valuable energy that could be used to work.[19] Health reformer Sylvester Graham went even further by asserting that one ounce of semen equaled forty ounces of blood. Sperm was men's very life force, such popularizers maintained, and therefore should not be expended casually.[20] Further, in keeping with this ideal of continence, men were warned not merely about the dangers of masturbation or of sex with prostitutes but also, from 1830 on, about the dangers of excessive sex even within marriage. Too much attention to sexuality distracted from more important matters—not merely work, but also men's responsibilities to the community or larger public world.

This public insistence on male purity and continence was the very lynchpin of the Victorian system of morality. Victorians were aware of the aggressive aspects of male sexuality. One "self-consciously horrified physician" in the early 1880s reported that "some fathers tickle the genital organs of their infant boys until a complete erection of the little penis ensued, which effect pleases the father as evidence of a robust boy."[21] Although the Victorian view of women as suffering from "passionlessness" should not be taken as a reflection of the reality of middle-class women's actual experience of sexuality in the nineteenth century, the development of this ideology is very revealing about the way Victorians assuaged their fears about male sexuality.[22] They understood that a rampant male sexuality was a threat to the moral order and to the family, on the maintenance of which the prosperity of the whole society depended. Many went further: they believed that civilization itself was bolstered by sexual control.[23]

Both the concept of "passionlessness" for women and of continence and purity for men must be seen in their context as being designed to protect middle-class women from the potential ravages of a male sexuality that was uncontrolled. "Passionlessness" in women was supposed to tame oversexed men, and therefore to help men maintain "character." Victorians grasped the need to protect women. Americans gave "tacit acceptance" to the red-light districts that sprang up in almost every city, or else "respectable women would not be safe."[24] The mayor of San Francisco said that because of the district "any woman could walk on the streets of San Francisco at any hour of the day or night without insult or embarrassment."[25] Mark Twain, in his 1880 story, "American Manners," insisted that in America, as opposed to Europe, "a lady may traverse our streets all day, going and coming as she chooses and she will never be molested by any man."[26] For Twain this was proof of the superior character of the American man to European men. The extent of a man's character was determined by how he treated women. Violence against women brought shame on a man. A rapist was the lowest of men because he had most sharply broken the code of "character." In the same story, Twain described the case of the English rapist Colonel Valentine Baker as an example of the disgrace brought on a man by such an act.[27] To be sure, this system ignored the concerns of working-class women, who were sometimes forced into prostitution, just as it denied the reality of middle-class women's sexuality, but its advantages for both sexes should be evident. Both men and women were protected from their worst selves—at little cost, for men anyway.

The Victorian ideology of sexuality was also bolstered by the conspiracy of silence, which was a further means of controlling sexuality by limiting discourse about it. The extent of the conspiracy can be exaggerated. Victorian marriage and sex manuals were notable for their "ambivalence and inconsistency," but they were at least consistent after 1830 in their vivid obsession with masturbation.[28] Further, there was communication about other areas of sexuality, too. But Victorians preferred to use euphemisms such as the need for "purity" or for "continence." Victorian society indeed deserves its reputation as a world characterized by reticence in discussing sexual matters publicly. Marriage manuals were hardly graphic about the sexual act itself. One such manual, inaccurately entitled *Plain Talks on Avoided Subjects*, still refrained from discussing sexual technique.[29] The conspiracy went beyond the famous observation of British visitor Captain Marryat of the covering of table legs for fear they imply the female limb.[30] Real evidence has survived of women's reticence in discussing sexual matters. Gynecologist Robert Latou Dickinson noted how the women he saw in the 1920s were more prepared to talk about sex in comparison with his female patients in the 1890s.[31] One authority described how "throughout the nineteenth century the taboo prevailed." He noted that "certain subjects were rarely mentioned in public and then only in euphemistic terms. The home, the church and the press joined in the conspiracy."[32] On the rare occasion when there was public discussion of sex, the discourse was squeamish, as when the Reverend Phillip Moxon spoke in 1890 to the White Cross Purity League of the YMCA, and declared that "this subject is not of my choosing, save as to the form in which it is put.... How shall I fitly and plainly say what needs to be said without revolting those who hear from a subject which every one of us would gladly drop into oblivion?"[33] While the extent of its influence can be exaggerated, the conspiracy of silence was nonetheless real, as was revealed by the shocked comments that greeted the burst of discourse on the subject of sex that streamed out in the second and third decades of the century.[34] For in Victorian America, gentlemen were not supposed to discuss sex with other men and certainly not with women: to do so would be the beginning of social anarchy.

It is the public system of morality of Victorian America that has received most attention from historians. Comparatively little is known about people's actual experience of sexuality in the private world of romantic love that recent research has shown to be important to Victorians. Yet this arena served, too, as much as the public world, to control male sexuality. Here the Christian Gentleman was also ascendant. The memoirist Henry Seidl Canby recalled in 1934 how men saw courtship at the turn of the century: "We tried to see our girls as romantic beauties and ourselves as gentlemen who lived by honor."[35] Walter Lippmann remembered that the "virtuous man, by popular standards, was one who before his marriage did not have sexual relations with a virtuous woman."[36] An elderly man interviewed in *Middletown* in the mid-1920s, who had been "a young buck about town in the eighties," said "the fellows nowadays don't seem to mind being seen on the street with a fast woman, but you bet we did then."[37] For if the codes were not as rigid as James Thurber's mother had experienced—"Why, when I was a girl, you didn't dare walk with a man after sunset, unless he was your husband, and even then there was talk"—they were still pretty strict.[38] The upper and middle classes in the cities in the 1880s relied upon the convention of the "call." A gentleman gave his card to a servant at the door, requesting to see the young lady in whom he was interested. If he was frequently received, he knew that he had her favor, but if she turned him down, he knew equally where he stood. This was a female-controlled ritual, a consequence of women's power in the domestic sphere.[39] Once the young couple saw each other a few times, they would be allowed out together, traditionally with a chaperone; for the time being, however, the affair must remain relatively sedate and unexciting. Yet, and this is important, men and women were permitted more than a little sexual experimentation in courtship after a while.[40] Young men and women could engage in an essentially female-controlled set of rituals that might include kissing, petting, and even, though less frequently, sexual intercourse. Such acts were permissible if the couple were in the throes of a romantic love—and there were plenty of older people looking on to assure that they were. So long as men acted and behaved as Christian Gentlemen—that is, as long as they loved and respected their lady friend, and at least had marriage as an ultimate goal—a wide range of acts was permissible.

Yet purity, as we understand it, was still an important aspect of romantic love.[41] Indeed, the vast majority of women entered marriage as virgins.[42] But men and women could also consider themselves pure, even if they had full sexual relations, so long as they entered into such acts with the attitude of romantic love. In such circumstances, sex could be a positive force for the good, and men still maintained "character." This female-controlled, structured private world complemented and fused into the public world's control of male sexuality. Here, even if the double standard often posed a challenge, gentlemanliness and "character" held ascendancy, and women were protected from the less savory aspects of Victorian masculinity.

Victorian society represented perhaps the strongest attempt ever to put reason over passion in human relations. Yet Victorians were hypocrites. There may have been a lofty morality in public and in middle-class heterosocial relations, but in other regards their system was far less salubrious. If Victorians accepted that men should be gentlemen, this was because they also understood men as primitives. If Victorians believed in purity, they also recognized what they called male "sexual necessity" and a double standard of morality: men could relieve their primitive desires and urges by having sex before and even after marriage with lower-class prostitutes.[43] Men, after all, had to sow their wild oats. Judge Lindsey, as late as the 1920s, surmised that 50 percent of men in Denver had been with prostitutes, an argument for reform of the sexual system he was not alone in using.[44] A study of seven hundred California couples in 1938 by psychologist Lewis Terman suggested that of people born before 1900, three times as many middle-class men as women had indulged in premarital sex as those born after, which suggests that some of the sex might have been with working-class prostitutes but which anyway confirms the pervasiveness of the double standard that dominated this system of morality of Victorian America.[45]

Here flourished the Victorian underworld where a third conception of the meaning of masculinity—what I am calling "underworld primitivism"—held sway.[46] The "Underworld Primitive" was the antithesis to the lofty ideals of the Christian Gentleman. He rejected repression and suppression of desires and abandoned respect for women in a flurry of aggressiveness associated with a violent homosocial culture. In particular, boxing was central to the underworld. With its ethos of braggadoccio, masculine prowess, and violent defense of honor, it fitted perfectly into the underworld male culture.[47] The sport of boxing fused into the underworld as one vice among many—prostitution, drinking, gambling; all flourished there. Here the Victorian working class—be it German, Irish, Anglo-Saxon, or black, whether in separate ethnic or racial groups or beginning to intermingle as "Americans"—played hard and furiously in the face of exploitation and subservience to the whims of ruthless and unscrupulous middle-class employers who all too often paid them minimal wages.

Yet the underworld was not confined merely to the working classes. Large numbers of middle-class men chose to participate in aspects of it at different times. The male middle class not only visited prostitutes; they could also indulge in male social life as spectators of boxing and baseball and participants in gambling and drinking. As men, they had access to the entire public world, and so they could enjoy themselves how they liked. The underworld also incorporated those we would today call "homosexuals," for whom there was no option but to enter into this society, since the Victorian public morality of manly love precluded consummation of homoerotic desire.[48] The mood and tenor of the underworld, according to one writer, was summed up in "crude nineteenth century potboilers which dealt with moral insanity, monomania, sex and sadism."[49] Pornography was rampant, with salacious literature like Maria Monk's *Awful Discourses of the Hotel Dieu Nunnery of Montreal.* Books like George G. Foster's *New York in Slices* (1849) and *New York by Gaslight* (1850), while claiming to condemn the underworld, only stimulated voyeuristic interest in it.[50] Further, from the mid-nineteenth century, dandies hung out on streetcorners blatantly ogling and verbally abusing passing women, or in theaters and concerts would train their opera glasses on ladies: a breach of decorum.[51] Above all, the underworld ethos after 1880 was captured in the *Police Gazette*, where spoofing of homosexuality went hand in hand with sports reports and pictures of scantily clad "ladies."[52] One hundred and fifty thousand men of the working and middle class read this publication: in this way, it represented a pivotal point, connecting in its darker and seamier side a standard of underworld primitivism that united American men across classes. Here, male primitivism, the very antithesis of the high ideals of the Christian Gentleman, ran rampant and unchecked. Here, in a lewd, crude, sordid, animal, and brutal world, "character" seemed irrelevant in the late nineteenth century. Yet—and this is important—the choices remained ultimately clear for Victorian men of the dominant class. The Christian Gentleman represented the correct and moral male ideal;

any other concept of manliness was wrong, and, if one was found out, one must face the consequences of the breaking of taboos. All the same, for most men the system had real advantages. If celibacy did not suit them, they could sow their wild oats. But sex with middle-class women was something special, almost sacred, to be savored only if in love. It was imbued with a mystery and spiritual worth that made it transcendent, beyond concerns of physical mechanics. Victorians no doubt did worry about sex. But sexual success was not of overwhelming importance to them. It was not deemed essential to the worth of a man. And it may well be, of course, that, without all the palaver that was to be associated with sex in the twentieth century, they actually enjoyed sex more.

After 1880, however, severe stresses appeared in the Victorian system of morality that heralded its demise. Self-control, discipline, delayed gratification, and self-sacrifice, ideal qualities in an economy geared towards production, seemed less appropriate in the late nineteenth century world of the national marketplace and of large bureaucratic corporations that undermined the small businessmen and farmers who had held sway in high Victorian America. The Self-Made Man with his firm sense of personal autonomy and independence gave way increasingly to the bureaucrat or manager and the salesman, who felt all the more enclosed and confined and limited in the corporations that were growing ever larger as the turn of the century loomed. Further, the closing of the frontier, with the concomitant crisis in America's sense of manifest destiny, only served to aggravate the middle class's sense of being hemmed in and trapped. The crisis of faith brought on by Darwinism and, above all, by the watering down of Protestantism, was significant. Liberal ministers like Henry Beecher and Lyman Abbott preached of a loving God who granted salvation to all. Protestantism degenerated into a vague and wishy-washy deism. Ministers downplayed the existence of hell and of a devil and celebrated material comfort as the rigorous Calvinist sanctions against sin disappeared.[53] This clouded the moral certainties that were the key to the firm Victorian sense of manhood and to the whole concept of "character" that held together the Victorian system of morality. In this context, for the middle class the crucial ethical question became, what was the point of a lofty Victorian morality when life seemed to lack transcendent meaning? Why accept such rigorous sanctions and maintain "character" when there was, as historian Jackson Lears memorably put it, "no place of grace"? Without religious structures, why not then behave badly?

No wonder these developments heralded for men a fundamental "masculinity crisis" as the Progressive era dawned after 1900. What new masculinities and moral systems could replace the Victorian as men's sense of identity became fragmented, and as the need for "character" became less evident? Faced with the breakdown of religious and moral certainties and faced, perhaps, with a sense of powerlessness in the workplace, where men were now cogs in a bureaucratic machine, commentators noticed an "American nervousness" afflicting both men and women. Seeking a remedy for such uncertainty, men searched for relief in intense experience to break the monotony. The most prominent manifestation of this was the obsession with the primitive that now openly and publicly swept into the middle class at the turn of the century in American society—that urge that historian John Higham first identified twenty-five years ago as the desire to be "young, masculine and adventurous."[54]

As of the early nineteenth century, a respectable form of primitivism had infused the public discourse of the American middle classes. Men admired, for example, the novels of James Fenimore Cooper with their depictions of white men like Natty Bumppo who were as brave as "savages." Physical vigor and stamina attained greater value as young men became increasingly concerned with the cultivation of their bodies. Urban gymnasiums sprang up all over the country around the time of the Civil War.[55] A graduate student writing home from Germany told his parents "the result of his self-imposed exercise program. He listed his chest, stomach, and hip measurements for them, exact to the quarter inch."[56] Male primitivism was popularized, too, in a number of male institutions such as the YMCA, which propagated a form of muscular Christianity. For bodily perfection remained "an essential part of Christian morality."[57] Yet, despite its emphasis on the body, primitivism continued as a part of respectable Victorian ideology. Victorians could cultivate their bodies in order to better compete in the marketplace as Masculine Achievers and to show they had the strength of "character" to be good Christian Gentlemen—not necessarily overtly to display their virility. The public advocates of primitivism in the middle class insisted on purity—as good Victorians. Yet in their implied rejection of civilization and in their glorification of the male body and of—albeit controlled—aggressiveness, the advocates of primitivism steered perilously close to the values of the underworld; in doing so, they helped to lay the foundations for the destruction of the Victorian system of manliness and morality.

For by the 1870s American primitivism had begun to break more openly with genteel traditions. First, the hugely popular dime novel heroes like Deadwood Dick and Gentleman Joe differed from the earlier gentlemanly heroes of Cooper in their use of openly crude language and public portrayal of violence.[58] By the turn of the century, five and a half million men were members of fraternal lodges, with their omnipresent and bizarre secret primitive rituals.[59] By 1890, the popularity of boxing grew beyond the underworld as John L. Sullivan became the first folk hero of the sport, and helped make popular with a mass audience the Irish male style of aggressiveness.[60] The controlled violence of football and other sports that developed into their modern forms in these years was representative also of the rise of primitivism.[61] Further, Afro-American musical forms were at this time first commercialized for white audiences, who often considered such music to be redolent of the savage and the exotic and the risqué.[62] Perhaps the advocacy of the primitive reached its apotheosis in the genre of the Western, which in Owen Wister's *The Virginian* attained its most characteristic and distinctive form. The Western hero was always a gentleman but was also "untamed" and a "primal savage."[63] Joe Knowles, who lived naked in the Maine wilderness for three months, transfixing 1913 Boston, helped turn male primitivism firmly against civilization, as did Edgar Rice Burroughs in his Tarzan stories.[64] The attainment of "character" remained the goal of this genre. But in the infusion into the mainstream of male toughness and aggression of a sort that had been confined before to the lower orders, the logic of the challenge that had always been posed to respectable Victorian manliness by primitivism began to work itself out.

This challenge was confirmed by Theodore Roosevelt's contemporary advocacy of the "strenuous life." Roosevelt shared and perhaps best articulated the men of his generation's confused sense of manliness. He strove for renewed meaning by glorifying the hard work and discipline of the vanished frontier. The future president advocated, in 1900, "the life of strenuous endeavor ... the life of toil and effort, of labor and strife to preach that highest form of success ... to the man who does not shrink from danger, from bitter toil and who out of these wins the ultimate endeavor."[65] For Roosevelt, the major role model for American men in the first twenty years of the century and beyond, the cowboys and hunters of the West best attained this "strenuous life," and therefore were the finest exemplars of American manhood. Having constantly to face the dangers of nature and its rigors, these men escaped from the confinements and effeteness that afflicted the Easterner. Their hardiness and physical vigor inspired Roosevelt, whose worldview should nevertheless be regarded with a great deal of suspicion. First, the "strenuous life" with its hustle and bustle involved only frantic avoidance of the psychic issues that confronted the middle class: it could only temporarily soothe the frustrations of men denied the autonomy of the Self-Made Man. Further, his emphasis on the significance of men's "virile fighting qualities" not only led to his rampant militarism but also to his popularization of boxing with his crass sparring session with boxer Mike Donovan in the White House in 1903. For if Roosevelt still emphasized the importance of "character," the cult of the "strenuous life" challenged it as the dominant ideal of American manliness because it helped bring aspects of the ethos of the underworld into the mainstream. Roosevelt was therefore surely not such a good role model for American men?

The logic of the cult of primitivism developed further as gentility lost ground as a guide to the social relations between the sexes. Work that was hardly respectable but was freely available and widely discussed now revealed the bitter hatreds that lay under the surface between the sexes. Jack London's rugged individualist and independent heroes fled from an effeminizing civilization, hearing the *Call of the Wild*. In his 1903 novel, London turned primitivism against women, especially with his portrayal of the female character, Mercedes, who having been "chivalrously treated all her days," still made the lives of her husband and brothers "unendurable" as a nag. London commented on this obsessively throughout the text, referring to the way in which she "interfered" and was "hysterical."[66] But London's blatant misogyny was nothing in comparison with that of Frank Norris, whose primitive characters represented a huge break from genteel literary traditions. In *McTeague* the brutal dentist of that name traps his girlfriend Trina on the operating chair. As he feels "the animal in the man" stirring, he struggles to control himself. On this occasion he succeeds but he wonders why he could not love her purely. After they marry he suffers a series of misfortunes and realizes that he cannot live with her civilization and sophistication. Frustrated, he turns increasingly to violence and eventually beats his wife to death.[67] The ethos of the Victorian underworld was in this way diffused more and more into the middle-class mainstream as men turned to primitivism as remedy and relief from the growing uncertainties of their lives.

This ever more public awareness of underworld primitivism at the turn of the century was of enormous importance for American society. It threatened the precarious balance between the Christian Gentleman and the Underworld Primitive that had driven the Victorian system of morality. Victorians in Great Britain and in the still essentially culturally British

United States well understood the centrality of the moral system to men's sense of themselves as men. They strove to rein in the irrational aspects of human society in an unprecedented way. The choices for Victorian males had been clear. A man of "character," a Christian Gentleman, controlled his sexuality both publicly and privately. If he could not control his sexual drives, he might visit a prostitute, but such behavior was only tolerated; it was never respectable. He must never admit it for fear that he might lose his "character"—that is, his very sense of what was best in himself as a man. Yet as late as 1910 the Christian Gentleman still tempered the excesses of primitivism and of the underworld. The single standard still held ascendancy over the double standard. And as late as the end of the first decade of the twentieth century, the Victorian system of morality remained intact, despite the stresses on it.

Yet, after about 1910, this sexual system crumbled. Writer Agnes Repplier declared the "repeal of reticence." Editor William Marion Moody announced it was "Sex O'Clock in America."[68] Put simply, society became more sexualized. After 1910, a vast corps of experts, be they corporate managers, ministers, doctors, advertisers, or marriage manual writers or dance-hall operators, began to offer new solutions to the nervousness and ethical confusion of Americans and in the process devised a new moral code for American society. This new morality stressed instant gratification and fulfillment through consumption and leisure as a means of assuaging the boredom and aimlessness of twentieth-century life and as a resolution to the seeming irrelevance of the older system and the dullness of corporate life and concomitant decline of personal autonomy. The growing hegemonic role of these experts in American life had enormous implications for the American sexual system.[69] They encouraged sexual expression rather than repression in an ideal that represented the solid beginnings of a liberation of sexuality from Victorian rigors. The implications for ideology and behavior of this revolutionary shift in sexual mores for American men are the subject of this book.

While the experts acted as a catalyst for the sexual revolution, it was facilitated, too, in a number of ways—first, by the growth of cities. By 1920, New York was becoming the world metropolis that it is today, a city of five and a half million people, when only three other cities had more than one million inhabitants. In this environment, many of the old strictures and controls over sexual behavior were breaking down. As newspapers pandered to a greater mass, they resorted to titillation in order to sell.[70] Leisure also grew among Americans, providing the time in which to consume. Mass entertainments—the movies, dance halls, amusements—all were set in sexualized environments in which an ever more middle-class audience could spend its money.[71] Even attempts to regulate sexuality in fact had the opposite affect. The American Social Hygiene Association's campaign against venereal diseases and prostitution helped open up a pandora's box of discourse on sex. This discourse, after 1910, seemed to aggravate an already sexually charged atmosphere and undermined the conspiracy of silence and the double standard, the great bulwarks of the Victorian system of morality.

Such changes must be understood, too, in the context of alterations in the meaning of youthfulness in American society that gave greater importance to the 15–24-year-old age group. Youth by the 1920s was moving towards our modern understanding of the period as a subculture, stimulated by G. Stanley Hall's identification of a period of "adolescence."[72] Young men could embark on leisure activities with their girlfriends and "dates" of the same class because the economy required less manpower and more young people were in school: the work week dropped from fifty-six hours in 1900 to forty-one hours by 1920.[73]

And courtship rituals changed steadily in response as urbanization proceeded and as the separation of spheres continued to break down. As from 1900 on teenagers began to go to high school and as more and more unmarried women obtained their own jobs, young people became more free to develop their own styles of courtship. Calling was hardly practicable for families crowded into one or two rooms. While it was true that girls of certain ethnic families were often kept secluded and chaperoned whatever their social status, more sought work outside of the home as well as amusement and leisure in the cheap dance halls that had long been features of male working-class urban life. A few of them became Charity Girls— young women who, in return for "treats," permitted the men who visited the dance halls a certain amount of casual sexual enjoyment—under the women's control.[74] But more "dated." The term "date" originated in working-class argot in Chicago in the 1890s, from which it was introduced to the middle classes by popular writer George Ade.[75] As the new century dawned, the middle classes in the cities began to adopt dating as the most convenient mode of courtship for independent young men and women; and by 1930, the modern dating system was firmly in place for high school students and for college youth. Courtship had been transformed from a system conducted in the home and under strict female-controlled conventions. Women surrendered the power that had gone with them in order to enjoy greater sexual freedom in the public heterosocial leisure world that replaced the previously extant homosocial one. Further, the shift in convention was reflected in changes in actual sexual behavior: women born after 1900 were two and a half times more likely to have had sex before marriage than those born before.[76] Evidently, this was a different world from Victorian America, one that suggested a whole new sexual system; and if a New Woman, then surely a New Man?

These changes raise serious questions about the construction of masculinity. What were the new masculinities that emerged in the leisure world of the sexualized society? How were ideals of male appearance altered? What were the new styles of masculinity in the world of youth? How did new male sexual ideology transform the male experience? How did men reared according to Victorian strictures respond to the New Woman? To what extent did they incorporate or differ from the Victorian ideal? Ultimately, how could one be a man in the twentieth century? Once again, the central question posed by this book is, who was the New Man to accompany the New Woman? Who, indeed, was the flapper's boyfriend?

The Masculine Image in an Age
of Cultural Revolution, 1910–1930

Nineteenth-century American men revealed their "character" through their appearance. Men dressed in dark, drab, and dour black and grey suits designed to create an aura of staidness and permanence. As much of the body as possible must be covered: to maintain dignity, layer upon layer of clothes were worn all year round with even a thin overcoat in the summer. By the second half of the century, men grew full beards and mustaches to accentuate a look of maturity. Even a certain portliness was acceptable. The gentleman thus contrasted with the dandy and the late—nineteenth-century dude, with their flamboyant and colorful mode of dressing that hinted at effeminacy. The respectable Victorian man must look the part of the Christian Gentleman: dignified and self-controlled, asexual and commanding. Quite simply, a man dressed as a gentleman because he was one. Clothes alone did not make the man but they did reflect his character: quiet and sober. What mattered was what a man did; he had no need to draw attention to himself. By contrast with the dandy or dude, he tried to be invisible and to merge with the crowd. Appearance was not terribly important to him: it could only reflect what was within him. For the substance of a man's character defined his worth.[1]

All the same, nineteenth-century American men were obsessed with their bodies. If, in the 1830s, the middle class shied away from public gymnastics because of their popularity with the working class, by the second half of the century body builders like Windship and boxers like Heenan increasingly became models of athleticism and strength.[2] By 1890, Eugene Sandow was the best-known example of the cult of the body, yet—and despite his excessive personal eating and drinking—he was still respectable enough to elicit the praise of YMCA leader Luther Gilick: helped, perhaps, by the classical poses that he struck.[3] This "cult of the body" was compatible with the concept of "character" because the development of muscularity was seen as part of the route to good health and all-around betterment, not necessarily as a means to virility. For, in 1910, the asexual man of "character," even with the growing contemporary interest in the body, remained the dominant concept of manhood in American culture.

But as the twentieth century progressed the man of character seemed more and more anomalous. The mass production of goods created a culture of abundance, plenty, and consumption that gave renewed importance to leisure. The heterosocial leisure world of youth that grew up in the cities gave young Americans a milieu in which to spend money they had not previously possessed in such quantities. The "culture of character" where men were expected to acquire above all "self-control" and discipline on the road to attaining manhood gave way to a "culture of personality." Here, as fad and fashion stimulated demand for ever newer products, the "performing self"—that is, "personal appearance and good manners" as well as "poise and charm"—gained increasing importance and relevance.[4] The presentation of self became vital in an arena where peers determined among themselves what constituted valued masculinity. Men now looked for symbols and signs of the latest trends to artifacts of the "culture of personality" such as movies, ads, and sex confession magazines. They found in these artifacts promises of pleasure and liberation but also sexual demands and expectations—of success with women—if they cultivated an appearance of youth and "sex appeal."

Youth became the central value of male appearance. It helped in the 1920s to be young because, as Gilman Ostrander has noted, there was in that decade a "glorification of youth."[5] Youth represented the very vanguard of the culture of personality, because youth was best able to live up to its demands. As never before, the period of youth began to be comprehended as a distinctive time of life with its own pattern of mores, norms, and values.[6] Popular literature and writing geared itself to the young of the middle class and reflected its mood as it prescribed its behavior. After the novels of F. Scott Fitzgerald, perhaps the most famous example of this to survive in the public's memory is Judge Ben B. Lindsey of Denver, Colorado's *The Revolt of Modern Youth*, a big seller in 1925.[7] Lindsey, the chief justice of the juvenile courts of Denver, produced the book with journalist and physical culturist Wainwright Evans in order to help adolescents who had gotten into some difficulties with the law. But their lawlessness does not appear to have colored Lindsey's appraisal of youth, which was always uniformly glowing. He explained,

> For twenty-five years, through more than ten of which I have had the sympathetic cooperation of my wife, whose desk is next to mine, and who there shares my confidences with youth, it has been my privilege and my delight to work in the midst of eternal childhood. Here, despite moments of blackness, the wind still blows in the willows, Pan still pipes in the Springtime, and the very sky takes on a deeper azure from the long, long thoughts of youth.[8]

Lindsey thus set the tone for this glorification of youth. And indeed, in testimony to the broad appeal of Lindsey's conception of youth, his *The Revolt of Modern Youth* was serialized, appropriately enough, in *Physical Culture*.

Images of male movie stars stressed youth and, also, physical attractiveness. Perhaps the embodiment of the new masculine ideal was Douglas Fairbanks, Sr., who, although around forty years old, played young, rebellious roles. On the screen, Fairbanks reveled in his continued youth and in his athleticism and physical appeal. Young men read avidly his popular tracts on how to attain success; "he was the dashing handsome boy, fearless, openly chivalrous," wrote pop psychologist James Oppenheim.[9] *Physical Culture*, in November 1921, featured an article, one of many in popular literature, on "Analyzing Douglas Fairbanks." It included a picture, "taken expressly for *Physical Culture*," of "Doug" jumping into the air. The author of the article proceeded, "What is Douglas Fairbanks anyway? He has 'a dash that represents the spirit of American youth'." The writer held Fairbanks up as a model for the American man: "And if you want to get the most out of life, even in respect to your physical condition, you could not do better than to cultivate first of all the Fairbanks psychology."[10] Though "Doug" was thirty-eight and had therefore reached the age where "so many men expand at the waistline—if not above the ears—and settle down to become ever softer and more physically flabby, Doug is as young as ever." Perhaps this was because "we have seen him fight whole bunches of villains, sometimes empty handed, sometimes with swords," but, crucially, "never with custard pies."[11]

Rudolph Valentino, like Fairbanks, was a model for young men through-out the twenties, especially as he, too, attracted women. *Physical Culture* also ran an article on Valentino that featured his "exceptional physique"— "the big hunky and all around athlete that he is. . . . Attention is especially called to the extraordinary development of the muscles across the small of the back, built up chiefly by rowing."[12] The two stars exemplified the central demands of the emerging culture of personality that men be young and that they have "sex appeal." As the critic Gilbert Seldes put it,

> sex appeal is in the main a masculine commodity and is perhaps the masculine revenge on the female of the movie species. He-vamp, sophisticated sinner, or great lover—it does not matter if he has sex appeal.[13]

Just as the movies screened out America's past, shifting American culture into a visual, image-led mode, so they helped give new definition to the renewed public importance of male appearance.

In this visual culture, advertising provided the motor for the new culture of personality. Nineteenth-century advertising was entirely compatible with the "culture of character." It was then seen as a little dubious, not entirely respectable. Victorians well understood that advertising, in its glorification of what was new and desirable, could represent a constant challenge to tradition, and, as such, a threat to social stability. Thus, ads were relatively inconspicuous; they were product oriented, and emphasized the practical uses of the item, not its benefits.[14] This remained the rule, even as, by the turn of the century, advertisers sought to sell their products by means of posters, jingles, and brand names. But after 1910, it became increasingly difficult to avoid exposure to ads. Total volume of advertising expenditure in 1914 was $682 million, in 1919 $1,409 million, and in 1929 $2,987 million.[15] Ads were, then, arguably more widely diffused than any other artifact of the culture of personality, yet their effect on meanings of manliness has been entirely missed by historians.

Ads more and more constituted what cultural historian Raymond Williams has termed a "magic system" of enticements and allurements to purchase products that were presented as sources of "pre-sexual and sexual satisfaction" in order to placate the consumer by clouding the way to more lasting and genuine means to happiness.[16] Put simply, advertisers promised fulfillment to men and women who would consume their products. One did not now buy merely a product but with it success, power, health, wealth, and beauty. The advertisers assured that gratification and relief from dull lives could be attained through consumption, but complete satisfaction and fulfillment must always stay short of attainment. The new advertising, in thus arousing male—and female—desires insidiously, subliminally and surreptitiously helped give greater importance to sexuality, though not yet as overtly as later in the century. Ads thus became more important in general as cultural artifacts—and harder to ignore. In this context, for men they also helped redefine ideals of male appearance in favor of an image of youth and "sex appeal" that contrasted sharply with Victorian staidness.[17]

Advertisers quite openly and frankly focused their attention on youth. One entrepreneur candidly noted of youth in the *Saturday Evening Post* that "the tremendous increase in the sales of cosmetics and silk stockings in the last ten years is a revelation of their [youth's] power. Their influence on clothing, corsets, shoes and lingerie has been revolutionary. Manufacturers of knickers and soft collars, sporting goods and automobiles know the value of their approval." With a shrewd eye for the main chance, this writer noted of youth that "today they are careless of tradition, heedless of responsibility. But tomorrow these . . . young men condition your business. They will buy enormous quantities of every conceivable kind of staple merchandise." He noted bluntly that "advertising that considers the preferences of the new generation not only returns a direct profit, but it may also be regarded as the soundest of investments. For the mind of the new generation is exactly like the mind of all preceding generations, 'wax to receive and marble to retain'."[18] Appropriately, an ad in *Life* therefore asked, "When do men start to get young?" The answer was, "When they shave with Barbasol."[19] Similarly, Colgate's "better shaving" could make "the middle aged man look young" if he used it every day.[20] One needed "the healthy MOUTH of youth." It was important to cultivate "that keen, youthful, athletic look."[21] If you patted a little Fougere Royale lotion on your face, in "ten seconds you can knock ten years off your appearance."[22] Aqua Velva could make you "young looking."[23] Hair should not be "lustreless" nor should it lack "the healthy, youthful look you wish for."[24] To make the face more attractive, men were encouraged to shave every day.[25] Gillette declared that "seventy out of every hundred men at Yale shave with a Gillette."[26] Everywhere in ads, it was young men who set the pace. Men should stay young.

It was after all young men who could best live up to the ideal of "sex appeal" that the ads stressed. Ads of all kinds advised men how they could draw women to them. Cigarettes gave accent to sex appeal. Milano pipes were advertised as "rakish and distinctive."[27] Smoking would make men attractive to women: the actress Billie Burke was called in to declare that she "loved to see a man smoke a pipe."[28] A 1926 *Collier's* ad used a quotation from a student at the University of California who had been converted to pipes when his girlfriend declared them to be "more manly looking than cigarettes."[29] Buckingham tobacco even claimed that other products encouraged "the womenfolk to withdraw from the room" when the men lighted up. But with the aroma of Buckingham, there was "no feminine retirement now," so "bewitching" was Buckingham.[30]

Advertisers for perfumes realized that they, perhaps, had the greatest challenge in convincing men that it was not effeminate or unmanly to use their products. However, in aiming their products at men, advertisers faced a dilemma. How could they encourage men to consume goods that might have been previously regarded as taboo or unrespectable, dubious, or, worse, effeminate? To sell their products they urged that men take care of their appearance as only dandies and dudes had done in the nineteenth century. Clothes, hair, and skin must show grooming, which needed the attention of the advertised products. Eau de cologne was the "only really masculine toilet water,"[31] while Williams perfume "delights with its man-style fragrance."[32] Men were advised to use talc:

> Men, always reluctant to try anything that makes them really comfortable, learned of the luxury of a Talcum shower after their bath—a silky film of Talcum that made clothes feel loose on a hot day, that prevented collar chafing and underwear from sticking.[33]

But it was still important that the talcum powder "didn't show."[34] Men were perhaps not ready yet to admit they used it.

Advertisers who marketed soap directed their ads at men, too. As one ad insisted, "The same fine palm and olive oil soap that has won recognition wherever beauty is prized in the world, is the favorite of men, too."[35] In one ad in *Physical Culture*, a woman was pictured next to her male dancing partner, thinking,

> "A Good Dancer But . . ."
> No excuse now for perspiration odor—just wash and bathe with the hygienic toilet soap that keeps pores purified.

> We naturally think of perspiration odor as something other people may be guilty of, but never ourselves.
>
> But the truth is that unless we are on our guard, everyone of us may offend at some time without knowing it. [Lifebuoy] purifies pores and gives lasting freedom from embarrassing odors.[36]

Men's skin became the focus of almost as much attention as women's. Men should "keep the skin fresh, ruddy, and vigorous."[37] "He could be so attractive," declared an ad in *Collier's* in 1926, but when girls would "look him over carefully" they would "just as carefully overlook him" because of his "grimy-looking skin spotted with blackheads and dull in appearance."[38] The solution to this dilemma was Pompeian Massage Cream, a sure cure for "Comedones" (blackheads): "Not a single dance with her. How he envied the other men as they gaily whirled her around on the floor. Somehow HE was always just too late. He suspected she was purposely declining his initiatives. But never for a moment did he guess that the reason was Comedones."[39] Bad breath, too, was undesirable:

> She hated to tell him. She was so proud of her big brother. But of late he seemed much discouraged. He was being left out of things—dances, dinners— and somehow "the girl" never had an open date.
>
> His sister knew the cause. She hated to tell him, because it was such a personal thing, but finally she did, and he was a good sport about it.[40]

Famously, advertisers devised the pseudo-illness, halitosis—"bad breath"— as a means of selling their mouthwashes.[41]

White teeth also increasingly became a concomitant of attractiveness. "Pepsodent [was] not for women only. Men's teeth also glisten now."[42] Pictures of young men with white teeth were used to illustrate the importance of dental hygiene: "Remove the dingy film that's clouding [your teeth] and you'll be surprised that your teeth are just as white and charming as any one's [if you brush with Pepsodent]."[43] Glossy, shiny, perfect teeth made you more, not less, of a man. In even a relatively sedate paper like the *Saturday Evening Post*, a bare-chested man was used to sell S.S. White toothpaste: "In Ancient Athens lithe youths ran races and performed wondrous feats in the arena for pure joy in their abounding vigor." The ad went on: "Without health vigor is not possible. When the strength of the body is sapped, vigor dwindles and is lost."[44] In this way even ads for toothpaste gained erotic connotations as they presented men with images of sexual success—and the implied message of failure if they did not buy the product.

Hair was similarly important. Dandruff must be avoided at all costs—"Have you ever noticed a white coat collar can mar the appearance of even the most fastidiously dressed man?"[45] Hair suddenly acquired "natural gloss and lustre" and if you purchased the right product "it is very easy to give it that rich, glossy, refined and orderly appearance, so essential to well-groomed men."[46] Hair must be kept "perfectly combed" or else "you cannot look well-groomed."[47] Any fears of effeminacy were allayed if you bought a "real, man's brush."[48] Ads concerned with balding were ubiquitous: "This new way MUST stop falling hair in three weeks. Must grow new hair in ninety days or your money refunded," declared one typical ad.[49] Yet advertisers—despicably—aggravated male anxieties, by devising pretended causes of baldness. One warned women, "your husband will be either bald or good-looking. It's largely up to you."[50] Another declared, "Oh, but he is handsome and you ARE beautiful. True—but Time will work its havoc on both of you. . . . If he neglects his hair, he may become bald."[51] Even dandruff was "a sign of an unhealthy scalp and a warning of possible baldness coming on."[52] Advertisers insisted that the balding man lacked sex appeal and could not be successful with women.

Youthful standards of looks and muscularity were intrinsic to the masculine ideals of the body in advertisements. Fat was to be avoided. Successful men were after all "slender men."[53] Such men realize "the danger of being stout—how excess weight saps their strength, slows down their thinking, mars their appearance, and hinders their advancement."[54] A good workout might help. Men were advised to get back their "winning muscles with Absorbine, Jr."[55] The Burdick Body Culturor would "hold your weight down—to keep your stomach flat and your waistline where it belongs."[56] Physically developed men were used to sell motorcar axles: "Confronted by new conditions, the world today as never before calls for concentration of thought and purpose in its industries."[57]

Even tanning began to become popular among the middle class in the 1920s, a practice previously confined to the working class. The formerly staid and straitlaced YMCA publication, *Association Men*, after the mid-1920s contained ads for tanning solariums that would make a man "look like six weeks in Florida" with a "deep healthy tan."[58] This contrasted sharply with the Victorian ideal that emphasized covering the body, and anyway valued white skin. By 1930, men wore swimming costumes that no longer covered the upper part of the body. Spalding suits declared rather ambiguously, "How well can you look in a swimming suit? You'll never know until you wear one of these new suits made by Spalding. . . . The ideal for swimming is NO SUIT AT ALL."[59] Another ad declared,

> The good old swimming days are here. Oh boy. But it's great to rip off your shirt, into your suit and splash. But what a shock to some of the poor girls when they see their heroes come out with flat chests and skinny arms, instead of the big husky frames they expected to see.

YOU ARE OUT OF LUCK.

> Don't try to make excuses. You are just plain out of luck. It's your own fault. You can't blame anyone but yourself. But what are you going to do? She is going to find you out.[60]

A swimming party might therefore be an "emotional moment in the life of a flapper." The solution when she saw her fiancé for the first time in his bathing suit was to "light a Murad"[61] (a cigarette). Constantly, advertisers played on male fears about their appearance as they played up a rugged, primitive image of the male body.

Much the same trend applied in clothing. Clothing increasingly was specifically aimed towards young men. Advertisers claimed to know "How Young Men Will Want Their Spring Clothes."[62] The wearer of Society Brand Clothes could be confident that he was wearing "clothes for young men and men who stay young." After all,

> Young men like these are going to wear clothes like these; they know what they want; they find it wherever our clothes are sold. . . . Double-breasted types; belted styles; high roll fronts, smart pockets, all-wool fabrics.[63]

Golden Arrow shirts declared that "it is ready for you today at the good men's outfitters. Young men will seize it. Frankly, Golden Arrow was made for them."[64] Clothes were designed to enhance physical attractiveness: "The shoulders will give you the look of a man who can pull an oar" and "the waistline of a commuter who can still run for his train."[65] Clothes could help you look young: " 'Why is your waistline so trim?' 'Because I've that wonderful new friction-fabric waistband'."[66]

Advertisers sought for men a more athletic, virile look that showed off the figure and was sufficiently manly to reassure men concerned about more flamboyant styles. In the *Saturday Evening Post*, a commentator noted how the "Milstande shoulder" had spread across the country that summer:

> Square, athletic, well-groomed looking, no finer interpretation of American briskness . . . has ever been developed . . . a shoulder that enhances the

erectness and set-up of the youthful figure by its clean, energetic, parade-ground contour.[67]

Hart, Marx, and Schaffner emphasized that

> Young men who are "up" on style—and most of them are—will see exactly what they've been looking for in these new suits. Wider shoulders, pockets and buttons are lower; the coats have a suggestion of a waistline; they are shorter and snug over the hips—"gathering" in slightly the hip-fullness of the trousers. They're smart and all right and our fine fabrics and needlework go with them.[68]

Even suits for dinner, previously symbolic of decorum, were influenced by this trend towards revealing the figure:

> The new DINNER SUIT by KUPPENHEIMER ... the athletic figure in silhouette ... broad shoulders tapering down to flat hips ... generous lapels ... low pockets ... wide, straight-hanging trousers. Tailored in the inimitable KUPPENHEIMER manner ... genuinely fine fabrics ... costliest silks ... richly finished throughout.[69]

Hats, too, were equated with masculinity: "Lion hats the right hat for Real Men."[70]

Further, in this period designers began to sell "athletic underwear," which was considerably lighter in weight and more practical than nineteenth-century underwear, which could weigh as much as four pounds.[71] "No, it isn't a new dance, merely underwear," declared one advertiser— "It's hard to achieve a rhythmic grace when your underwear threatens to cut you in two":

> Underwear for men, never mentioned save with blushes, has recently become less of an outlaw in the scheme of attire. Artistic ether has seeped into the world of unmentionables and imparted poetry to the most drab of all elements of dress. ... Men are drugging their senses with batik designs in sleeping apparel and inhaling the stimulation of contrasting shades of underclothes.[72]

Advertisements for BVDs had to assure men that their products would not suggest effeteness: "Or are you afraid of being suspected of effeminacy? Some men are, as amused haberdashers tell us" said an ad for Champknit athletic underwear. The appropriately named Joe Ruddy was brought in to prove that BVDs were in fact emblematic of virility:

> Joe Ruddy, holder of more than seven hundred trophies in twenty-six
> fields of athletic endeavor, and including two Olympic championships, wears
> CHAMPKNIT. So does Tom Thorpe, football authority and referee.... So
> do many of the brawniest men you meet in your travels.[73]

So said the ad, no doubt much to its readers' relief.

From the 1890s, sportswear became more and more popular for casual
wear when shirt styles previously worn for sports replaced older styles of
shirts.[74] Men's clothes at last loosened up and became practical for sum-
mertime:

> The National Summer Suit for men. You can't look hot and look well-dressed,
> but you can look well-dressed and BE cool. Keep-Kool is the answer. In a
> Keep-Kool suit a fellow can feel delightfully comfortable the length and
> breadth of a hot Summer day.
> Light in weight—tailored in the best of fashion—correct in style and fit.[75]

Canvas shoes and sweaters also formerly worn for sports passed into casual
wear. This created a more sporty and virile image in ordinary life that
guaranteed stylishness but not at the cost of effeminacy. The Arrow Man
who advertised Arrow shirts became the first in a long line of models to
be seen as sex symbols: from 1905 on, the model received love letters from
young women.[76] Doubtless their gentlemen friends were jealous. These
styles extended and developed to an ever wider audience the athletic, firm,
clean-shaven image of Richard Harding Davis, the Gibson Man, who had
been popular in the first decade of the century. Several articles celebrated
the more flamboyant styles that prevailed in certain circles:

> They are looking back to the days when Solomon was arrayed in considerable
> glory—or, with less strain to the eyesight, a time when it was not unusual
> for the stronger sex to sport yellow breeches, a red waistcoat, a frilled shirt,
> a plum-colored coat, and a pearl gray top hat.[77]

Fashion commentator Paul Nystrom, in 1928, predicted that if this trend
continued, the "vivid colors of the eighteenth century might return to
men's clothing."[78] This did not quite happen, but in the celebrated mid-
1920s study of Muncie, Indiana, *Middletown*, "Even among the men ... it
is apparently less common today than in the nineties to renounce any effort
at appearing well-dressed by speaking scornfully of 'dudes.' They're no
longer content with plain, substantial, low-priced goods but demand 'nifty'

suits that look like those everyone else buys and like they see in the movies."[79] Styles of appearance that had been regarded as risqué in the nineteenth century among youth became the norm as the visual culture grew in influence. This resulted in an increase in sexual demands and expectations. A public culture rose to hegemony that stressed youth and sex appeal as ideals for men, and that stressed "appearance" and "personality." The term "sex appeal," which was often used, summed up the new ideal of male appearance perfectly. The suggestiveness of the word "sex" was tempered by the word "appeal," which implied a gentle, even innocent, eroticism that was not—as yet—too overt or threatening. This was safe sexiness by the standards of the late twentieth century, but it was a major shift in public ideology from Victorian mores for the men of the 1920s.

Yet, too, men were caught up in a contradiction that—perhaps reflecting the confusion of the advertisers themselves—is difficult to unravel: not only were they expected to attain sexiness and power over women, but they were also supposed to look (and smell) democratic: like women, to cultivate their bodies and looks, in order to be presentable.

Advertisers presented a further paradox that can only have aggravated anxieties. While claiming their products would give men individuality and personality, they also imposed a kind of wholesome, crass, corn-fed, clean-cut conformity on young males that may have fitted in perfectly with the peer-led, other-directed youth culture but that boded badly for the genuine individualism of the Victorians—for "character." For success as a man now turned on the superficialities of dress and appearance.

The genre of the sex confession magazines extended this sexualization of male images. Bernarr Macfadden, publisher of *Physical Culture* and confession magazines such as *True Story*, was a pivotal figure in effecting and reflecting these changes. Macfadden was the sickly child of Missouri settlers who left him to fend for himself while he was young. He had found a life of strenuous exercise and careful eating a solution to his poor health and his emotional problems. In the 1890s, he gave one-man shows, in which he posed his excellent physical development for what he regarded as frustratingly limited audiences. Determined to spread the word of his exercise techniques, he took over the exercise magazine *Physical Culture* in 1899. The Macfadden version of the journal was an immediate hit, reaching an audience of about 150,000 by 1906. Macfadden attempted with his most enthusiastic readers to start a Physical Culture City in New Jersey, where the physical culture way could be lived. He gave his journal the flagmast: "Weakness is a crime." Here he could rail at his enemies—"Corsets, muscular inactivity, gluttony, drugs and alcohol." But worst of all was "prudery"—"the most important of all evils."[80] However, (quite well-founded) rumors of prurience and nudity at Physical Culture City led to an investigation that culminated in Macfadden's being sentenced to prison for putting obscenities in the mail. Though President Taft pardoned him, *Physical Culture* went into a decline. Macfadden himself relinquished the editorship in 1912 and went to proselytize his ideas in England for two years. Though he resumed the editorship in 1916, the circulation was at 110,000 in 1919, no greater than it had been in 1906. In response, Macfadden founded a new outlet for his ideas, *True Story* magazine, in 1919. This journal advocated his physical ideals in lurid "sex" confession stories devised by a group of hack writers around Macfadden, many borrowed from *Physical Culture*, though Macfadden claimed that the stories were sent in by readers. *True Story* was an immediate success, and it spread the physical culture ideal to a whole generation of readers, both women and men—predominantly young—and of both the working and the "new middle class." By 1926—when the editor decided to reduce the stories' all but explicit sexual content in favor of "romance" stories—each issue of the journal was selling two million: *True Story*, like *Physical Culture*, was reaching between one in five and one in ten of the homes in the mid-1920s in Muncie, Indiana (Middletown). *True Story* spawned a host of imitators, both from the Macfadden camp and elsewhere. It also stimulated sales of *Physical Culture* itself, which virtually quadrupled, reaching four hundred thousand by 1926. This was one-fifth the circulation of *True Story* but still a major seller of the time, if not quite the publication phenomenon that describes *True Story*.[81] *Physical Culture* especially was read avidly by a whole generation of boys and young men across the country. Through these journals the physical culture way was offered as inspirational for an appropriate way of life for young American males of the working and, most significantly, of the middle classes, for whom they offered a standard of male appearance that would not previously have been respectable.

In these influential journals, youth and physical attraction were equated and made into doubled benchmarks for happiness. As in ads, men had to be young and good-looking. *Physical Culture* was littered with pictures of almost naked but decidedly young-looking men—their ages emphasized in the blurbs beneath the pictures—as apparently exemplary examples of physical development, described thus typically as "a sculptural and magnificent photograph of a hundred percent physique" or "Leonard St. Leo, dancer in the Music Box Revue, presents a fine study of masculine beauty. The pose suggests his exceptional athletic make-up." To emphasize the youthful theme, a group of Oklahoma high school boys posed quite naked and were photographed from behind following an "Apollo contest."[82] "Fatal beauty" was a distinct advantage as was being "handsome in a tall, slim, boyish way with a wonderful lot of black, soft hair."[83] The hero of one story, "The Price," was "wonderful to look at, so big in body and somehow one knew he was big in mind and soul as well." His eyes were "the eyes of a boy, blue as a cornflower, and honest and open as a child's." To be "startlingly boyish" was an advantage.[84] Youth set the pace. Confession magazines featured stories in which an older man was devalued in comparison with a more youthful counterpart. For example, in one story, 70-year-old Dascom Fielding persuades the heroine to marry him, but after producing a eugenically defective child who dies, she divorces him and marries a younger man; on the day they marry, Fielding commits suicide clutching his dead son's shoe.[85] In *Physical Culture*, the value of a man at sixty was based on how much like a 25-year-old he looked. Heaven forbid that one look one's age. Men, when older, had to try to stay young. Thomas Marvin, in *True Story*'s "After the Eleventh Hour," may have had hair sprinkled with gray, "yet he was not old-looking,"[86] while Colonel Harry Stevens of Chicago, at seventy-nine, has "more youth per year than any other man we have met."[87] Dwight Clark was "eighty-nine years young," while underneath a picture of one man was posed the question, "How would you like to look like this at fifty years of age?" Another man was forty-nine years old and "spry as a boy."[88] Further, men were constantly warned in the pages of Macfadden's journal that "early old age shows at the waistline."[89] Thus, "one must buy a new youth-giving belt."[90] An editorial in January 1924 implored,

> Young men, do you get up in the morning, look in the mirror and remark how young you are? If not, it will be worth your while to do so. By young men I mean those from forty to a hundred.
> Look yourself over in the mirror and ask yourself, "Am I Getting Old?" If you are, then decide to drop fifteen to twenty years. You can do it. [91]

Further, Wainwright Evans explained "Why Athletes Grow Old at Thirty."[92] If one followed the physical culture way, then "all the fire, snap and sparkle of youth will be yours once more by methods acknowledged superior to everything previously offered."[93] Thus, one writer could proclaim, "My youth has come back to me."[94] Another claimed that one must maintain "the pep of youth."[95] Throughout these journals, the need to be young or stay young was hammered home to readers, a reminder that youth was best able to flourish in the culture of personality.

Macfadden encouraged an ethos in his publications to men that the way to attain success with women was through charm, popularity, and "sex appeal." While Macfadden's stories were often little morality tales in which a rake was contrasted with the hero, it is often difficult to differentiate between the two: both had "sex appeal." If a man followed the physical culture way, "those who now laugh at you and smile will envy you for your physical charms."[96] Rose, in "The Heart of a Wife," meets Larry at a wild party; he is "fascinating and handsome."[97] Because of this he can "vamp any woman this side of heaven." Though Apollo is a "lady-bug," he is still "a fascinating devil."[98] Ultimately, in these magazines, what was most important was to have "good looks and charm": one must be "charming and fascinating."[99] One needed a "magnetic touch" to be physically attractive in the culture of personality,[100] for ultimately "personality" meant "sex appeal." So powerful was this force that in "Lover or Husband," the heroine vows that having been scorned by a flighty but attractive lover, she would marry "the first man who asked me, provided he did not carry that 'sex appeal'."[101] In "Just a Showgirl," the heroine speculates as to whether or not it was "the hero's physical attractiveness that came under my notice first," while another heroine laments that what she thought was love was "nothing but physical attraction."[102]

Those men who did have sex appeal were compared favorably against those who did not—that is, the "dead wood."[103] One should on no account be a "fat boob" or a "young hippo."[104] Professor Henry Titus declared that his graduates "were not merely pretty boys. They are strong."[105] However, if one worked out properly, one might see "the Regeneration of a 'Big Slob.' "[106] One writer compared himself unfavorably as "fat and bald" to the hero "with curly hair and soulful eyes."[107] Another writer, Todd Robbins, even felt it necessary to prove his own credentials for writing an appropriate *Physical Culture* story by posing in the nude in the pages of the paper.[108]

He indeed followed the lead of Macfadden himself, who endeavored to practice what he preached by becoming the living embodiment of the *Physical Culture* ideal. He would pose in the pages of his journal practically nude as the epitome of youth and beauty—well into his sixties. One eyewitness reported that

> When lecturing Macfadden would employ his well-defined figure to fortify his message. Turning from the audience, the well-conditioned crusader

would keep time with his back muscles to the music of the orchestra. It was all very impressive to the viewer.[109]

He had, as one commentator noted, a "magnificent body."[110] According to his biographer, Clifford Waugh, Macfadden said, "If my friends should refer to me as the old editor . . . I want them to understand that I am still YOUNG [he was fifty]."[111] Macfadden carried his own obsession with youth to absurd extremes. When he married for the fourth time at the age of eighty in 1948, he would not allow his youngest child—at twenty-three—to attend for fear people would think him an old man.[112]

Death was of course the weak point of such an ethos. When Theodore Roosevelt died in February 1919 at only sixty-two, *Physical Culture* asked, "Did Mr. Roosevelt's extra weight in any way lessen his length of life? What were the causes of his untimely death?"[113] More sinister was the response of the Macfadden publications to the death of Valentino. When Valentino died in October 1926, *Physical Culture* ran an article on "What Really Killed Valentino," articulating the shock that many experienced when such a leading exponent of the emerging cult of youth and beauty for men had died, especially when it was revealed that he "had not taken such good care of himself as he should have done" (this despite the fact that the star had died of peritonitis).[114]

But Macfadden's journals developed an element of the ideology of masculinity—that is, they extended more overtly than the ads the equation of "sex appeal" and manliness with muscles. Macfadden carried on this American "cult of the body" in many ways and not unlike the Victorian, though his wide distribution gave him unprecedented access to his target audience. *Physical Culture* is famous as the pioneer of the physique magazines of the thirties, forties, and fifties and hence it featured models and readers displaying their physical development. This was self-consciously presented as worthy of emulation to middle-class youth. For example, the photo of one Mr. Frank Sobota presented "a pleasing combination of muscular development and artistic posing."[115] Admirably, Mr. Andrews "gained twenty pounds of solid muscle in four years."[116] There was a sculptural beauty in the symmetrical development of Gaspar Di Giovanna of Brooklyn, New York. "Surely this is Apollo come to life again," declared one blurb.[117] Of the athlete Adolph Nordquest, it was written,

> I know other strong men and athletes with arms, chests and legs just as big as Nordquest's. I know men who excel his measurements in parts of the body, but I have never seen in the flesh or in portraits more than half a dozen men who approach him in all around development.[118]

The pages of *Physical Culture* were full of vivid descriptions of male physiques. Men were advised on "strengthening the shoulders—Exercises by Clevio Massimo."[119] The Milo Bar-Bell Company declared, "We can make you the man we would like you to be."[120] "Have you a body to be proud of?" asked one ad written by an exercise specialist.[121] Earl Liederman, perhaps the most advertised strong man of the twenties, declared, "When I'm through with you you're a real man. The kind that can prove it."[122] And Charles Atlas, later so extensively advertised, emerged at this time, too. In March 1826, the journal sponsored a male beauty contest:

> Remember the purpose is not the frivolous one of gratifying personal vanity. Not merely that of decorating our pages in future with beautiful photographs. The purpose is that of improving the human race, holding forth ideals that will stimulate personal improvement and so help us to make the human race what it should be and may be.[123]

In each and every issue, Macfadden advertised his *Manhood and Marriage*, in which he expounded further on the equation between true manhood and the ideology of physical culture:

> Am I a complete man?
> It is certainly a good plan for a young man when he is doubtful upon such an important matter to ask himself some very plain questions. He should have a good plain talk with himself. "Do I possess all the strength, health, and manhood that I can attain? Have I wasted my vitality and vigor? In what way am I wanting? In what way am I defective? Am I doing all I can to build up superior virility? Am I as good a man as I can be?"[124]

One reader agreed with Macfadden: "I believe we should prepare ourselves for companionship so I have tried to make an all-round man of myself, swimming, diving, wrestling, light gymnastics and walking are my physical enjoyments."[125]

"Physical attraction" was indeed seen as being synonymous with muscularity, and he who lacked muscles was lacking in manhood. But what was so strikingly different about Macfadden's philosophy in this period was the equation of sexual success and, indeed, of sex appeal with the right physical attributes. In the 1920s, Macfadden was able to be more explicit than he had been earlier about the chances of sexual success that his ethos could offer. Hence he helped accelerate further sexual demands on middle-class men. Material geared to the Victorian lower classes had carried such a message, as did material available in the "Victorian underworld."[126] But middle-class readers especially knew that, ultimately, such material was salacious and improper. If it was widely available, the message was firmly countered by the prescription that "character" was most important in attaining a wife. Yet never was such material so respectable and openly and widely read as it was in the emerging culture of personality and in the youth subculture that represented its cutting edge. Not only was Macfadden at his commercial peak after World War I, but also he got into far less trouble with the censors and keepers of the moral flame in the 1920s than he had before the breaching of the "conspiracy of silence" after 1910.[127] If when Macfadden first began he was an oddity, by the 1920s he was mainstream—especially among youth.

Thus, by the 1920s, in *True Story* and *Physical Culture* Macfadden was able to emphasize ever more explicitly that it was always the physical culturist who got the girl. In the story "Her Morning After," the male character is described as having a "sleek plumpness" that "struck just the wrong note."[128] Hence he is rejected. The tale "A Greased Pig and My Romance" is the story of how an "all round physically perfect man" finds his feminine ideal.[129] In "Love's Turmoil," Roscoe Warren, the physical culturist with the "rough bristles" on his "cheek" and the "stiff strong beard," is successful with women.[130] And in *Physical Culture*, Jack "Cyclone" Adams, Athlete Detective, is described on account of his physical perfection as a "demi-God, to be looked up to, admired and worshipped."[131] Thus, when he meets the beautiful Elsie, "Both of them were embarrassed for a moment, but desire was too strong for any convention and they were soon in each other's arms."[132] Macfadden gave advice in the pages of *Physical Culture* on selecting a husband:

> Don't marry a clothing-dummy, a mannikin, a make-believe.
> But when you are looking for a husband, beware of the white-collar weaklings. They may be alright in the drawing-room. Their English may be perfect.
> But for husbands. Ah that's different. [sic][133]

But perhaps more disturbing for men were articles like "I Want a Physical Culture Man says this Modern Girl":

> Because I have read so many articles by both men and women on the modern girl, and very few, if any on that great and wonderful creation, man, I am impelled to write this letter.

1. He must be physically clean. . . . But he MUST be an athlete.
2. He must be mentally strong.[134]

Further, in the November 1918 issue of *Physical Culture*, men were offered "Her Choice between a Man and a Weakling."[135] Thus, Macfadden's message was clear and unequivocal as it perfectly fitted the emerging culture of personality. Men were valued increasingly for what was outward, superficial, impermanent, and fleeting. Not only were men expected to be young, to remain young, to be physically attractive and magnetic and to have sex appeal, but they also were to be muscular—like movie stars. If they failed to live up to this ideal, they rightly deserved ridicule and further risked sexual failure. Again, Macfadden's slogan resonates over the decades—"Weakness is a crime."

Macfadden's ideals represented a subtle difference from those of advertisers. A clear emphasis on youth and sex appeal gained ascendancy, but so did the focus on primitive muscularity—reminiscent of the values of the underworld. But together the ideology of the advertisers and of Macfadden amounted to the same thing: a fundamental redefinition of the public ideals of American masculinity that gave greater importance to male appearance. Thus the emerging culture of personality imposed new demands on men in the most intimate areas of their lives. Wherever they turned, be it to the movies, the Macfadden publications, or advertisements, they were confronted with ideals that stressed that men should be valued for attaining and maintaining sexual attractiveness and youth, a goal that, ultimately, all men must fail to realize. Under the old Victorian system, the young man who came to call had to project an aura of respectability and solidity and permanence. He had to look like a good potential patriarch, a solid breadwinner for his wife and future family, but he did not have to worry so much about his "sex appeal" as he did in the twentieth century "culture of personality." For casual dating and for the romantic, gently eroticized styles of courtship that were well in the process of development by the 1920s, having "sex appeal" was a major asset in a competitive game.[136]

While some aspects of the sexual revolution no doubt benefited men, the new sexual demands undermined male power by putting a premium on youth and good looks for men, too, as well as for women. Nor should their impact on men be exaggerated: they may have applied in dating, but when women were questioned about the characteristics of ideal husbands, they deemphasized looks, although they mentioned them as a criterion in choosing men.[137] If the emphasis on male appearance was all the rage in

New York, it was new in *Middletown*; but increasingly, it is clear, men were expected to have "sex appeal." Physical considerations thus loomed larger than ever in the ideals of what constituted an attractive man in this culture of personality and consumption.

Styles of Masculinity in the
World of Youth, 1910–1930

The culture of personality placed greater stress on appearance, but it also redefined models of male behavior. The popular literature of the youth culture introduced two new styles of masculinity, the male flapper and the tramp Bohemian. The male flapper of popular novels of the 1920s was in effect an attempt to fuse the Victorian Christian Gentleman with the culture of personality. He was coy, sensitive, gentle, but capable of being sexual. He was ultimately responsible but, tantalizingly, hinted at irresponsibility and unwillingness to commit to a relationship. He was also capable of violence, not in defense of women, but rather against them. Despite his superficial resemblance to the Christian Gentleman, he did not therefore adequately play the role of the foil and check to the second style of the youth culture, the tramp Bohemian. This model celebrated overt irresponsibility and violence against women in a blatant glorification of the Victorian underworld styles of masculinity. Together, these two models of manliness set the pace and the trends of the emerging peer-led youth culture. They competed with and increasingly gained ascendancy over the older Victorian styles in the American middle class.

The roots of the new public models of masculinity lay in the Bohemian sexual avant-garde in New York's Greenwich Village in the second decade of the twentieth century.[1] The proliferation of memoirs published in the 1920s and 1930s, and especially Floyd Dell's *Love in Greenwich Village*, discussed sexuality in some detail.[2] In the renowned salon of Mabel Dodge Luhan, the ideas of Freud and Havelock Ellis, the "free love" ideals of the English Socialist Edward Carpenter, and the theories of the Swedish feminist Ellen Key were discussed regularly.[3] Within the Village, men and women struggled in deadly earnest to overcome their Victorian inhibitions and to practice free love. But they also looked to the inhabitants of South Manhattan and to other parts of New York City—to the working-class leisure subculture—for models of sexual behavior that seemed very like those advocated by their European intellectual mentors. Some of them, too, such as Harry Kemp and Clement Wood, were graduates of Bernarr Macfadden's Physical Culture College. In Greenwich Village, the atmosphere was right for experimental relationships that sought actively to break the supposed bonds of Victorianism—albeit with limited success. A whole host of names stand out, but among the men, Floyd Dell, Max Eastman, Hutchins Hapgood, and John Reed remain the most famous.

For intellectual historians, however, one very significant figure was Randolph Bourne, whose 1913 *Youth and Life* celebrated the youthful experience that he himself was so long denied. Bourne captured the mood and tenor of the Village at this time—and the ethos that it later helped spread to the larger society. He articulated the ascendancy of the 1920s "glorification of youth": "Old men cherish a fond delusion that there is something mystically valuable in mere quantity of experience. Now the fact is, of course, it is the young people who have all the really valuable experience."[4] He thus also recommended a redefinition of morality to suit the needs of youth. He railed at "the rigid self-control that used to be preached." Far better was the new morality that was "a more positive ideal than the rigid mastery which self-control implies."[5] Bourne, with this freewheeling rejection of tradition, here staked his claim as, perhaps, the leading intellectual precursor of twentieth-century youth culture. And certainly his work set the tone for what followed in the next decade.

But until World War I, the Greenwich Village Bohemians received little public attention. Their great journal, *The Masses*, was not widely read outside of the Village, and their free love antics were not broadcast beyond Washington Square except, perhaps, by way of ridicule. However, the opposition of some of them to the war and their willingness to stand trial to defend their opinions attracted attention. Further, during the Red Scare that followed the war, the Bohemians were satirized widely in popular journals as suspected Bolshevik sympathizers. But the influence of the

Greenwich Village Bohemians of the second decade of the twentieth century was to be much more pervasive in the 1920s. For, once the high period of Village life was over, the Villagers settled down to write a series of novels and memoirs in which they presented themselves self-consciously as precursors of the emerging youth culture.[6] In 1921, Carl Van Doren identified this genre of books as the "revolt from the village."[7] Works of this type—often autobiographical—became standards for the emerging city/college youth subculture and set the tone for their generation much as *On the Road* or *Catcher in the Rye* did for the 1950s generation of youth. In this way, the styles and patterns and models of masculinity celebrated in the Village were diffused into the broader culture—with revolutionary implications for the construction of American masculinity.

While F. Scott Fitzgerald remains, rightly, the most famous of the writers of this genre, there were several others who astutely and perceptively commented on the new meanings and definitions of masculinity. Bohemian and Socialist Floyd Dell was perhaps the best but Carl Van Vechten, Stephen Benet, Ludwig Lewisohn, and the young Ben Hecht were good, too, as were observers of college youth Warner Fabian and Percy Marks.

The efforts of these youth culture writers redefined the meaning of American manliness. The first product of these writers' analysis of men's problems was the male flapper. It was Fitzgerald's Jay Gatsby who has gained most fame with his tragically adolescent faith that his youth and beauty could be retained by wealth. Yet the most famous lines reflecting the glorification of youthful styles of manliness belong to Gatsby's narrator, Nick Carraway: "I was thirty," he declares. "Before me stretched the portentous, menacing road of a new decade. . . . Thirty—the promise of a decade of loneliness, a thinning list of single men to know, a thinning briefcase of enthusiasm, thinning hair."[8]

Floyd Dell developed such characters in three autobiographical novels. His hero, Felix Fay, frets over the desperate search for a woman who "can be talked to, and that can be kissed."[9] After kissing, Fay and his girlfriend discuss their positions as members of the younger generation. They had "scorned the older generation. And we are ashamed, coming back to face them, because we've nothing better—really—to show for our lives than they have."[10] By the time of *Souvenir* in 1927, disillusionment and the fear of growing older set in as Felix Fay, like Dell, enters his late thirties. At one point Fay begs his wife, "Don't let me get old."[11] Dell himself continued to glorify youth, even as he came to fear its irresponsible side. In his *Moon-Calf* dedication to his wife, B. Marie Gage, for example, he referred to "the fantastic beauty of American youth."[12]

The male flapper style of masculinity had other components besides its emphasis on the continuation of youth. Felix Fay speculates about the traditional prescriptions for an American male. As a Bohemian, he seeks artistic and creative satisfaction and regards the accumulation of money as unimportant. One of his girlfriends asks him,

> "Do you want to make a million dollars?"
> He replied,
> "No, not at all."
> "Then of course you're a freak."[13]

Even more important than his lack of interest in making money is his questioning of the work ethic. In the novel *Moon-Calf*, Fay takes a job in a factory where he is immediately hired at seven dollars a week so that a young man who has worked there since the previous summer could be laid off, as his wage has risen to fifteen dollars a week.[14] Along with his relationship with Comrade Franz Vogelsang, this experience helps sensitize Fay to socialism. Fay increasingly detests his job as a press-feeder at the printing press, saying that "it was easy enough work, but the air of the little coop was filled with the fine floating bronze-dust. He breathed it into his lungs, and his throat became sore with it."[15] After a week of this work, Fay rebels and leaves the job. According to Franz, his Socialist mentor, this is the first step towards a Socialist consciousness: "I've been waiting to see you throw up the job. You hate work, and so you do whatever comes along. That is silly. One must choose. You have begun, by choosing NOT to do something. Now see if you can take the next step—choose to do something."[16] As a Socialist Fay rebels against mindless capitalist labor and tries to choose his line of work. Fay chooses to become a reporter. For while Fay rebels at certain aspects of the demand that he work, there are limitations to his revolt. So immersed is he in the American work ethic that he is ambivalent even about the worth of factory work: "The trouble is that performing some of the idiotic motions conduce to my own sense of collective self-respect."[17] Fay's rebellion entails questioning the work ethic but does not extend to rejection of it.

Others developed this theme. Carl Van Vechten, in his "biography" of the fictional *Peter Whiffle*, advocated the questioning of the work ethic: "He had no desire to work, in fact his repugnance for work was his strongest feeling."[18] The narrator follows the dilettante Whiffle around Europe on his aimless treks. The character Ted in Stephen Vincent Benet's *Young People's Pride* satirizes expectations of American men. Surely a man should go and make money in advertising? Why then does he "insist on writing novels when he ought to be reading, 'How I Sold America on Ossified Oats,' he wondered."[19] Ted's revolt against expectations, which is reflected in his being a writer, does not go very far: he still doubts the worth of writing as a career.

The male flapper also differed from the tramp Bohemian in his extreme sensitivity. Dell's Fay coyly analyzes and torments over every move. He dreads a date:

> Painfully he groped among the thorny realities, trying to find a path. . . . Yes, and he would have to take her home from the party. Then he would have to stand there by the gate and talk to her—a long time. And then. O! Yes, this especially—he would have to "treat" her.[20]

For Fay sexuality is a complex matter worthy of serious intellectual attention. Of his girlfriend he says that "he wanted her to believe in his theories."[21] So intense is he that he often becomes deeply depressed. He is bewildered, lost, confused; he notes of one crisis that "it was time for him to learn to be like other people—to take such things more lightly."[22] In *Janet March*, the hero Roger, after many affairs, feels that "love . . . had come to seem ugly to him. It had taken on the respectable dullness of the world in which it existed." The solution for the male flapper is to "think about it."[23] Dell presented in Felix Fay and Roger in *Janet March* an image of male youth that was sensitive, gentle, and vulnerable to the rough and tumble of the modern search for a girl who could both "be talked to and be kissed."[24] The male flapper was therefore no stoic patriarch, but really rather fluffy.

Other writers developed this construction of manliness under the influence of Dell and Fitzgerald. The hero, Hugh, in Percy Marks's *The Plastic Age* is an especially good example of the male flapper genre. He displays sensitivity and guilt about his actions with women during the period of "play-need" before marriage. For several days Hugh is tortured by doubt and indecision: there are times when he thinks he loves Cynthia, times when he is sure that he doesn't—when he had just about made up his mind that "he hated her." Hugh is so upset that he even wishes at one point to cry. This would mean breaking one of the greatest taboos, so "there were no tears."[25] Yet Marks had established his sensitivity.

In Stephen Benet's *The Beginning of Wisdom*, the hero Phillip is "sensitive, worshiping beauty, humor, and friendliness as a Parsee worships the sun."[26] When walking up from the railroad station to meet his girlfriend's mother, he is "nervously alert, with a boyish feeling." He is "as patient as a lost dog these weeks, and as gentle, as if all life he had had been taken away from him like the air under the glass of a vacuum-pump."[27] Ludwig Lewisohn's *Stephen Escott*, like Felix Fay, is tormented by sexual conflicts that result from his upbringing. He writes that "since all the moral ideas amid which I had been brought up and to which I had no reason not to consent were wholly at variance with human nature and rigidly refused to take it into account, the result of my inner life was shame and confusion."[28] Later, Lewisohn admits the consequences of his inhibitions: he "had been wretchedly lonely, unmothered, cut loose from human ties; I was without admitting it to myself, sex-starved; more than that; nothing had fed the sexual self-estimation of the budding man."[29] Escott, poor fellow, travels, like Fay before him, to New York's Bohemia, in an effort to find liberation. But this does not work either:

> But I was in reality an underdeveloped and inexperienced country boy. All the influences of my life had been in favor of the frugal, the repressive, and the decent. I instinctively identified all that I saw on Broadway with the life of sin, of drunkenness, of death.[30]

Like Fay, this sensitive young man finds his sexuality a source of torment and anxiety. Fitzgerald's Amory Blaine, from *This Side of Paradise*, displays not only this sensitivity but gentleness as well. He is smitten with a "Puritan conscience" that "at fifteen ... made him consider himself a great deal worse than other boys," so that he is disturbed when he "saw girls doing things that even in his memory would have been impossible."[31] This does not, as it turns out, prevent him from indulging in pleasures, but, still, his guilt does not diminish at all.

If the male flapper was youthful and sensitive, he was also more egalitarian in his relations with women. Dell, as ever, set the pace. The ideal woman for the male flapper was, after all, a girl who could "be talked to, and that can be kissed."[32] For Dell, a relationship of companionship and of "friendship" replaced Victorian patriarchal roles.[33] Women were entitled to have as much fun as men: "I don't see why a girl isn't as much entitled to her fling as a boy," says Fay.[34] In his autobiography *Homecoming* Dell rails at the attitude of other men that "girls are things."[35] According to Stephen in *The Beginning of Wisdom*, one of the criteria for the male flapper is to have a "genius for comradeship" with women.[36] "Good Lord. She's a lovely companionable person," he says of one potential girlfriend.[37] In Katherine Brush's *Young Man of Manhattan*, the hero pleads with his girlfriend that, should they get married, he will, above all, not be "domineering."[38] For the male flapper must not only be able to discuss "the sunset" with his girlfriend, like Dell's couple from *Janet March*, Jack and Pansy, but also "the universe"—that is, they must be intellectual equals.[39] In Ludwig Lewisohn's *Stephen Escott*, one of the characters, David, warns Stephen Escott of his choice of wife that "the modern man wants more in the way of intellectual sympathy from his wife than that type of girl can give."[40] As a result, Escott does not marry this girl. Thus, in the popular novels of the youth culture of the 1920s, the Victorian patriarch lost ground. The male flapper had to be, if not yet exactly egalitarian, then at least more democratic in his relations with women.

How could such a dull, self-absorbed figure still remain interesting? Because he more than hints that he fears commitment. He cannot be tied down. Dell discussed at length the problem of what he called men's "play-need"—that is, the desire for experimentation with different relationships with women before marriage.[41] Casualness was the right pose for a male flapper during this period. Roger in *Janet March* indulges in "harmless, boyish kisses with an air of bored indifference."[42] Writing retrospectively in the 1920s, Dell focuses in the Felix Fay trilogy as in his other work, on how the "play-need" tends to encourage irresponsibility in men. Yet he recognizes the value to Fay of this experimental period. He moves from one intense involvement to another, torn between the ultimate urge to commit himself and his wish for freedom. Of one relationship, he observes, "She is right. She wants her happiness now. Why don't I? It's so easy to fall in love. I'm more than half in love with her now and she with me. That's why we're quarreling. We want each other. Well, why don't we take each other?"[43] But Fay is not ready to commit himself. At twenty, he embarks on an affair with a 35-year-old woman. Next he dates a woman he meets in an amusement park, whom he decides he loves.[44] Still, Fay hesitates to become involved: "Yet, even erect and proud, as he thought of her, his mind braced itself, would not quite surrender to the profound restfulness of happiness, but held itself erect and proud as though indeed his soul perceived in her a beautiful and sweet antagonist."[45] He knows that although this is the first time he has fallen in love, it will not be his last. Ultimately, however, he does settle down, albeit in what turns out to be a disastrous marriage, indeed, a *Briary-Bush*.[46] For when he marries Rose-Ann, he rejects the freedom of the period of play-need as irresponsible. "Freedom," Dell wrote, "It's not a nice word, not a pretty word . . . to me . . . don't offer me freedom, Rose-Ann."[47] One of Dell's characters in *An Unmarried Father* (1925) rails against marriage but with the honest addendum that his distrust of the institution is because "I've not quite grown up."[48] For, ultimately, hard though it was, the goal was to grow up. For like Dell himself, the male flapper, unlike the tramp Bohemian, was a conformist who would eventually settle down. Dell was very clear about this, especially by the late 1920s.

Fitzgerald's Amory Blaine also insists on having a good time; he is so fly-by-night that his lover Rosalind contemplates not marrying him in favor of "reliable" Dawson Ryder.[49] Like Fay, Hugh in the *Plastic Age* is unwilling to become seriously involved with his girlfriend during the period of "play-need." This does not "seem quite right when—I don't really love her."[50] When he kisses his girlfriend for the last time before going to college, "he had a distinct feeling of relief. Well, that would be off his mind for a while anyway."[51] Something prevented him from committing: "I don't know what love is. . . . I can't find out."[52] Hugh's ultimate goal, like Fay's, however, is love, but only when he is ready. Hugh declares, "Whether love was merely sexual attraction or not, he wanted something more than that; his every instinct demanded something more."[53] And by the end of the novel, he has regained his self-respect and has learned to love. While he is mildly irresponsible, in the long term he aims at responsibility.

In the case of Lewisohn's hero Stephen Escott, it is only when his first wife, Dorothy, dies that he is able to satisfy his "play-need." His girlfriend, Beatrice, is experienced, and has had many lovers. She can practice freedom only because of male willingness to accept women's right to it. This New Man of the world of youth was therefore the appropriate companion to the New Woman. As Lewisohn wrote, "The casual man was necessary, doubtless. Without him her triumph could not exist."[54]

Yet, intriguingly, the emphasis on male sensitivity and democratic relations with women did not preclude aggressiveness and even violence. Male behavior could easily deteriorate into violence. Even the hypersensitive Philip in *The Beginning of Wisdom*, when his relationship comes to a crisis, "shakes Sylvia violently."[55] Dell's Roger from *Janet March* lets his embrace of his girlfriend "become an unseemly scuffle. . . . 'Let me go!' she pleaded. 'Kiss me!' he demanded."[56] And it does not take long for Fitzgerald's heroes to become angry with their flappers. Anthony Patch, in *The Beautiful and Damned*, knows what he wants—to assert his will against "this cool and impervious girl, to obtain with one magnificent effort a mastery."[57] And, indeed, in an intense fight in a railroad station, he succeeds: "He had sustained his will with violence. Let leniency walk in the wake of victory."[58] A Christian Gentleman would never have considered such behavior except in order to protect a girl.

In this way, the male flapper of 1920s popular literature represented an attempt on the part of writers to create a New Man to accompany the New Woman. He was in some ways a direct descendant of the Christian Gentleman, especially in his gentleness and sensitivity. But the male flapper's very self-conscious youthfulness was the key to understanding how the model differed from the genre of the Christian Gentleman. For, far from being repressed, the male flapper was intent on sexual exploration and relished the period of "play-need." If, like the Christian Gentleman, he was, at least ultimately, determined to be responsible, this could be delayed. If the male flapper was somehow more interesting in the light subversiveness of his ambivalence about commitment and conformity to the breadwinner role, then, unlike the Christian Gentleman, he was companionable with women. But, in the final analysis, he remained firmly dominant and capable of violence against women.

This New Man was therefore a very precarious construct. As an attempt to convert an essentially Victorian man into one more suitable for the modern world, this was an ideal that was still vague and in flux. As the male flapper lacked the force of tradition behind him, it was all too likely that men—confused—would choose the second great ideal of masculinity, one that drew directly on underworld primitivism.

American writing in the 1920s has also been associated with the phenomenon of literary primitivism. Writers of this genre, in attempting to deflate and pinprick imagined middle-class strictures and structures, looked to the underworld for new ideas about an appropriate moral system for the social relations between the sexes. In doing so, they adopted a spurious glorification of what they considered "working-class" mores, of black culture, and of a malicious view of women. In this context, violence against women was presented uncritically, even as titillating; and commitment to relationships was more firmly discouraged than by the advocates of the male flapper ideal. Writers of this mode looked, bizarrely, to the underworld tramp and hobo for inspiration. Drawing on earlier works like Jack London's *Vagabondia* and W. H. Davies' *Autobiography of a Supertramp*, this tramp Bohemian ideal represented not only an idealization of underworld styles of masculinity but also a specific adaptation of those styles for the middle class. Floyd Dell, the best advocate of the sensitive male flapper style, was also responsible in another context for the idealization of the tramp style. Dell entitled one of his studies of Greenwich Village *Intellectual Vagabondage*. He also published a well-known story, "Hallelujah, I'm a Bum," which celebrated the life of the tramp.[59] Self-consciously, he took this style from well-known works like Hovey's *Songs from Vagabondia*. To be sure, there was nothing new in the idealization of the tramp, but what was new—and so inflammatory—was the meeting of this genre with an emerging heterosocial youth culture.

Jasper Weed, Dell's hero, took on perhaps the most distinctive feature of this style of masculinity. If the male flapper was, for a while, a rebel, in the end he settled down to love and marriage. Not so Jasper Weed, the tramp. When an old man suggests that he get married, this is enough for him to run:

> No doubt the old man meant well, but it scared me. I saw myself settling down in that little town and buying a house for that girl to live in, and spending the rest of my life paying off the mortgage. The truth was, I was almost crazy enough about her to do something like that, and that was what scared me.[60]

Further, in *Souvenir*, Fay's son, Prentice Fay, sees "opportunities for enacting the role of charming vagabond."[61] Dell presented men with another alternative style of masculinity. But the pragmatic Dell's focus in the 1920s was now on the sensitive and ultimately conformist male flapper. His advocacy of tramp styles represented his fantasy of another ideal masculine style, one that he aspired to but did not practice. Yet, he helped spread both the styles within the youth culture.

In contrast, far and away the best example of the tramp genre was Harry Kemp, the "Don Juan of Greenwich Village," author of the autobiographical *Tramping on Life*. This work directly inspired Jack Kerouac's *On the Road* in the 1950s.[62] *Tramping on Life* (1922) and its less commercial successor, *More Miles* (1926), are fascinating celebrations of this Bohemian style of masculinity. Using pseudonyms, Kemp discussed various important figures in the Village, as well as Bernarr Macfadden (given the pseudonym

Stephen Barton). Kemp's *Tramping on Life* and *More Miles* are paeans to life on the road. They self-consciously advocate the tramp style. Indeed, as one reviewer wrote of him, "One does not get the feeling that Kemp is in the confessional. Rather he is on the rostrum."[63]

Like Dell's Felix Fay, Harry Kemp embarked on his career as a tramp as a revolt against the work strictures for American men. In his case, however, there was more of an element of abject laziness in his rebellion:

> Once I worked, plowing—to drive the horses as far as a tall tree for shade, at the end of the third day, sneak back to the house ... and out to the highway with my bundle and my belongings, kicking up my heels ecstatically, glad to be free from work.[64]

He preferred to read:

> With a second-hand Shakespeare, in one volume, of wretched print, with a much-abused school-copy of Caesar, in the Latin (of whose idiomatic Latin I have never tired), an extra suit of khaki, a razor, tooth-brush and tooth-powder and a cake of soap—all wrapped up in my army blankets. I set forth on my peregrinations as blanket stiff or "bindle-bum."[65]

Kemp embarked on his life as a tramp—albeit a clean one—in order to celebrate lower class/underworld primitive styles of masculinity:

> Paul and Josh were "puddlers"—when they worked ... in the open furnaces that were in use in those days ... when you saw huge, magnificent men, naked to the belt, whose muscles rippled in coils as they toiled away in the midst of the living red of the flowing metal.[66]

Kemp worked hard as a sailor and, for a time, even himself became a tramp living in a boxcar. He strove for the sailor's muscularity, and worked out profusely after he was described as the "Skinny Yankee" and was given only a ginger ale while his companion was made a "man's drink" by a barmaid.[67] Later, in *More Miles*, when he took up boxing he wrote that he "was a bit frightened, but I pitched my timidity out. I summoned up all the lean, hard wolf in me that my daily regimen of exercise, my solitary outdoor life had fostered."[68] *Tramping on Life* and *More Miles* were celebrations not merely of the perceived physical aspects of lower class/underworld primitive styles of masculinity but also of what Bohemians imagined were lower-class styles of relationships with women. Kemp enthused about the joys of the single life, of short, sharp, sweet liaisons that did not involve marriage. He declared proudly at one point that "at the table [he] delivered a long harangue against marriage."[69] What is striking, though, in Kemp's work, apart from a rejection of marriage and commitment, is how unimportant women were to him. Although not from choice, he was a lonely fellow and, like many Bohemians of the time, he remained celibate until his late twenties on account of confusion about his sexuality.

Kemp's relationships, however fleeting, had the element of perhaps the most sinister aspect of the tramp styles of masculinity—that is, the open depiction of violence against women. When he accused his lover Opal of interest in another man, he declared,

"To hell with the rest of the people in the House!" I caught her violently into my arms. I would plead and whine no more. I would take her by force. She fought hardily against me.
"I'll call for help, if you don't let me go,—this instant."[70]

He continued by stating forcefully that "I love you and I'll kill you—or myself—or both of us—you've got to become my sweetheart."[71] Kemp's violence even extended to kissing. When he first kissed one girl, he reveled in her "shrill exclamation of virginal fright, not at me,—but at my abrupt, hungry masculinity."[72] Obviously, in his work Kemp hardly set a healthy example for the young.

Kemp was not, however, alone. Sherwood Anderson, for historian Oscar Cargill, was the "epitome of primitivism."[73] Anderson's chilling *Winesburg, Ohio* (1919), the author's self-conscious effort to come to terms with his own myth-laden flight from the responsibilities of his small-town Ohio family, showcased the hero, George Willard, as a link between various loosely connected short stories. These feature several "grotesques" for whom "youth and life" is long over, from the frustrated Alice Hindman, whose lover had deserted her, to Wing Biddlebaum, the broken protagonist of "Hands," whose career as a schoolteacher had ended after he was suspected of molesting his male students. These represent a sharp contrast to George Willard who, because of his "animalism of youth," is able to escape the stifling small-town life of Winesburg and avoid the fate of these "grotesques." Yet the style of manliness of *Winesburg, Ohio* is again an aggressively masculine one. As Willard thinks of his lover, Belle Carpenter, he is "half drunk with the sense of masculine power."[74]

The hero, John Webster, of Anderson's bizarre autobiographical *Many Marriages* (1923), like Anderson himself, abandons career responsibilities: "I have decided to no longer concern myself with this buying and selling. . . . And what do you do? You take the slips, read them and run around town . . . you're so impotent you don't even write your own stuff." He is therefore "cutting out."[75] This idea excites him. He can now remove the strappings of civilization. As he says, "I guess I'm a primitive man."[76] As Anderson himself commented, "He had a vague notion that he, in common with almost all American men had got out of touch with things."[77] Like Kemp, Anderson looked to the working class for inspiration in stimulating men's primitive selves: "Workmen were like that, they thought of women only in one way. There was a kind of terrible matter-of-factness about working men."[78] Anderson's John Webster reminds us of many of the obsessions of Kemp's John Gregory. Webster is obsessed with his body. He, like Gregory, walks around naked. But this novel is much more blatant in its celebration of the violent aspects of masculinity. Webster symbolically rapes his daughter to make amends for her mother's unwillingness to have sexual intercourse with him. Anderson thought that this was justifiable behavior because "there was a kind of cruelty in nature and at the proper time that cruelty became a part of one's manhood."[79] Such an overt celebration of rape was not part of high Victorian ideology. And critics, noticing this, railed at Anderson at the time; one observed the book as a deviation from the "completely accepted code for the social relations between the sexes."[80]

Ben Hecht's *Erik Dorn* echoes these themes. Dorn steadily becomes entrapped in an unsatisfactory marriage. After he embarks on an affair, he fantasizes about murdering his wife, Anna: he says he "must kill her swiftly, before she could know that prayers were vain."[81] Dorn sets a low value on marriage: "Two little husks boring metronomically in a vacuum and anointing each other with pompous adjectives."[82] When he leaves Anna he sets off on the life of the tramp; he has been on the road "since the night he had walked out of his home and there had been no looking back."[83] But this does not change his contempt for women. He describes a girl he meets in a dance hall by writing that, "She's not a woman. . . . She's a lust. No brain. No heart. A stark unhuman piece of flesh with a shark's hunger inside it." It is "amusing to converse professionally with a pretty woman whose sole contributions to any dialogue are a bit of silk hose and an oscillation of the breast," Hecht wrote.[84] This kind of comment would hardly have been acceptable in Victorian America.

In Warner Fabian's notorious *Flaming Youth*, there are several characters from the world of upper-class youth. These included Leo Stanak, a Russian anarchist, who has "no belief in or use for society's instituted formulas: marriage, laws, government—nothing but the eternal right of the individual to express himself to the utmost in his chosen medium of life."[85] In Carl Van Vechten's *Firecrackers*, the Danish acrobat, Gunnar O'Grady, laments falling in love because he and his lover might meet the fate of many couples who have. He declares that "he [had] lost his freedom again." After all, "What was there to do in life? Conform to the action of the puppets, dull one's perceptions."[86] No, O'Grady desires complete freedom.

O'Grady is indeed a "Don Juan," a term that was often used in popular novels and one analogous to the tramp Bohemian style. In Gladys Johnson's *Desire* (1929), the aptly named Don Chansellor appears irresistible to women, taking them away from less attractive men. Johnson described how on the "first whistle from Don Chansellor" the heroine "was away— with no thought of this other tried but true friend."[87] In Percy Marks's *The Plastic Age*, the hero, Hugh, meets his new college roommate, whose exploits impress him: "Carl dazzled and confused him. He had often listened to the recitals of their exploits by the Merrytown Don Juans, but this good-looking, sophisticated lad evidently had a technique and breadth of experience quite unknown to Merrytown."[88] Carl's exploits continue to dazzle and confuse Hugh throughout the novel. Although the Don Juan was widely discussed, he remained just beyond the bound of respectability. Yet his success with women gained him admiration and envy. The tramp Bohemian who did not want to commit himself to marriage or to the role of breadwinner appeared in the writing of the youth culture, also, in the guise of the Don Juan, who was, of course, not a new figure in literature. But in the 1920s youth culture he gained renewed admiration.

Literary primitivism was perpetrated and reflected in the discovery of black culture by 1920s writers. Unquestionably, this work by white writers and black writers associated with the Harlem Renaissance enriched American culture as a whole and had a long-term positive effect in helping to turn the cultural and political tide in favor of blacks. But in looking at black men, as men, they all too often resorted to stereotypes; and, further, black women tended to appear as sex objects. Indeed, this genre aggravated the general cultural trend towards celebrating lower-class cultural models of masculinity, especially as it came at a very important time when blacks were migrating from the South to northern cities in general, and could begin to influence northern urban life. Eugene O'Neill is, perhaps, the most famous writer of this genre. In plays like *The Hairy Ape* and *Emperor Jones* he was one of the first to bring not only black culture but also the underworld ethos to the stage.[89] However, writers of lesser, but significant, talent, like Carl Van Vechten, DuBose Heyward, Sherwood Anderson, and Waldo Frank also explored black culture in their works. They openly celebrated black culture as more vital and spontaneous than white culture—as more instinctive and "sensual."[90] Sherwood Anderson insisted in *Dark Laughter* that the black man shared "an unconscious love of inanimate things lost to the whites—skies, the river, a moving boat—black mysticism."[91] Anderson's hero, Bruce, goes off in search of black life in New Orleans as a means of finding his primitive roots: "Perhaps the white man's getting on so fast in life . . . has cost them more than they had gained. They hadn't gained much."[92] Carl Van Vechten's search for authenticity in black New York attained such notoriety that in the contemporary popular song, "Go Harlem," the singer urged people to "go inspectin' " like Carl Van Vechten.[93] One of the white characters in his controversial *Nigger Heaven* (1925) declares that "the low life of your people is exotic. It has a splendid, fantastic quality. And the humour. How vital it is, how rich in idiom."[94] DuBose Heyward in *Porgy* wrote of blacks as emerging "out of the fetters of civilisation. Exotic as the Congo."[95] The black man was the ultimate primitive. Physically, he was more muscular, more masculine than the white man. Black men were, for Waldo Frank, "big fellows with flourishing mustaches, bushy brows. They are obscene with brutal energy."[96] Sherwood Anderson even more overtly referred to the "slender flanks. Like running horses—bodies like young Gods" of black men in New Orleans.[97] Similar descriptions of white men would not have been so acceptable, unless they were of the working class.

Similarly, stereotypical descriptions of black male attitudes towards women predominated. Violence towards women was the norm. In DuBose Heyward's *Porgy*, the protagonist, Crown, "snatched" the heroine "with such force that her breath was forced from her in a sharp gasp."[98] But women were meant to enjoy it—"Then she inhaled deeply, threw back her head and sent a wild laugh out."[99] Similarly, one of Van Vechten's female characters begs her violent boyfriend, "I'm your slave, your own Nigger. Beat me. I'm yours to do with what you please."[100] This was much stronger stuff than most of the images of the tramp Bohemian, but it indicated one direction in which the glorification of perceived working-class models of manliness were headed by the late 1920s: towards an imagined more virile, spontaneous, sexual, yet violent model that derived from perceptions of black manliness.

In this way, a group of writers associated with the youth culture of the 1920s advocated styles of manliness that were heavily influenced by the underworld styles of masculinity that they openly admired. They showed little respect for women. They were, at best, flippant about violence against women; at worst, they presented it as titillating. Further, they displayed ambivalence about commitment to getting or staying married. Though writing about their Greenwich Village experiences in the 1910s, the ex-Bohemians celebrated and sentimentalized their past while simultaneously spreading it as a spurious example to middle-class youth. In the form of the tramp Bohemian, styles of masculinity that had not been openly encouraged before, or that had been frowned upon, gained greater respectability as they became ascendant in the incipient youth culture. Significantly, they more and more overwhelmed the wimpy male flapper. After all, as critic Frederic Hoffman has noted, "There were probably more Erik Dorns than Amory Blaines or Felix Fays among the younger generation."[101]

This genre was also adopted by writers who have gained some notoriety for their attitude towards women. Hemingway's macho, boxing, bull-fighting characters, with what we would regard as their egregiously sexist attitudes, and Faulkner, who only respected postmenopausal women in his work, are the best examples.[102] And by 1930 the genre reached its acme, its apotheosis, in the tough-guy writers of the 1930s.[103] But literary primitivism reached broader social groups through the Western. Owen Wister's *The Virginian* (1902) had been considered quite risqué, but it was the work of Zane Grey that was the most popular of the Western mode in the 1920s. The earlier Westerns had been among the first areas of the culture to abandon more genteel mores, and Zane Grey's work continued in this tradition. Grey was remarkably Victorian. He saw himself as an opponent of the revolution in morals. He thus believed in chastity for women and chivalry for men. He published his stories in conservative journals like *The Country Gentleman* and *McCall's*: if the desert dropped men down to the "level of beasts," he wrote, then "primitive instincts" must be overcome.[104] Yet Grey was more complex: as regards models of masculinity, he often advocated something closer to underworld primitivism in that his tales were very violent. After all, he also published in youth culture journals like *Collier's*. He presented tough, virile cowboys—"hicks"—as heroes, and "cavemen."[105] For example, in *Stairs of Sand*, the hero's brother, thwarted by a woman, announces to her, "I want to beat you, violate you. . . . I'll make you cringe and crawl."[106] Randolph, the hero of *Lost Pueblo*, announces he will "take that young lady across my knee and spank her soundly."[107] The women love this, of course: "Be a brute to me," begs the heroine of this novel.[108] Grey's characters lack genteel pretensions. Sam, in *Under the Tonto Rim*, drawls, "She's a looker."[109] Savages though they are, Grey's protagonists are "somehow the better for it."[110] Zane Grey's Westerns enjoyed an enormous working- and middle-class audience. Although they were highly moralistic as regards sexuality, they still moved precariously between respectable and underworld primitive models. Literary primitivism pervades stories in the *Saturday Evening Post*. Violence is treated with flippancy in periodical literature that had once been a haven of respectability. Ben Hecht could celebrate "The Wife-Beating Wave" in *Collier's*, while Nina Putnam could flippantly comment on domestic violence in the *American Monthly* in the colorfully titled "Say It with Bricks."[111] Katherine Gerould, in an article entitled "Treat 'em Rough" in the October 1922 issue of *Harper's*, noted the larger shift in literature towards "the increasing prominence of the caveman." In the past, "We did not take away for Summer reading novels that showed gentlemen with the full approval of the author swinging their clubs like cavemen." Noting the popularity of the "Sheik," she observed that "twenty years ago, no popular author would have permitted an ultra-civilized hero to drag an egotistical wife into the solitudes and beat her." But in 1922 a million people read the novel and even more people saw the film.[112]

Such models of masculinity reached an even broader audience through the medium of *True Story*, the most popular pulp magazine of the 1920s. Macfadden spread underworld and Bohemian styles of masculinity to an ever-widening audience of working- and, most significantly, middle-class youth. The portrayals of men in these stories are a rich resource. They present a cultural ideal of masculine behavior that is quite consistent with the Bohemian styles characteristic of the emerging youth culture. *True Story*, after all, reached a large audience. Designed for both men and women, it affected both male readers and men involved with its predominantly female readership. Macfadden's confession magazines helped set the pace for the social relations between the sexes in the 1920s, when their outrageousness made them widely known. They presented underworld styles of behavior to both the youth of the working class and the consumer-oriented "new middle class" for whom their very nonrespectability heightened their appeal. The stories, scenes from the new public, heterosocial, youth-oriented leisure world, represented the intersection of the mores of the youth of the working and new middle classes in this period.

True Story presented the tramp Bohemian ideal in a less sophisticated, cruder manner, using vernacular. A typical story featured dissolute male

characters whom the heroine finds irresistibly attractive; the story, however, was ostensibly a warning that such men were to be avoided. Yet the
tramp Bohemians helped provide the spice that sold the stories and the
titillation that was Macfadden's underlying goal.

Significantly, Bohemians from Greenwich Village appeared in several
stories. In "How Life's Lessons Came to Me," the heroine avoids a Bohemian about whom she is warned by a friend:

> Allan is not a one woman man. He can love one woman but he cannot be
> true to her. That is his great weakness and it is such a great weakness that
> he cannot overcome it. If he marries again, he will be faithful to his wife
> for a while; but the lure to intimate associations with more than one woman
> will be too strong.[113]

In typical Bohemian fashion, Allan is quite unable to commit to one relationship, much less to marriage. In the "Little Cloud," the heroine is
stuck with a formerly monogamous husband who is converted to Greenwich Village–style relationships, much to her chagrin. In "Renee Finds
a Link," the heroine moves to the Village only to find that "offers of
marriage in the village were few."[114] Bohemian men were notoriously
unreliable, if always exciting. In "A Secondhand Bride," the heroine, bored
in her marriage to her husband George, meets an exciting Bohemian who
is "so different from anyone I had ever known before."[115] They exchange
both ideas and books. However, when the Bohemian falls in love with
her, this is the signal for him to flee to the mecca for all his ilk—Paris.
True Story presented a model of masculinity reminiscent of the tramp
Bohemian—unwilling to commit to more than short, sharp, sporadic relationships.

Such models of manliness were endemic in *True Story*. Macfadden's
writers specialized in tales of the horrors of Broadway life. In 1922, Macfadden devoted a lot of space over several months to the saga, "A Chorus
Girl Confesses," which details the dangers for women of male predators
on Broadway from the point of view of a woman who has passed her
prime. For example, when the heroine joins forces for a double act, her
partner, Rex, insists on having an affair with her since he has had affairs
with other partners.[116] This was after all, Broadway, where, as one *True
Story* puts it, a woman could go to date "swells" just like in the movies.[117]
But she could not expect love and commitment. The most pervasive Broadway character is the "Stage-Door Johnnie," the male groupie whom every
chorus girl feared:

Often, as I passed them, I noticed that they were gazing at me with an air of appraisal that began at my feet and ended with an interesting stare at my face. I pretended not to see them at all, however, and passed on with my head held high. Once I saw some young fellow nudge another and heard him say "Some looker." Inwardly I raged. What right had these men to stand there and look me over that way?[118]

When a woman became involved with one of these men, he would kiss her "against her will."[119] For the Stage-Door Johnnie was quite incorrigible. In "His Yesterdays," the hero, Livingston, has "innumerable love affairs" that bring his family newspaper notoriety.[120] Even when Livingston actually falls in love, stops drinking, and begins to show an interest in business, his friends suspect his reformation will not last. And it doesn't.[121] By the end of the story, he is keeping a Spanish dancer.

True Story is full of men who are unable to commit themselves to love or who, once married, no longer wish to stay so. Significantly, many of these men are not just exotic Bohemians or Stage-Door Johnnies but ordinary men. In "Can a Woman Come Back?" the heroine involves herself in a sorry affair with such a man: "As time went on, I found that love had indeed no deeper meaning to him. He seemed utterly incapable of seeing its spiritual aspect. Openly he boasted to me of his affairs with other women before we were married."[122] Another woman marries a "lady bug." As she resignedly puts it, "I suppose I must accept my husband for what he is— a lady-Bug."[123] It is hardly surprising that the "rolling stone" so admired by a later youth culture appeared here too.[124]

Macfadden's celebration of underworld and Bohemian styles of masculinity could not avoid a new and striking element that entered the ideology of masculinity. As never before in ideology that was read and digested by young Americans, especially those of the middle class, violence was, if not exactly glorified, then presented as a frequent part of interaction between men and women.

For the system that had long been designed to protect women broke down in Macfadden's world. Women always lived under the threat of violence in *True Story*. In "Suppose Your Husband Did This?" the wife of the hero, Richard, begins "to flirt in a mild way in order to keep the interest of the man," which stimulates the apparently exemplary Richard to declare, "I said I would spank you and I will."[125] He does. Yet, though this inevitably causes problems in their relationship, Richard gets away with such behavior when his wife again capitulates to his charms. Violence pays. Richard in this way escapes from the implications of his behavior.

And this story was not an anomaly in Macfadden's publications. The hero of "Nearly Trapped," Phillip Gaylor, to all intents and purposes rapes the heroine. He places her in a compromising situation and declares,

> "Say ... I've been wondering right along whether all that innocent stuff you've been pulling is a fake or not. ... What are you going to do now? You're all alone with me, remember. You could yell yourself hoarse without anybody ever hearing you."[126]

Macfadden's writers often presented aggressive male lovemaking as appropriate and attractive. In "Through the Valley of Death," the heroine's lover, Fred, is an "ardent, aggressive lover" who "swept [me] along with him."[127] In "The Fickleness of Men," the hero seizes the heroine:

> I snatched her into my arms and held her as in a vise. I smothered her face with my kisses. I was madly infatuated, infatuated beyond vision or hope. I could hold bounds no longer, nor did I want to. I thrust her from me, tingling in every atom of my being.[128]

In "The Girl Who Claimed My Husband," the heroine's ex-husband storms into her room, and she recalls that "the man then went mad. He seized my two hands and forcibly wrenched the telephone from my grasp."[129] Diligently, she awaits his return to her after he leaves her. In "Her Caveman Wooing," what appears to be a rape is presented in very positive terms:

> It was the early dusk of a February day as I hastened home from my Philosophy lecture. An auto passed at the curb, and before I knew what was happening to me, I was struggling vainly in an iron grip. The door slammed, the car started. ... Desperately I tried to keep my senses, everything was going black. "Do I have to chloroform you or will you promise not to scream?" a not unpleasing but firm voice asked.[130]

After this abduction, the hero declares, "I did not ask you to marry me. I said you were going to." However, it all turns out so well in the end, when the heroine insists, "Now we are just the lovingest family."[131] In a fit of passion in "Out of the Shadow," Lucifer Tombs grabs his girlfriend Effie: "Let me go. Lucifer you are hurting me," she screams.[132] Effie's pleadings are in vain: in Macfadden's dreamworld women are supposed to enjoy a little violence.

The Victorian Underworld Primitive had been checked by the "conspiracy of silence" as well as by the ideology of the Christian Gentleman who had seen himself as determinedly reverent to the women of his own class. This had perhaps limited and confined and oppressed women, but it had protected them from the worst men. But now these new styles attained relative respectability and were prescribed as appropriate behavior with middle-class women. This was ultimately pernicious, because such models encouraged youthful male irresponsibility and, most unpleasantly, presented violence against women positively. The rough and aggressive ideals of the youth culture of the 1920s were checked only by the male flapper who, while he was gentle and sensitive and more democratic, otherwise shared the characteristics of the tramp Bohemian. Women, and particularly New Women who could be assumed to be sexually independent, were left to the vagaries and whims of men, and men to their own worst behavior. Such conduct was, after all, presented as positive and attractive, which placed demands on men to act thus rather than according to the traditional codes of gentlemanly good behavior. In such an environment, it, of course, became harder to maintain "character."

Male Ideology and the Roots of
the Sexualized Society, 1910–1930

W hen James Thurber and E. B. White in 1929 asked the question *Is Sex Necessary?*, they encapsulated the confusion and frustration that many American men felt at the growing sexual demands of the previous two decades.[1] In a crescendo of sex films, sex plays, sex books, and sex education, the conspiracy of silence lost force, while the Victorian system of morality, designed to control male sexuality, cracked open in the 1910s.[2] If Victorian males feared both their potency and their impotency and both feared and celebrated their sexuality, now a public ethic that emphasized heterosexual sexual expression and performance rather than repression, and male potency over impotency, gained ascendancy.

By the 1920s there was widespread discussion of sex in American society. Writers exaggerated and accentuated the extent to which their attitudes towards sex had progressed from the Victorians. Floyd Dell, in particular, liked to elaborate on how the modern sexual world had advanced from the Victorian. Typically he referred to Victorians as "Puritans," as if there were no difference between the two. So, in *Janet March*, Dell's scandalous attempt to analyze the recent history of the American family, the hero,

Roger, is "too much of a Puritan" because he has his misgivings about sexual openness.[3] Dell railed at examples of such "Puritans": "the ascetic reformer or cleric who professes complete sexual holiness and occasionally is guilty of homosexual practices which he promptly crosses off his record because he is 'not really that kind of person' or 'the conventional girl who professes complete chastity and is able to forget and deny her occasional lapses when under the sudden and overwhelming domination of her repressed sexuality.' " Like others in the 1890–1940 period, he used the word "Puritan" to refer to a "sterile moralism": that is, as an all-encompassing critique of the Victorian sexual system and, in particular, against the public emphasis on purity.[4] For Dell advocated what he would have called "healthy sex adjustment," which meant that he encouraged, above all, uninhibited heterosexual expression, by exaggerating the extent to which Victorians believed in sexual repression.

Historian Christina Simmons has referred to this phenomenon of exaggerating Victorian prudery in the interests of advocating sexual expressiveness as the "myth of Victorian repression."[5] Other writers encouraged this myth. Ben Hecht was an especially good example. In *Erik Dorn*, one main character, Hazlitt, is described as a "Prude" to underline his undesirability: "For the paradox of Hazlitt was not that he was a thinker but a dreamer. His Puritanism had put an end to his brain."[6] One writer termed "Puritanism" a "dignified neurosis"—the Puritan was sexually obsessed and perverse: "No normal craving can be normally repressed. Nor can it be normally sublimated. Sexual desire cannot be transformed into artistic achievement, philanthropy, social usefulness."[7] One of the characters in Ludwig Lewisohn's *Stephen Escott* remarks on sex as "a sensation, mind you, which he himself, in the Puritan pervert way, considers dirty. And therefore he considers women dirty."[8] Repression had no value or worth.

The ubiquitous discussion of sex aggravated the pressures on men to act out by constantly inciting desire. The greater public visibility of the erotic that characterized the "repeal of reticence" has long been appreciated as a feature of 1920s culture. The promise of sexual satisfaction encouraged people to purchase the products of mass production. Sexual release and relief was the carrot that substituted for the loss of the autonomy that "character" had given the Self-Made Man. The preoccupation of youth with pleasure and private life kept the young firmly subdued and placated and refocused their attention away from citizenship and responsibility towards hedonism. In this way, elites and experts maintained their hegemony and control.

Therefore, writers who often imagined themselves to be subversive, in reality only helped to prop up American capitalism, and indeed helped it renew itself. Of course, explicit sex did not appear in mainstream literature at this time. Vivid descriptions of kisses were as far as most writers went. But such scenes were considered risqué. Fitzgerald was renowned for this. Typical was "the long fantastic kiss" Stephen Benet permitted the protagonists in *The Beginning of Wisdom*.[9] Hugh in *The Plastic Age* neglects "to mention the kiss" to his friends. "Shyness overcame any desire he had to strut. Besides, there was something about that kiss that made it impossible to tell anyone."[10] There was stronger material. Hecht in *Erik Dorn* had one of his women characters remove her "waist and shoes. . . . Shoulders suddenly bare."[11] Warner Fabian's lamely risqué *Flaming Youth* was described with wonderful innocence as "hot stuff" in a prominent review.[12] More deserving of this phrase was the genuinely scandalous *Jurgen*. Set in medieval times, this tale of a bold knight of old was mildly pornographic even by today's standards. In one scene, for example, a group of nymphettes "bathed" "Jurgen." They gave him "astonishing caresses . . . with the tongue, the hair, the fingernails, and the tips of the breasts,—and they anointed him with four oils, they dressed him again in his glittering shirt."[13] But *Jurgen* was a cause célèbre, not mainstream.

Usually this trend has been associated with the influence of Freud and the popularizers of instinct theory in general. They accepted the centrality of sexuality in human life. As George Henry Green explained, "Sex colours the whole of life, and the powerful instinct draws into its service practically every other instinct with which we are acquainted."[14] Therefore, "the problem of sex expression in youth" was one of the "first importance."[15] "Are you shackled by repressed desires?" asked one ad: "Psychoanalysis, the new miracle science, proves that most people live only half-power lives because of repressed sex instincts."[16] "Sex expression" was a panacea for some commentators. Yet the 1920s popularizers of instinct theory and of Freud left aside his respect for the power and force of male sexuality and his awareness of its need to be controlled if civilization were to be preserved. They misinterpreted Freud's insight that psychological adjustment and heterosexual adjustment were one to mean that healthy psychological adjustment was facilitated by having lots of sex.[17] An ideology that urged sexual expression in this way gained ascendancy over an ideology that emphasized repression.

The Freudian popularizers thus brilliantly adapted Freud to the hedonistic consumption-oriented mood of the 1920s. They assured that now "the center of gravity shifted from procreation to recreation."[18] This was the era of "passion's coming of age."[19] In this way, sexual demands and expectations on men increased during this period as experts insisted on the importance of good sex for psychological health. Not only could American men see youthful male heterosexual expression celebrated and glorified and equated with the attainment of manliness, but they also saw purity denigrated as "neurosis" and even "psychosis." It is no exaggeration to say that this refocusing of sexual ideology constituted a genuine sexual revolution.

Bernarr Macfadden, unsurprisingly, played a part in this development by actively encouraging sexual acting out. *True Story* and other confession magazines were often called the "sex appeal" magazines, especially until 1926, when they shifted focus in favor of "romance" over "sex." *Nation* editor Oswald Garrison Villard colorfully described them as "veracious narratives of titillating human experiences thrilling literally millions of readers."[20] Frederic Lewis Allen, the definer of the American 1920s, noted the cultural importance of *True Story* as part of the revolution in morals that he identified in his *Only Yesterday* (1931).[21] In "A Midnight's Memories" the heroine is swept away by the hero's passion. The author describes how "lower and lower the man's face dropped, while the woman waited in suspenseful bliss for the touch of his lips. They brushed hers softly and her being thrilled."[22] In the "Jungle's Shadow," the heroine is fortunate enough to have a lover "like a tropical thunderstorm in his wooing."[23] In "Keeping Up with the Crowd," the subject of premarital pregnancy, which a mere ten years before would have been unmentionable, is raised. Berry and his flapper stop off by a lake in an automobile: "It was still light when we stopped there, but we stayed on and made love under the moon. Those kisses seemed so innocent and perhaps would have been had our passions not been inflamed by drink."[24] The heroine becomes pregnant out of wedlock, though her reputation is fortunately saved by the hero's willingness to marry her.

But the confession magazines were only the beginning. In keeping with the unprecedented public obsession with sex in the 1920s, the period after World War I featured open and mass market erotica (if not pornography) on an unprecedented and recognizably modern scale, facilitated by modern mass production and marketing techniques. "Sex" was increasingly, as historians John D'Emilio and Estelle Freedman have observed, "on display."[25] Macfadden himself was able, after the 1924 founding of the *New York Evening Graphic*, to go several steps lower on the level of smut than he had dared to go in his confession magazines or in *Physical Culture*. Here any pretense at morality was cast to the winds. It should be noted that the readership of this "newspaper" was predominantly working class, far more than was the case with *True Story* or even *Physical Culture*. But a significant number of its readers were middle class.[26] And, unlike earlier material aimed at the working class, the paper was widely known because of the increasing intermingling of classes in New York. Because it was everywhere available for whomever wanted to buy it, its notoriety spread; indeed, it was known popularly with great accuracy as the "pornographic."[27] The editors sought to appeal to the red-blooded heterosexual male. One scandalous divorce case that featured domestic violence elicited from the *Graphic* a composite of the husband beating up his wife.[28] Macfadden even had his editor include a striptease in reverse in one issue under the guise of the "proper way to dress for the street."[29] Amid the increasingly sensational journalism of the 1920s, the *Graphic* stood out and was indeed widely reviled for its efforts to arouse and incite mass male desire.[30]

Sensational journalism such as that of the *Graphic* was one thing, but the wide availability of sexually explicit material was quite another. The Victorian underworld *Police Gazette* was the forerunner of the modern "girlie" magazine.[31] But by the turn of the century, even relatively respectable magazines like *Munsey's* and *Cosmopolitan* featured scantily clad women. Indeed, even the sensual, hourglass figure of Charles Dana Gibson's "Gibson Girl" in *Life* broke away ever more decisively from the restraints of the Cult of True Womanhood and of Victorianism in general.[32] But after 1910, the *Police Gazette* went into sharp decline in an environment of increasing openness about sexuality and as an accompanying burst of more outrageous magazines focused, significantly, on younger male readers.[33] For what was available by the 1920s was something different altogether.

Oswald Garrison Villard, in a 1926 *Atlantic Monthly* article, "Sex, Art, Truth, and Magazines," expanded on four types of sexually explicit material that were widely distributed by the middle 1920s.[34] The first was *True Story* itself. The second was the "Snappy Story" group. This was headed by William Randolph Hearst's *Snappy Stories* itself, with a circulation of 125,000. As early as 1914, this journal featured girls in bathing suits on its front cover. *Breezy Stories* had a similar circulation.

Villard identified a third, more explicitly sexual group of magazines, the "Artists and Models" variety, which presented nudity in the guise of art. Joseph Hershey, in his analysis of these magazines in *Pulpwood Editor*,

expanded in some detail on these journals. They included titles such as
Art Studies, *Art Poses*, *Art Models*, and *Art Albums*, which justified the
baring of female breasts in the name of art.[35] Journalist Will Irwin commented on how "the perils of young girls who hired out as artists' models
served for years as a recurring theme."[36] Increasingly, however, by the
late 1920s, such magazines as these and various movie magazines abandoned
the pretense of having a moral purpose and simply offered "plain and simple
pictures of nudes with no special technical or formal merit."[37] In doing
so they threw out a further vestige of moralistic Victorianism and added
to the sexualization of American society. There is some evidence that even
Villard's fourth variety, which was the most intriguing and, easily, the most
modern, also became widely available. This group he dismissed with the
conclusion that a representative issue was "the acme of vulgarity; its pages
are lined with the kind of jokes commercial travelers have always revelled
in, and the coarse humor to be found in low music-halls the world over."[38]
This is not surprising, because these magazines came closest to traversing
the delicate line between erotica and pornography. They represented, in
many ways, a constant that never changed. If Villard railed at them in the
1920s, Anthony Comstock had fought them in the previous two generations.
Yet Villard's insistence on their wide availability suggests that it became
harder for a respectable young man not to be lured by their temptations.
These magazines included *Hot Dog* and also *Whizz Bang*, *Paris Nights*, *Hi-
Jinks*, *Happy Howls*, and *Red Pepper*, which "struck to the burlesque theme
with huge success."[39] *Hot Dog* sold hundreds of thousands of copies at a
quarter apiece. According to Villard, such magazines were "openly displayed on hundreds of stands."[40] Nor were most of these stands merely
in New York but, quite the contrary, if Villard is to be believed, they were
available throughout the country:

> Let any Doubting Thomas go on a tour of inspection and see for himself.
> Mr. Frank Kent took a venturesome journey last Summer into a hitherto
> terra incognita—the five thousand inhabited towns between the *Baltimore
> Sun* and San Francisco, our only bulwark against the unmoral Japanese.[41]

Mr. Kent, the famous journalist, testified to his horror that "a lot of these
little towns seem literally saturated with sex."[42] If anything, this material
was even better received among the middle classes of Middletown than
on the East Coast because "the small town people . . . respond more keenly
to the new literature because they, having more leisure than big town

dwellers, are always more avid readers of all sorts of periodicals."[43] He reported that in Steubenville, Ohio, "Out of 110 publications in a single store 68 were either out-and-out smut or bordering on the line."[44] Villard concluded that "what Mr. Kent represents of the five-thousand-person town is true all the way up. The new publications are to be found everywhere."[45] This was therefore hardly a phenomenon that was confined to big-city dens of iniquity but one that had infiltrated even the rural Midwest.

Material that had previously been confined to the Victorian underworld was now relatively more openly displayed and widely distributed among the middle classes. It was more difficult for men of the middle classes, wherever they were in the United States, to avoid such encouragements of sexual arousal and sex expression. These magazines helped accentuate and accelerate the sexual demands on men after the war. In general, the demands were for heterosexual expression. In one area only, and then only rarely and marginally, did the glorification of male sexual expression not identify as vehemently and aggressively heterosexual. This was in portrayals of masturbation. Mostly, writers at this time remained as strong in their opposition to masturbation as had the Victorians. Social hygienist Winfield Scott Hall, for example, declared that the "natural process of development from youth to manhood could be seriously interfered with by the act of masturbation or self-abuse."[46] Indeed, if he continued to practice it, "the youth might almost have no testicles."[47] Further, according to sex educator E. B. Lowry, "older boys who are masturbating usually get a sallow look and have a hang-dog expression."[48] Clearly, there was disapproval in sex manuals of this kind of sexual practice; this was a continuation of Victorian patterns. In some manuals, however, there were signs of liberalization. Social hygienist Frederic Gerrish, in his *A Talk to College Boys*, admitted that "in general the health is not ruined, as is alleged in the quack adverts that deface and disgrace some journals." Still, he opposed onanism; for Gerrish "the fact remains that the practice is low, filthy, bestial and degrading."[49] But others were much less equivocal. Leading liberalizer W. J. Robinson was even relatively enthusiastic:

> The evil results of masturbation have been shamefully and stupidly exaggerated. In the vast majority of cases masturbation leads to no disastrous results and it is better for a man who cannot satisfy his sex instinct naturally to indulge in occasional masturbation.[50]

Sex manual writer W. H. Robie followed up this pragmatic approach: "Occasional masturbation is for many single people a necessity to prevent

marital disorders or the moral contamination of promiscuous sex relations."[51] But he also acknowledged that "the fact remains that most of the
peculiarities and new disturbances of youth and many of those of adult
years are due to masturbation." How could this paradox be explained?
"Quite easily. Practically all young people masturbate at one time or
another"[52]—which sounds strikingly modern. This was a very significant
admission. Masturbation was perhaps the greatest taboo in Victorian sex
manuals, which devoted pages and pages to its ill effects and delineated it
as if the practice were the root of all evil. Although elements of the older
attitude remained predominant, by the 1920s the solitary vice was, if certainly not encouraged, much more tolerated. Even in this area, then, men
began to sense some demand to express themselves sexually.

If masturbation did not explicitly presume heterosexuality, the vast majority of writings on sexuality did. In the 1920s, the term "heterosexual"
came into widespread public use. Floyd Dell used it throughout his *Love
in the Machine Age* (1930).[53] And in 1925, over twenty years before Kinsey,
Joseph Collins set the heterosexual ideal firmly against the homosexual in
his popular sex manual, *The Doctor Looks at Love and Life*.[54] The writers
of the youth culture, too, in their advocacy of heterosexuality, railed against
homosexuality. The categorization of a homosexual person was a relatively
new phenomenon. Until Victorian times, homosexuality was regarded in
the West as a sin that anybody could commit: homosexual acts did not
define a whole person. Victorians kept quiet about their homoerotic desires
and relegated them with their other desires to the underworld.[55] In the
late nineteenth century, German technical writers Karl Ulrich and Richard
von Krafft-Ebing first devised the "medical model" of homosexuality,
which attempted to identify particular types of persons who were homosexuals. By 1898, English sexologist Havelock Ellis, in his *Sexual Inversion*,
was discussing different types of homosexuals: in such literature a person's
homosexuality became central to his (or indeed her) identity.[56] As philos-
opher Michel Foucault put it so well, "The Sodomite had been a temporary
aberration: the homosexual was now a species."[57] In effect, these writers
took their ideas from underworld concepts of homosexuality, where the
existence of a "homosexual pervert" was well understood.[58] Ellis was extremely influential in the United States during this period, especially among
sex manual writers. Indeed, his influence is a far more direct one than
Freud's, whose ideas about the universal prevalence of bisexuality at certain
stages of life were truly sensational at the time.[59]

The extent to which the medical model actually influenced popular
discourse and practice remains unclear. But what is most important is that

a view of the homosexual as defining a whole person—a view prevalent both in the medical model and in the underworld sexual subculture—appeared in respectable literature that was read by the young of the middle classes at this time. Further, the homosexual was specifically presented as the antithesis of the heterosexual, the male ideal. Indeed, in many ways, by the 1920s, men's fear of effeminacy, which had characterized the "masculinity crisis" of the Progressive Era, was diffused into a fear of the new category, the homosexual. This added a whole new dimension to the sexual demands and expectations on men. For in the modern world, not only were men pressured to be sexual more than ever, but any impotence or effeminacy was equated with homosexuality. In public discourse this was now regarded as defining a whole person. Therefore any homosexual desire a young man might feel now caused him to fear that he was a homosexual person rather than someone tempted merely to commit a sin, albeit a rather venal one.

Floyd Dell, for example, who found that his psychoanalysis revealed that he himself had "a great deal of unconscious homosexuality, and a variety of other frightful-sounding traits," featured occasional homosexual characters in his fiction to set against the heterosexual ideal.[60] In *The Briary-Bush*, Felix Fay, new to Chicago, after encountering one of the hazards of the city, a rather effeminate homosexual, discusses him with a girlfriend:

> "But are these airs natural to him or is he just putting them on to impress people? Where is he from?"
> "Guess?"
> Felix thought he saw a light.
> "London?"
> The girl laughed again.
> "Arkansas or what?"[61]

Harry Kemp, too, featured several effeminate characters who were presented as the opposite of the "physical culture" ideal. One character, Jack Matthewson, "possessed a slight effeminateness about his too regular classic features—but the effeminacy extended no further than his features."[62] In Percy Marks's *The Plastic Age*, the hero, Hugh, speculates on why the fraternity initiation demands "the freshmen strip." He concludes that "there was something phallic about the proceedings that disgusted him," which implies disgust at the homoerotic implications of the ceremony.[63] There are several such characters in the fiction of F. Scott Fitzgerald, who was himself suspected of having homosexual tendencies by his wife Zelda, according to Gore Vidal.[64] In *Tender Is the Night*, the monocled Campion at least manages "somehow to restrain his most blatant effeminacy."[65] But later he lets go: "'I can't stand it,' he squeaked, almost voiceless; 'It's too much. This will cost me.'"[66] Later, psychologist Dick Diver interviews the young character Francisco with Freudian aplomb about his homosexuality. In this case, "there was some manliness in the boy, perverted now into an active resistance to his father. But he had that typically roguish look in his eyes that homosexuals assume in discussing the subject."[67]

Sinclair Lewis also loathed homosexuals, although he added the typical twist of seeing the phenomenon as part and parcel of a decadent Europe. His semi-autobiographical *Dodsworth* (1929) features the upright, uptight all-American, Sam Dodsworth, being dragged by the dubious German, Kurt, into what sounds like a gay bar:

> Their new venture in restaurants was called "Die Neuste Ehe,"—"The Latest Style in Marriage"—and after two minutes' view of it, Sam concluded that he preferred the old style. Here, in a city in which, according to the sentiment of the American comic weeklies, all males were thick as pancakes and stolid as plow-horses, was a mass of delicate young men with the voices of chorus girls, dancing together and whispering in corners, young men with scarves of violet and rose, wearing bracelets and heavy symbolic rings. And there was a girl in lavender chiffon—only from the set of her shoulders Sam was sure that she was a man.

There is worse in store for poor, beleaguered Sam:

> As they entered, the bartender, and a very pretty and pink-cheeked bartender he was, waved his towel at them and said something in a shrill playful German which Sam took to signify that Kurt was a charming person worthy of closer acquaintance, that he himself was a tower of steel and a glory upon the mountains. It was new to Sam.
>
> He stood gaping. His fists half clenched. The thick, reddish hair on the back of his hands bristled. But it was not belligerence he felt—it was fear of something unholy. He saw that Fran was equally aghast, proudly he saw that she drew nearer his stalwartness.[68]

Robert McAlmon, in his short story "Distinguished Air," adopted a similar device but was even more viciously homophobic. He featured two Americans on a tour of Berlin gay bars with what he called a "fag artist," Foster:

"Goodness me, Marjorie, I just love art. I love art," Foster minced, unable to be directed for over a moment. "Will there be some pictures of naked boys? I just love art. It's too exquisite. So glad you asked me along."[69]

The narrator also goes to Berlin, where he meets more such people:

"Whoops, dearie, I see you," sounded a falsetto voice, faking feminine tones. "Sisters Adlon are with us." The speaker, I noticed, was a man who had dined at a table near ours when we were at the Adlon Hotel. "I'll show these boys that us Americans aren't tight with money."

While he was there an elderly fairy, well known to various psychoanalysts in Germany, came into the place. This night he was dressed up as a blond-haired doll, and his fat old body looked in its doll's dress much like that of a barn-storming burlesque sobrette grown a generation or so too old.[70]

Writers often speculated about and perceived an increase in homosexuality as an unfavorable development against the desirable heterosexual goal. Ludwig Lewisohn, in *Stephen Escott* (1930), included a lengthy discussion that directly suggests that the changes in women's roles would lead to an increase in homosexuality among men. If women could no longer uplift men, the result would be homosexuality:

"Primitive men in the tribes I've mentioned would never sustain that wound nor require its healing, nor would an Arab who saves money and buys a wife and saves more money and buys another. It is we who seek the angel image; it is we who need our mates to uplift us from the crushed estate of our youth. Or else the men of the West, like the men of Greece, will find another object for their ideal cravings and seek another Eros." He stopped short. "Am I shocking you?" David had grown very grave. "Not in the least. There is a distinct increase in homosexuality already. Go on."[71]

As these witnesses and many more suggest, by the 1920s, men's fear of effeminacy was diffused into a vilification of homosexuality in the literature of the youth culture. Effeminacy of any kind was placed under suspicion, for some of men's fear of impotence, by the 1920s, took the form of a fear of homosexuality.

Similar evidence appeared in the sex and marriage manuals and the work of the Freudian popularizers of the 1920s. The ending of the conspiracy of silence about sexuality in general also meant the ending of the conspiracy of silence about homosexuality. The sex manual writers, like the youth culture writers, seized on the Underworld Masculine Primitive ideal and medical model of the homosexual as a person defined by his sexuality and made this model public. One popularizer, for example, diagnosed "the passive male homosexual" as "in every case the son of a widow or divorced mother, separated from her husband by death, desertion or legal proceedings soon after the boy's birth."[72] The flamboyant Samuel Schmalhausen was convinced that "for aught I know homosexuals may be winning armies of new recruits." He warned boys not to "frequent public toilets, for many perverts watch these places and entice boys into submitting to their desires."[73] Even more influential, because of the millions of copies sold, were the works of Clement Wood, James Oppenheim, and William J. Fielding. Oppenheim, having referred positively to some homosexuals in *The Common Sense of Sex*, speculated on the cause of homosexuality as "an excessive sexual craving."[74] But what was perhaps even more disturbing to the middle classes was the widespread discussion of the prevalence of homosexuality in adolescence. Clement Wood, for example, went into great detail about this. He even provided figures. Thus in *Manhood: The Facts of Life Presented to Men*, he wrote of the boy of twelve's sex interests:

Autosexuality	40%
Homosexuality	50%
Heterosexuality	10%

At puberty, the red-blooded heterosexual fathers had less to fear of their sons:

Autosexuality	20%
Homosexuality	30%
Heterosexuality	50%[75]

It was, however, Joseph Collins's *The Doctor Looks at Love and Life* that was one of the biggest sellers among sex manuals in the 1920s. Yet Collins devoted relatively little space to heterosexuality: a third of the book was given over to homosexuality, which firmly brought the subject into the American middle-class home a full generation before Kinsey. Collins stimulated the fear among young men that they, too, could be homosexual:

There are persons who indulge in unnatural sexual relations who are not homosexuals. They are the real degenerates. There are many potential and actual homosexuals whose intercourse with persons of their own sex is confined to emotional and intellectual contact; to establish romantic friendship with them.[76]

Collins generally regarded the homosexual as effeminate. Any effeminacy in a man could make his sexual orientation suspect. But what was worse was that Collins established that one could be both masculine and homosexual. Any homosexual desire a young man might feel could make him suspect that he was a homosexual person:

Strangely enough, many people think that masculine [i.e. male] homosexuals are invariably timid, shy, retiring, fastidious, dainty even, and what is popularly called effeminate. Some are but many are not. I have known husky, articulate, self-opinionated and even domineering ones. Indeed, most of them ... have what is known as a superiority complex which they conceal.[77]

Contrasted to this, according to Collins, was "the other extreme ... the man of broad hips and mincing gait, who vocalizes like a lady and articulates like a chatterbox, who likes to sew and knit, to ornament his clothing and decorate his face."[78] What is so striking in Collins's discussion is his suggestion that homosexuals were literally everywhere, which revelation can only have added to male anxieties:

I know that my counsel as physician has frequently been sought by them and that I see many persons in clubs, churches, theaters, busses and the street who have somatic and gestural manifestations which are frequently associated with it, and voices and manners that its victims often have.[79]

Historian Gilman Ostrander has commented, rightly, on how, too, the openness about adolescent homosexual desire was genuinely new at the time, and it therefore added to sexual anxieties.[80]

The portrayal of homosexuality was sometimes relatively sympathetic. McAlmon, showing the ambivalence that many Americans felt within their homophobia, in "Distinguished Air" featured two of his heterosexual characters discussing their observation of homosexuals and concluding, "Nothing to be added, I guess. We all do what we do and will do, so it might as well be flagrant, I suppose."[81] Oppenheim referred to "a certain percentage of men, relatively small, who seem more like the victims than the willing practitioners of homosexuality. The overwhelming prejudice against them, the fact that they cannot escape their doom, the often effeminate traits that give them away, make them as a rule, pitiable objects."[82] While W. J. Robinson thought homosexuality "a sign of degeneracy," he called for an end "to all stupid laws against homosexuality."[83] Further, at this time the Chicago Society for Human Rights was formed, the first homosexual advocacy group.[84] While undoubtedly the 1920s, therefore, saw the beginning of a liberal view of homosexuality, the overwhelming tenor was still what we would call homophobic, because of the pressure to be heterosexual.

The emphasis on heterosexuality reached its acme in a celebration of male potency. Judge Lindsey reveled in adolescent male sexuality, describing it as "animal" and therefore healthy.[85] Popular writers titillated their readers with descriptions of excited men. In Percy Marks's spoof of college life, *The Plastic Age*, the hero, Hugh, is "lashed by desire, he was burning with curiosity" at the prospect of visiting a prostitute.[86] Warner Fabian's *Flaming Youth* is full of males who experience their sexuality somewhat melodramatically as their strongest urge: "The terrible fiery desire seized him to claim her there and then and there, to bid her leave everything for love and go with him to the ends of the earth, to overwhelm her with the force of his desire."[87] Fabian portrayed male potency positively, but not every writer was as explicit or romantic as Samuel Schmalhausen, who implored,

> Can't youth be taught to accept his sex more sweetly? More proudly and more reverently? The wonderful phenomenon of his sexuality, wonderful as science, as poetry, as mysticism are love worthy! His body is lovable, his young manhood inspiring, his sexual yearning the source of poetry and dream and gentleness.

With growing clamor, he went on:

> In man's quivering limbs the fire of life burns luminous and strong. His sexual potency is remarkable,—if anything, in excess of human nature's civil demands. . . . Sexually, man is still a wonderfully potent savage.[88]

Male sexuality was thus publicly celebrated. Previously such an extremely positive view of male potency would have been confined to the Underworld Primitive ideal. Though this view was still not entirely respectable, its public visibility marked a sharp contrast from Victorian mores. No wonder one writer has quoted a wit as saying that Schmalhausen's tract *Why We Misbehave* should have been retitled "Why We Should

Misbehave."[89] Quite simply, male potency was celebrated more and more as it was feared less.

This trend continued in sex/marriage manuals. These mass-produced best-sellers, especially those of the Haldeman-Julius Company, publicly advocated the Underworld Primitive style of male sexuality. W. J. Fielding wrote that "in man the sexual impulse takes a more dynamic turn than is the case with women."[90] William Robinson described male sexuality as "man's most dynamic urge." He wrote that "in man the sex instinct is primary and the paternal instinct secondary and latent while in woman the maternal instinct is primary and the sex instinct secondary and latent."[91] James Oppenheim wrote similarly that "the man is swift, ready, and active, the woman slow, unresponsive and passive."[92] Also, as Clement Wood put it, "the average man comes to his passion quickly and after his orgasm, it dies as quickly. The average woman mounts far more slowly towards the crest of her passion."[93] Victorians had held a similar view of the dynamism of male sexuality but regarded this as proof its power should be checked; there was none of this here, only an uncritical celebration of potency. Perhaps because of the high value placed on male sexuality in these same popularizations, effeminization was man's worst fear. As Jungian popularizer James Oppenheim explained, "If the fear of impregnation is woman's chief fear that of man is often the fear of impotence."[94] Oppenheim thought that this was an appropriate fear because "the so-called he-men of America are fond of affirming that they are red-blooded and masculine through and through. Neither of these statements can bear any serious consideration."[95] William Robinson was even more trenchant about this question when he wrote, "And I repeat . . . an impotent man is a more pitiable man than a venereally infected one."[96]

The hugely influential Margaret Sanger saw the effeminization of men as a problem, too, observing that "the great danger in this day is not that it [sex] be too recklessly romantic, but that it [sex] be too tamely accepted, too anaemic, too lifeless. The woman pursuing, the man passively accepting."[97] Victorian repression lay at the root of such effeminacy because "inhibited and restrained by the false restrictions of so-called polite society, too many repressed young men take up the task of love-making in too tame and effete a style."[98] On top of the pressure to have sex and to be heterosexual there therefore appeared also the pressure to be potent.

No wonder two groups of writers were especially concerned with the social relations between the sexes: in the 1910–1920 decade, the social hygienists, and in the 1920–1930 decade, the companionate marriage writers.

According to historian Christina Simmons, the social hygienists, while trying to preserve the old system of morality, in fact inadvertently helped stimulate a new morality, while the companionate marriage writers tried to devise new controls over male sexuality to replace the crumbling barriers.[99]

The American Social Hygiene Association was a product of the growing awareness of the presence of venereal diseases among prostitutes and the realization that through the prevailing double standard of morality it was highly likely that men who had visited prostitutes could transmit venereal diseases to their wives and offspring. The organization attempted to spread knowledge about the terrible effects of venereal diseases and, given this concern, they encouraged purity as an ideal for men. They insisted that "the prospective husband should be sexually just as pure as he expects his future wife to be."[100] In other words, a single standard of morality was to be rigorously enforced. Thomas Galloway recommended "a continent life."[101] Irving Steinhardt was more unequivocal: "The sexual relation is absolutely unnecessary to you or to any other man."[102] But similarities with Victorian purity advocates were only superficial, for social hygienists were one of the first groups to deride Victorianism by emphasizing the "myth of Victorian repression." They in fact mocked the lofty Victorian ideal of asceticism and purity as irrational. They preferred to enforce purity by rigorous social control. Whereas Victorians regarded male sexuality as dangerous, the social hygienists denied any religious or moral reasons for sexual control. As major social hygiene writer Max Exner put it, that sexual desire might be a "sin or a cause for self-reproach and shame is false and pernicious. Youth must not be taught that the sex nature is to be repressed because it is shameful but that it must be controlled and refined because of its dignity and power."[103] Social hygienists therefore celebrated male sexuality. They favored purity before marriage, but only as a means of better enjoying disease-free fulfillment *in* marriage. This, following the pattern of the time, accelerated demands on men: put simply, sexual pleasure in marriage was a desirable goal.

Also, ironically, as the first organization to breach publicly the conspiracy of silence about sex, most especially by giving sex education to children outside the home, the American Social Hygiene Association represents the very cutting edge of the revolution in morals for men. By breaking this central tenet of the Victorian system of morality, it brought the Underworld Masculine Primitive right out on the center stage of public discussion. Despite the emphasis on purity, social hygiene writers did not argue with the Underworld Primitive understanding of masculinity. Winfield Scott Hall, for example, declared,

> Manhood has been called virility. For want of a better word this term has been applied to the sum total of the male qualities of any animal whatsoever, so that the male qualities of the stallion are also encompassed in the term virility.[104]

Thomas Galloway wrote that "in man . . . desires are strongly defined, can be aroused almost any time when in health."[105] Thus the social hygienists tried to establish a feeble public ethic based on rationality that demanded male continence without the safety valve of prostitution.

But perhaps even more significant was the almost cavalier way in which the social hygienists went about their sex education. True, much sexual instruction remained euphemistic and squeamish, though, crucially, it was even then innovative in that it was always public, but as historian John Burnham has shown, "the most pious and unsubstantial purity pamphlet might stand next to detailed medical works on sexual perversion by Richard von Krafft-Ebing and Venyamin Tarmowsky."[106] This was unprecedented: here was a major, respectable organization that openly encouraged sexual fulfillment. In this way, the social hygienists inadvertently contributed to the breaching of the conspiracy of silence. Hence they undermined the controls over male sexuality and accelerated demands on men by suggesting the desirability of erotic liberation in a way not so entirely distant from that advocated by Greenwich Village Bohemians.

This was, after all, one of the great propaganda campaigns of American history. In particular, it is likely that the social hygienists' direct influence on the revolution in morals was not so much through sex education for children begun in 1913 but through their enrollment in the extraordinary anti–venereal disease campaign of the American army in World War I.[107] This is worth examining in some detail. By this time the social hygienists had virtually become a branch of the government and had taken several organizations under their wing. They had therefore gained confidence. The American Expeditionary Force adopted an elaborate policy designed to prevent men from taking advantage of French prostitution. Demands on men were again accelerated by the manner in which the social hygienists emphasized purity as utility: obviously, the AEF had indeed to be "fit to fight," but also they encouraged airmen, soldiers, and sailors to be chaste to preserve their health. Ultimately, the justification for avoiding venereal disease was to gain fulfillment in marriage later on. But in the meantime, the lurid discussion of sexual disease broke the conspiracy of silence.

The strictures against VD were very powerful. Men could be prosecuted or court-martialed just for having a venereal disease, and they were subjected to vigorous propaganda to keep them celibate. "Will you be a free Man or in Chains?" declared one poster, while another, picturing a family, ordered, "Get back to them Physically Fit and Morally Clean."[108] Here they were successful. The incidence of venereal disease in the U.S. Army in the world war was remarkably low, although this may not have reflected the success of the social hygienists so much as the discipline of the army. One-third of unmarried white men were chaste, one survey showed, while for the year ending August 31, 1918, only 126 out of a thousand men were treated for venereal disease.[109] Educator G. Stanley Hall was brought in to discuss how sports could reduce sex urges, for "every young man has athletic sympathies and he can be shown that purity is the best way of keeping the body at the very top of its condition."[110] The social hygienists conducted studies of sexual behavior, distributed sex information to the troops, and made the film, *Fit to Fight,* which was unequivocal in its message and was one among many facets of the campaign. According to John B. Watson, who was involved in the making of the film, it sought to teach

1. That continence is in no way injurious to health. . . .
2. That seminal emissions are not harmful unless occurring more frequently than twice a week.
3. That venereal diseases are very serious and may lead to total disability.
4. That venereal diseases are the result of infection by microorganisms.[111]

The film went on to show how syphilis could be transmitted "by a kiss from a prostitute."[112] The movie also discussed the fact "that both gonorrhea and syphilis required persistent and long-continued treatment."[113] The hygienists advised that "the government maintains recreation rooms for soldiers and that various forms of wholesome recreation may serve as a substitute for the bawdy house."[114] These strictures were certainly powerful. They reinforced "the old Puritan view that crime and punishment were mechanically related."[115] Yet the threat that one might get a venereal disease was not as strong as the fear that one might, for example, go to hell.

Further, some more traditional purity campaigners were highly suspicious that many social hygiene administrators were "insensitive to moral considerations."[116] To some extent this was justified. One hygienist in effect all but encouraged his soldiers to indulge: "Does any red-blooded man feel any doubt of his ability to preserve his manhood though tempted by the alluring seductions of voluptuous and beautiful women in the whirl and excitement of the gay metropolis, or the fascinations that may come to you from delicate and devoted attentions in the solitude of remote billets?"[117] However, sexual demands were most clearly accentuated in the sheer emphasis on ultimate sexual pleasure—"supreme experience"—which continence in the present would facilitate in the future.[118] Men's sweethearts were shown awaiting their arrival home still pure and undiseased. For social hygienists in the war were able to emphasize sexual pleasure in marriage to ever-larger groups; as one pamphlet put it, "Sex power is not lost by laying off"—that is, pleasure was only to be deferred.[119] In this way, through the film and the whole campaign in general, it was quite impossible for a doughboy not to know about the centrality of passion and orgasm to sex. The organization thus set the scene for the 1920s.

For in the materialistic, hedonistic, consumption-oriented twenties, the breaking of the old sexual system accelerated. To cope with the "revolt of youth," the changing position of women, and the greater availability of birth control, a number of reformers attempted to redefine the sexual system.[120] Like the social hygienists and Victorians before them, they found it desirable to control male sexuality. They therefore advocated purity for men before marriage.

But sex as erotic pleasure as well as spiritual union nevertheless came to play a greater part in marriage ideology in the 1920s. This is entirely consistent with the larger cultural celebration of sex expression. This further exacerbated the sexual demands and expectations on men by stressing male performance. Samuel Schmalhausen, for example, asked, "What in truth is the meaning of marriage if it is not sexual felicity?"[121] Haldeman-Julius Company sex manual writer William Fielding declared, "But what is love, even in its noblest form, but the supreme refinement of the sexual impulse?"[122] While the spiritual side remained important, the erotic side of sexuality was more and more emphasized. Marriage counselor Ira Wile wrote,

Sex communion possesses esthetic and spiritual attributes that are far more significant perhaps than the sensual phases which at the present time are seemingly in the foreground of public thought. This does not, however, mean that the physical side of sex life is not of tremendous importance.[123]

Margaret Sanger declared that for "enduring happiness in marriage" to be attained, "Love is essential. Passion is essential. Virility is essential."[124] In this world erotic sex was given an increasingly central role in marriage.

These developments alone exacerbated demands and expectations on men. But, in addition, much of the onus for the success of the sex act was placed on men. Men were expected to stimulate women. Marriage counselor Paul Popenoe declared in 1925 that "after marriage it is the husband's part to show his aptitude in arousing and maintaining the responsiveness of his wife."[125] Indeed, "the woman's desire needs to be actively aroused."[126] Above all, the emphasis in the manuals was on sex expression as pleasure for its own sake. In contrast, the late Victorian marriage manuals had emphasized spiritual union and referred to the physical aspects of sexuality euphemistically and not in the increasingly specific detail of the 1930s.[127]

Writers in the 1920s attempted to devise a new masculine sexual ideal that was subtle, intricate, and complex. It was also genuinely demanding. Indeed, if men were to take the ideal seriously, it would require almost superhuman concentration and assurance. Directly influenced by the British writer Havelock Ellis, whose chapter 6 of *The Psychology of Sex* was entitled "The Art of Love," writers of marriage/sex manuals repeatedly emphasized the concept of "artfulness" and of "skillfulness."[128] Thus, several writers followed Ellis in entitling a chapter of their manuals "The Art of Love."[129] Writer Charles Malchow declared that if a man did not continue when a woman begged him not to, he had then "not progressed very far in 'the art of love'." In this way he encouraged rape.[130] Sanger insisted that a man be a "skillful husband."[131] He must not "neglect the task of preparing his beloved for their mutual flight together. . . . He must awaken her senses and her soul. . . . He alone can accomplish this." Further, he must, "like a skillful driver, at every moment hold herself under intelligent control." For the Binkleys, the act of sex should be "fully developed aesthetically" and should reach its "full beauty."[132]

While this demand was onerous enough, the increasingly specific instructions for men required attention. Men were required to perform in bed. Men were to be masterly. Every young husband had to learn that "to be the master of his passion instead of its slave is the first essential rule in love etiquette every young husband must learn."[133] He must juggle "passion with compassion."[134] A "magic male manipulation" of women was the secret of the success of the sex act.[135] This should be no hardship for the husband "if he be a true lover."[136] But while being masterly, he was also supposed to display "tenderness" and "gentle manhood."[137] He should thus be extra careful "not to permit the weight of his body to hold down his wife."[138] The husband's caresses could be likened to the gentle touches of a "composer whose fingers begin an improvisation on a keyboard of his piano." He should "take plenty of time,"[139] "avoid hurry," "avoid violence," yet "remember that true strength may and should express itself gently."[140] A lack of tenderness could cause "alterations in the love-life" for the worse.[141] Indeed, "only disaster can result."[142] Not all of the experts brought out the contradiction in the ideal as clearly as Sanger, who at one point called for "aggressive gentleness."[143]

Ultimately, the call for "mutuality" was the most pervasive in the manuals, and this served to accelerate the tensions and anxieties. The marriage manuals reflect the fact that women were expected to demand greater sexual satisfaction. Gone at last was the ideology of Victorian "passionlessness." Thus, for Paul Popenoe, after marriage, "Sexual intercourse plays fully as large a part in the life of the average wife as it does in that of the average husband."[144] Poet and sex manual writer Clement Wood feared a "passion that leaves the woman unsatisfied."[145] YMCA marriage expert Sherwood Eddy asked whether the sex act be "mutual or one-sided and does it mean the same thing to both parts?"[146] For Paul Popenoe, complete "mutuality" was essential.[147] This idea culminated in what Michael Gordon has called the "cult of the mutual orgasm."[148] In the future, even the wedding night would be blissful:

> Such a first meeting of bride and bridegroom will be no raping affair. They will mingle in a unity the most perfect and blissful that can ever be experienced by human beings in this world.[149]

For the Binkleys, the most central part of the entire "artistry of marriage" was the mutual orgasm:

> If the man reaches the orgasm too quickly the woman will fail to experience it at all. The man who understands the physiology of sex can often correct such disharmonies by taking pains more amply to stimulate the tumescent process in the woman, while restraining the process in himself, thus compensating for physiological differences.[150]

The secret of "happiness in marriage" was male control. Ira Wile well understood that for men, "real sex communion called for self-control and for consideration of the interests of the loved one."[151] For Margaret Sanger, the man's role was the most "controlled part of the act of sex."[152] As these writers called for a modern man, they expected him to control his sexuality, which, like the Victorians before them, they saw as "active," "dynamic," and "urgent."[153] They stereotyped their Victorian fathers and grandfathers as "derogatory, dominant and brutal," and hoped that there would be an end to the "master-slave relationship" they claimed had characterized relations between men and women in the past.[154] They railed against "petty household tyrants" and hoped for a "modern man" who could conform to the new masculine sexual ideal.[155] Sanger really believed that "[the Victorian] type of man is gradually disappearing."[156] Sherwood Eddy insisted that "man is not a beast" if "woman is not an iceberg."[157] Even a cautious writer like Heinrich Wolf insisted that " 'the New Man' is being born."[158]

The modern masculine sexual ideal called for self-control as in the Victorian system, but in the context of an environment that made this more and more difficult to attain. And, in addition, men were expected now to have acquired skills in bed. Purity and prostitution were deemphasized. Men and women were placed in the bedroom where, if women were not making greater demands for sex expression and performance, the marriage manuals certainly were. There men were expected to be masterly yet tender and above all mutual, even to the point of orgasm. As artifacts of the culture of personality, the sex/marriage manuals stressed male performance. The public and open environment of sex discussion and sex demands that pervaded the United States in the 1910–1930 period pressured men publicly to express themselves sexually, specifically heterosexually, as never before. Social commentator Theodore Newcomb noted that "there is considerable evidence that among some groups at least the newer codes of a decade ago were actually compulsive, that individuals in considerable numbers felt themselves in danger of losing caste if the new freedom was not explored."[159] Male sexual potency was celebrated as male impotency was shunned and equated with homosexuality. Suppliers of erotica brought their wares aboveground and onto the newsstands. Freudian popularizers insisted that everything was sexual and that thus good sex was vital to healthy psychological adjustment. So insistent were they on the need for orgasmic expression that the last and greatest taboo, that against masturbation, began to break down. But this was the exception rather than the rule. In general, the accelerating demands for male potency were vehemently heterosexual. Men were taught to judge their manliness against the unmanliness of the homosexual. The accelerated fear of impotency only added to the celebration of potency and the undermining of the older controls over male sexuality. If the Victorians were taught to fear both their potency and their impotency, increasingly the young men of the 1920s youth culture were taught to fear clumsiness as well as impotency—that is, they were encouraged more and more to be sexual athletes. These prescriptions took the place of the older Victorian public moral strictures, and now set the agenda for the construction of masculinity that was valued in the peer-led youth culture. This modern man was thus a precarious construct, caught between the demand that he both control and express his sexuality. Symbolic of this sexual conflict, the hero of *Is Sex Necessary?* decides that he is "not cut out for kissing" after reading the new sex manuals; he leaves the city to raise fruit in Oregon.[160] Such might have been the fate of many young American men in the 1920s had they taken the ideology of the sexualized society seriously.

CHAPTER FIVE

The Working-Class, Public, Youth-Oriented World of Leisure: Chicago and New York, 1900–1930

Within the working class in the cities in the early twentieth century, there arose a public, youth-oriented, heterosocial leisure world. Here a vast array of amusements, dance halls, and movie theaters provided the backdrop for the redefinition of American heterosociality.[1] In this social milieu, there appeared the earliest version of the New Woman; in New York, the "Charity Girl," who differed from a prostitute in that she demanded not money but presents and a good time from her male friends; and the "woman adrift" of Chicago, who, like the Charity Girl, was a self-supporting single woman.[2] Such independence for women was hardly new in itself; nor was her sexual precocity. While a rigid double standard existed in the working classes, with a clear distinction between "good" and "bad" women, that distinction was always blurred to some extent by working women's greater personal autonomy. For most working women, vital alterations in premarital sexual behavior were being experienced by the late nineteenth century. Premarital sexual behavior in largely working-class Hingham, Massachusetts, increased from 8.5 percent of women (1841–1860) to 16.0 percent (1861–1880) and in Lexington jumped from 3.6 percent (1854–1866) to 19.3 percent in 1885 to 1895, as measured by premarital pregnancy.[3] This suggests a greater willingness among working-class women to "go all the way" in the late nineteenth century. It confirms that, especially as regards behavior, some modification of the double standard occurred among the working classes earlier than it did among the middle classes. These figures are important. While we should not exaggerate the extent to which working-class sexuality changed, the erotic pace indeed accelerated at this time as the public, youth-oriented, heterosocial leisure world grew out of the Victorian underworld. If working-class women had often had the independence to be sexually expressive with men, they now had still greater independence because they had more economic autonomy.[4] And this sexual freedom was reflected in the declining double standard. Further, many of these women lived apart from their families, which gave them even more bargaining power than their Victorian precursors, who had invariably lived at home. Thus, the Charity Girl and "woman adrift" was a genuine New Woman for the working classes in the city, the precursor of the mainstream middle-class New Woman of the 1920s.

The social relations between the sexes of the Victorian underworld provide the crucial backdrop to the early twentieth-century heterosocial leisure world. To say the least, here the social relations between the sexes lacked the decorousness that characterized the Victorian middle classes. The prevalence of prostitution captures much of the sordid essence of this subculture, but there was in New York an elaborate system of amusements where young men and women of the working class controlled the processes of courtship in a competitive game. A wide range of physical contacts were deemed appropriate: the options for sexual gratification for working-class men ran the gamut from prostitution through the "taxi-dancer" who required payment from men for limited "thrills" through to women who asked nothing in return for dates and relationships. Heterosocial relations in New York in the mid—nineteenth century were remarkably similar to those fifty years later. In the New York of the 1850s, new employment opportunities occurred beyond domestic service and this increased young women's leisure time and earnings and extended sexual freedom. In this new space, a youth-oriented leisure world grew up because young women were freed from domestic duties by their greater purchasing power.[5] Differences with the public world that emerged fifty years later should not be exaggerated. Yet this was still a precarious world for women. Single women abandoned the protections that the family and local people had provided to control male behavior. Further, because the emerging heterosocial marketplace stayed linked to the older world of the "bawdy" houses, new styles of relationships between men and women had small opportunity to develop.[6] For, above all, working-class sexuality in New York remained part of the underworld, the antithesis and foil to the lofty, if hypocritical, middle-class system of morality.

Yet, after 1900, several important changes transformed the Victorian underworld. There is evidence that in New York and in Chicago and other U.S. urban centers, prostitution went into a sharp decline in the second decade of the twentieth century, in large part because of the efforts of reformers: "In 1912, prostitution was open, organised, aggressive, and prosperous; in 1916 it was furtive, disorganised, precarious, unsuccessful."[7] Further, the report of the Committee of Fifteen in Chicago in April 1930 noted the decline of the "brothel" and the ascendancy of the dance halls as a pattern of the previous twenty years.[8] The attention that this change received from social hygienists helped bring working-class sexuality and the underworld to greater public visibility. In the great cities, amusement parks sprang up where young men and women went on dates. Entrepreneurs appreciated the potential in dance halls and ballrooms, which grew larger and more elaborate and glitzy than in Victorian times.[9] Further, movie theaters appeared after 1900, where young working-class men and women were the first to go on dates and to be stimulated by the darkened atmosphere and by the eroticism of the movies.[10]

The expanding subculture was transformed, too, by immigration.[11] The working class of mid-Victorian America was largely Anglo-Saxon, Irish, German, and black: by 1900 it was also Southern and Eastern European, especially in New York and Chicago. These first- and second-generation Jewish, Slavonic, and Italian immigrants, eager for assimilation, saw the dance halls, movie theaters, and amusements as quintessentially American, because they often contrasted so sharply and, for them, refreshingly with the mores of their indigenous cultures. Differences in ethnicity do not emerge as a major factor, for the dance halls seemed to offer greater possibility of sexual freedom for men who came from, to one degree or another, male-dominant cultures where a rigid double standard applied. In the United States, for immigrant men of whatever ethnicity of origin, there seemed ample opportunity to take advantage of the "bad" women of the dance halls; women were not so available on this scale in their indigenous cultures. This enthusiasm to conform to what they saw as American mores only helped to accelerate the erotic pace.

The dance halls perhaps epitomized the coming world of commercial amusements.[12] As prostitution declined, there developed what can most tactfully be described as sleazy and less sleazy places. Most notorious, perhaps, were the "taxi-dance halls" and the closed dance halls that admitted only men (although women, of course, worked there). As sociologist Harvey Zorbaugh bluntly noted, "their appeal is frankly sexual."[13] Here men could buy tickets that entitled them to a dance or to an occasional "thrill" with a taxi-dancer. The practice at these institutions acted as a grotesque parody of the dating system that was beginning to take shape at this time, especially as real relationships were formed sometimes from these liaisons: as in "dating" in general, the men paid and, in return, received "thrills," at the whim of women. Other types of dance halls, while they left some investigators aghast, do not shock us seventy years later. Investigator Walter Reckless, in his social hygiene classic, *Vice in Chicago*, described such a place:

> Young people, some visibly under the influence of liquor, others apparently sober, were repeatedly seen to dance or whirl about the floor with their bodies pressed tightly together, shaking, moving and rotating their lower portions in a way that undoubtedly roused their sex impulses. Some even were seen to engage in "soul kissing" and "biting" one another in the lobes of the ears and upon the neck.[14]

And there were other, less sleazy places in Chicago, like the Erie Cafe where, apparently, "the owners [are] more circumspect about selling liquor; the patrons [are] more orderly, there is less 'rough' dancing on the floor, there is better ventilation, the women are not so easy to 'pick up'."[15]

Trying to summarize the differences between these places, historian John Modell has suggested that what distinguished the working-class dance halls and middle-class dance palaces underlined the greater sexualization that existed in the working class: working-class males tended to go to dance halls in order to "pick up" women, while the middle class usually went to their places with their "dates."[16] This is a useful but overly simplistic differentiation, especially as there was some class intermingling. In reality, the dance halls provided the cultural space for the operation of all three of the dance-hall subculture's forms of heterosexuality—serial monogamy, polygamy, and prostitution. A young man could bring his date to a dance hall, he could meet a "date" at a dance hall, or, he could make a "pick up" at one. Whatever the case, the same kind of exchange went on: men paid women for treats in return for sexual favors, which were controlled by women.

The men of this working-class, public, heterosocial leisure world were on the cutting edge of change, and therefore, along with the New Men discussed in the next chapters, served as a vanguard in the revolution in morals. If young middle-class men sometimes frequented the working-class dives in the nineteenth century, increasingly they had no need to, because entrepreneurs devised movie theaters, amusement parks, and dance palaces especially to be frequented by young middle-class men and their middle-class dates along with an often working-class clientele.[17] These institutions helped redefine middle-class sexuality on terms similar to those common in the working class. I have shown already how the working class influenced ideology directed at the new middle class and how middle-class men were infatuated with working-class sexuality. This alone validates a study of working-class male sexuality.

Most intriguingly, the evidence supports a "trickle-up" theory.[18] Middle-class youth did not necessarily consciously copy working-class sexuality. Yet some kind of cultural diffusion clearly occurred. For they were influenced by the working class through their environment and subconsciously. One further point: this is not a study of all of working-class sexuality. That would, for a start, be a huge topic. The working class in general, especially labor elites, possibly followed the Victorian system of sexual morality. My study focuses on the men of a particular group: that is, unskilled and semi-skilled laborers, as well as skilled workers involved in the youth-oriented, heterosocial, public leisure world that grew out of the Victorian underworld within the working class in the large cities.

There are surely serious questions to be raised about the men of this emerging public world. How did they respond to the challenge to their power posed by women's greater freedom? How did men who were used to a rigid double standard of sexual morality that enabled them to indulge in sex with prostitutes or "bad" women before marriage respond when the New Woman blurred distinctions between the "good" and the "bad" woman by taking on greater control of sexual interactions? Such were the questions faced by the men who represented one major influence that, along with popular ideology and elite feminism, by the 1920s helped create what I am calling modern American male sexuality.[19]

The great Kinsey sex survey of 1948 made a significant attempt to gather a working-class sample. He defined the working class as encompassing those who had only received an education up to the eighth grade or those who were in blue-collar positions. We cannot know for certain, of course, that this was the group that actually frequented the dance halls and other amusements of the city. But the qualitative studies bear out that these were the kind of men who did so, and Kinsey is a rich source on male sexuality in America as it was around 1940. He also provided a generational comparison, the first generation of which averaged 43.1 years of age at the time of their interviews and were thus the individuals who "were responsible for the reputation of the 'roaring twenties' "—that is, they were in their "youth and therefore sexually most active from 1910 to 1925."[20] Unfortunately, in the generational comparison, Kinsey divided the groups only by educational level. But this is still useful, as working-class males were more likely to be educated only up to or below the eighth grade.

These figures reveal a society in which premarital intercourse was much more common for men than in the college-educated group. Those less well educated, that is, those educated only up to eighth grade, tended to "go all the way" in premarital intercourse with companions. Thus, premarital intercourse, as table 5.1 shows, was a more common part of working-class life for men and was also practiced earlier than among Kinsey's college-educated groups, as table 5.2 reveals. In general, working-class men preferred to have full intercourse rather than to pet to climax by com-

TABLE 5.1
Percentage of Men Who Experienced Premarital Intercourse

	Least-Educated	College-Educated
Adol.–15*	37.1%	9.3%
16–20	74.3%	37.0%
21–25	72.5%	56.4%

SOURCE: Kinsey, *Sexual Behavior in the Human Male*, 412. Reprinted by permission of The Kinsey Institute for Research in Sex, Gender, and Reproduction, Inc.

* Adolescence here means onset of puberty.

TABLE 5.2
Percentage of Men Who Petted to Climax

	Least-Educated	College-Educated
16–20	13%	39.3%
21–25	11.4%	51.8%

SOURCE: Kinsey, *Sexual Behavior in the Human Male*, 412. Reprinted by permission of The Kinsey Institute for Research in Sex, Gender, and Reproduction, Inc.

parison with college-educated groups. Kinsey noted that it was usual for the men in the less-educated group to achieve an orgasm as soon as possible after effecting genital union. There was thus little concern for the niceties of foreplay. This suggests an experience of sexual intercourse among the working classes that was very much geared to male satisfaction, enjoyment, and pleasure.

The Kinsey data reveal also some differences in attitudes between the classes and generations as regards premarital intercourse. Among the least educated, 33.9 percent of those aged 46+ at time of interview disapproved of premarital intercourse, while of those aged from "adolescence" to 25, only 18.9 percent did (the college group averaged 61.4 percent disapproval).[21] Clearly, the working class had fewer inhibitions about premarital intercourse. Only 13.5 percent of the whole sample, older and younger, feared public opinion (compared to 22.8 percent of the college educated), while 41.9 percent lacked interest in having more (18.8 percent of the college educated).[22] These figures are too striking to be dismissed. They suggest that the working class tended to see sex as something to be taken for granted as early as possible; and they imply that this group probably lacked the moral and religious inhibitions that generally helped define middle-class men's and women's behavior, which much more readily stopped at petting. The figures suggest that male sexuality was relatively less controlled and guided among the working classes than among the middle classes and that the tendency was for it to become, if anything, even less so.

All the frequenters of the taxi-dance halls and the other working-class heterosocial institutions had one thing in common: the seeking in leisure of relief from the grueling tedium of their work. As famous reformer Jane Addams perceptively and understandingly noted, "'Looping the loop' amid shrieks of simulated terror or dancing in disorderly saloon halls, are perhaps the natural reactions to a day spent in noisy factories and in trolley cars whirling through the distracting streets."[23] Similarly, New York observer Richard Henry Edwards declared that the wildness of youth "is the result of unbearable strains which a complexity of exploitations puts upon it. These young people are not infrequently exploited in their homes. They are widely exploited in their work and set to mechanical routines."[24] Social hygienist Eleanor Rowland Wembridge sensitively observed that

> the ignorant boy and girl, untrained to look forward to any constructive outlet of their feelings, find it only in the immediate fact, which is usually

illicit and underhand. They find no joy in their work and see little of it in family life. Yet they long for joy as passionately as the rest of the world. How can the driving force of youth be harnessed to clean romance and family happiness, in one as in the other?[25]

Ultimately, the economic conditions that these men experienced provide the crucial backdrop to any examination of their leisure life. Leisure provided relief from a hard life: "Coming from the monotony of work and sometimes dreary home surroundings, the dance hall with its lights, gay music, refreshments and attractive surroundings seems everything that is bright and beautiful."[26]

The heterosexual relations of the dance halls must be understood as a part of a male-dominated culture that began with the teenage "gang." This was a mainstay of the working-class male subculture of this time. Within this social world, the men prided themselves on their success with women. A report on the Weiss Candy Store at 4101 West Fifth Avenue saw it as "a congregating place for great numbers of boys and girls who used very improper language toward each other."[27] As sociologist Paul Cressey put it, "the boy's gang may lead to actual immorality."[28] Another report commented on "much foul talk and boastful talk of sex conquests in the presence of girls by boys not over sixteen years of age," while the boys themselves were "given to betting on the color of girls' garters. . . . Then when she is close someone contrives to raise her shirt—if necessary—and the awards are made."[29] The Bureau of Social Hygiene reported that in more houses, men would insult "the females especally young girls:—accidentally on purpose."[30] Frederic Thrasher talked of how in the gang,

> Stories of the most obscene character are related by a woman to a crowd of men and boys. Indescribably filthy jokes are perpetuated by a ventriloquist with the aid of a puppet. Dancing vile beyond description is indulged in by girls some of whom are apparently scarcely out of their teens, while a woman gives nude an unbelievably debasing dance.[31]

As Cressey reported of another group, they were, "to put it plainly—moral degenerates. They have had the audacity to display their nakedness under the lamplight. Last night they had several young girls not over thirteen there with them whom they were very evidently trying to get in a state of excitement."[32] The gang around the Vernon Athletic Club had "its own girl" who "comes to meet its especial fellows. . . . These girls must not dance with anyone outside of the clique, and any outsider who presumes to transgress this rule is waylaid outside and convinced physically of the error of his ways."[33] In the gang, male teenagers learned the moves that in youth and early adulthood they were to display in the dance halls.

Here, men confirmed their masculinity among other men by discussing their conquests. One dancemaster was an assiduous date maker who would "go the limit."[34] A group of clerks interviewed by sociology students Alinsky and Weinberger "seemed rather doubtful about getting it because they haven't a car. One said that if he had a car there wouldn't be a virgin left in town."[35] An investigator recorded a conversation: "Whaddya say, Jim, pick 'em up? Y' betcha life, whispers Jim."[36] Investigator Louise de Koven Bowen observed in Chicago dance halls that "obscene language is permitted, and even the girls among the habitués carry on indecent conversations."[37] One remarked proudly that he "took a girl out boat-riding in the park and screwed her three times in a boat."[38] Perhaps the epitome of this kind of self-confidence was reformer Hutchins Hapgood's "tough" from his *Types from City Streets*: "But the tough is sure. He does not hold off from satisfaction. He reposes on the firm bosom of the early need of the race, where there is no tremulousness or uncertainty. His footing is as firm as that of the aristocrat."[39] The "tough" and his compatriots could here indulge their primitive urges unchecked.

Indeed, for these men, women were simply objects for sexual gratification, if men's language was to be believed. A Committee of Fourteen investigator paraphrased a discussion he had with one man:

> Twenty cunts hanging around here. I said last year there was always a chance of picking up a piece of gash in here, he said you can do it now, too, I said how, he said if they know you, you can go over and sit down with them or else take them for a dance.[40]

Men inquired of one another as to whether they "had gotten that chicken yet. . . . Can you fix it for me Henry?" while another affirmed that a girl "was a fine chicken."[41] In Chicago in the 1920s, the term "hot babe" kept recurring; one fellow advised that "if you find a good hot baby that will show you a good time it's better to go to some hall like the Marigold or the Columbia. There are a lot of hot babies, that go up there regularly."[42] At the New American, it was possible to get some real "hot birds."[43] This language demonstrates colorfully the sexual objectification of women that was part and parcel of male homosocial behavior. Now, while this could merely reflect rhetoric and the imperatives of peer bonding, its prevalence suggests it often reflected men's real feelings, and an intensely felt desire for dominance over the New Woman. This language was anyway, distasteful.

These men supplemented their nocturnal activities with pornography. Saloons had pictures of naked women on their walls. The Bureau of Social Hygiene reported on one "Joe Pete" who did not do much reading except sex books; he bought those "books that show all dirty pictures from friends of his that come around and sell them at a quarter a book."[44] He discussed buying a lot of "Artist and Model Books to see how the models look in the nude," hence gaining his nickname of "Joe the Chronic Masturbator."[45] Another Bureau of Social Hygiene investigator noted that "'French pictures' ... are passed around frequently in the pool halls and 'gin mills' "[46] while Thrasher noted in his study of *The Gang*, "There was a large amount of obscene material and art, which was circulated very freely among the boys, copied many times over and handed down to the next 'generation' as a social legacy."[47]

Men's attitudes towards women encouraged violent behavior. The Bureau of Social Hygiene conducted an investigation in the New York University Boy's Club and concluded that "The Neighbourhood Credo" entailed that "most boys of this community believe that: the girls who accept gifts willingly give themselves up to be attacked."[48] Violence directed at women was inherent in the working-class male sexual subculture. Several investigators commented on the "rough and uncouth" clientele of the places they visited. An investigator for the Committee of Fourteen commented that at Gilligan's Cafe, "there is an indescribable air of hardness or toughness in their mannerism and personal conduct."[49] Such sordidness was perhaps most accentuated in the observations of one investigator in Chicago who observed behavior that most strongly contrasted to Victorian ideals. He described various "boys ... [who] micturated while in the full view of the dancers," while, to their credit, "the more modest ones retired to a more secluded part of the field behind a dilapidated bandstand."[50] Apparently the women did not in this case see the men's behavior as particularly peculiar. Indeed, they even walked up to a man and chatted with him "as though there were nothing unusual or embarrassing in his activities of the moment."[51] Here decorum was clearly not of the essence. A Committee of Fourteen investigator noted the violence of the social interaction between the sexes at a dancing school:

> About 8.00 pm I arrived at Public School number 65 where I attended a dance. Conditions didn't improved [sic] here. Girls are still abused, insulted

and hit if they disobey the orders of the loafers who hang out in this school. While I was here I was told, that some boys are using itching powder while they dance with girls in here. They were cought [sic] last week with that powder on them, but no action was taken.[52]

Bizarre individuals frequented the dance halls. Cressey described one experience of a taxi-dancer who on a date stopped the car and proceeded to declare that he wanted to brand his girlfriend: "He was the queerest fellow I ever knew. . . . He didn't seem to want to make love. He seemed to want nothing sometimes but go around hurting girls."[53] The dance halls, however, encouraged an environment where violence could flourish. Two investigators from the Committee of Fourteen "struck up an acquaintance with a young man who declared, "Well anything goes here," which included "tough dancing," which often caused the patrons to become so "obstreperous" that a youth had to be ejected.[54] Nevertheless, we should be careful of the evidence about violence, as investigators were likely to exaggerate its prevalence. Still, they show that it existed, which is, ultimately, what is most important.

Men regarded a "bad" woman as fit for anything. What is striking is that rape was regarded as quite a normal, almost routine, part of life in this subculture. A disturbingly common example was one investigator's discovery of the "line-up," when a "girl or a woman . . . is induced to go in the back of a poolroom, down a cellar, up on a roof, or into an empty apartment. With utter disregard for the laws of nature, the young men violate her one after another until she can't stand any more."[55] One of the most celebrated of the investigators, Louise de Koven Bowen, observed in Chicago in 1912 how "in one case where the girl screamed the men choked her."[56] At the Lafayette Casino on Saturday, June 1, 1912, an investigator watched as "one girl was forced down on her back on a table by a man and kissed."[57] Among sociologist William Foote Whyte's Italians, examined in mid-1930s Boston, the virginity of a "teaser" was "thought to be only a technicality and if she is raped it serves her right."[58] The Syracuse Morals Commission noted the case of a man who treated one woman "to ice cream and took her to a nearby resort. There he attempted to assault her and she screamed."[59] Thrasher described the phenomenon of the "gang shag" as beginning early in adolescence:

> The gang shag is an institution peculiar to the gangs and clubs of this neighbourhood. There are few sex perverts among the boys, but there is a great deal of immorality. . . . This number of boys have relations with the

women in the course of a few hours. There is a common practice among young men in Chicago, and this is by no means confined to boys of the gangs or the underprivileged classes, of picking up girls, utter strangers, on the street and taking them for a ride in an automobile. During the course of this ride it is customary to indulge in passionate petting, and often the affair culminates in the sex act. If the girl refuses, it is commonly supposed that she is put out of the car some place in the country and asked to walk back. So widespread is this practice that allusions to it have become a common joke on the vaudeville stage.[60]

The dance-hall environment encouraged a single standard that left the distinctions between the good woman and the bad woman blurred, underscoring the arbitrariness of the categories:

> It is a rare case of any young girl making a clean getaway after attending halls of this character. There are so many young men on the march that a chaste girl will generally fall and a great many cases are forcible seduction, then the girl becomes an habitual rounder of this class of dance hall.[61]

A Committee of Fourteen investigator noted in detail the story of one "Newry," who encouraged his girl Alice to give up her job to live with him: he kept her away for two weeks. "He ruined this girl."[62] Later he "raped another girl, Jessie Schneider, seventeen and a half years of age, who lived with her parents in the vicinity of 18th. Street and 3rd. Avenue and worked as a waitress. He pretended to be in a position to [give] theatre passes. This won her over and he eventually ruined this girl."[63] Many accounts of this kind of treatment of women were given verbatim to investigators:

> I had spent all kinds of money on her and would get her in a hotel do or die. I said further that I would take her to Pabsts' Harlem some night, get her under the influence of liquor, take a taxi and rush her into a hotel before she would realize it.[64]

This same man had had to take one woman out twenty times before she would have sexual intercourse with him. But then he simply "finally met her one day without [?] and took her to Brooklyn Hotel where [he] had intercourse," this without the formality of a date.[65] One Chicago man told an investigator how he had taken a woman on a boat:

> He had been loving her up and asked for coitus. She refused and said she would call out. He said he would capsize the boat if she did and drown them

both. She begged and pleaded with him. But he said he must have it. Finally, in spite of her protestations, he threw up her clothes. She cried at first and then suddenly burst out laughing and enjoyed. He felt she had been stalking him.[66]

One investigator reported one of his interviewees as suggesting to him, "I'm afraid to take a chance in the grass or a hallway as she might yell and have me pinched. The only thing to do is to get her in this backroom, force her upstairs and then she couldn't squeal. Can you fix it for me, Henry?"[67] This investigator was able to pull out of a barman advice on how to get his girl to succumb to his wiles when she would not enter a hotel for fear of being observed by a friend or acquaintance:

> Oh, it's easy with cases of that "kind" and I've been up against them. All you have to do is to take her upstairs by the 124th. Street entrance and she won't be wise. Just register, go in your room, lock the door and then you've got her right.[68]

Thus the bad woman or the good who had merely taken a favor was fair game for any kind of treatment, however forcible or violent it might have been. Without the conventions of the middle class, rape was accepted as a normal way of life in the public world of youthful leisure so that, ultimately, any assertion—or perceived assertion—of her sexuality on a woman's part left her vulnerable; and with such a strong male desire for dominance in a context of few controls, women simply had to take their chances.

It would be naive and erroneous to suggest that all of the men necessarily shared these views. Evidence suggests that men made distinctions at the time. In Chicago, a man declared to Alinsky and Weinberger, for example, that the Dreamland crowd was "too tough."[69] Paul Cressey identified the "slummer" as a man who frequented the dance halls out of a search for experience.[70] But, as he put it,

> Many young men who came expecting to be shocked are so disgusted by the experience that they do not return. . . . "A friend of mine told me about this place and I thought I'd come up here to see what it was like. Gosh, this is awful, it's disgusting. . . . It's a joke to see that sign up there. 'No improper Dancing Allowed.' This is no place for me. I wouldn't hang around a dump like this for anything . . . once is enough."[71]

When one investigator for the Committee of Fourteen declared that he was going to leave for "Diggs' Place," "the man looked surprised and said that was too tough for us, that he never went there, because he was afraid of getting into trouble."[72] An older man declared to Cressey that "their [sic] too tough for me. I was out to the New American one night. That was enough."[73]

If the males of the dance-hall subculture thrived on braggadocio and violence, they also defined themselves against the homosexual communities that coexisted in the large cities. There were homosexual bars and networks in New York as early as the 1870s.[74] The Chicago Vice Commission Report had identified a homosexual community in Chicago around 1911.[75] The men of the world of youthful, working-class leisure were aware of this milieu. Indeed, homoerotic experience was growing among the working class at this time, as table 5.3 shows.

In large part, the presence of a homosexual community unsettled the heterosexual working class, which defined its own community sharply against the homoerotic world even as the two communities interacted. One active dance-hall goer announced his feelings about "queers" to an investigator in Chicago, declaring that "when they shake hands with you they have that peculiar look in their eyes that have a wanting feeling of expression."[76] The men of the dance-hall subculture had their own models of homosexual persons. The working class established the model of the masculine man who only temporarily practiced his proclivities for same-sex activity. He was known as a "straight," which confirmed that he was not differentiated from other men. In the long term he was to be heterosexual. There was, in addition, the effeminate man who was permanently homosexual. Both groups were the butt of prejudice in the dance-hall subculture. The Bureau of Social Hygiene's study of boys' clubs noted that men with "full faces, long delicate fingers, tweezed eyebrows and well-shaped lips are inverts."[77] One young man reported on one Chicago hotel:

TABLE 5.3
Percentage of Men with Homoerotic Experience to Orgasm

Educ. Level 0–8	Older Generation	Younger Generation
Adol. to 15	17.1%	29.0%
16–20	17.9%	33.7%
21– 25	16.65%	32.6%

SOURCE: Kinsey, *Sexual Behavior in the Human Male*, 412. Reprinted by permission of The Kinsey Institute for Research in Sex, Gender, and Reproduction, Inc.

A fellow doesn't make acquaintances easy at the hotel except with a bunch of fellows that he doesn't care to meet up with. They are easy, too easy, to get acquainted with. There is a bunch of prick-lickers at the hotel. They are steady roomers, they don't come and go like most of the fellows.[78]

This man described one experience he had of an attempted seduction by a homosexual to which he reacted violently:

One day he was in my room and was rocking himself back and forth, while sitting down on the bed. He began by praising my figure. "What a fine physique you have. What wide shoulders." He got up and put one hand on my chest and the other on my back. "How broad you are through the chest." Then he unbuttoned one or two of the buttons of my shirt. "What well developed breasts."[79]

The man responded to this attempted seduction by declaring, "I said hold off what are you trying to do? . . . You red haired bastard. I told him to stop that or I [would] beat [him] up."[80] There were several other examples of this kind of reaction reported to investigators. One boy said, "Fuck you." The man said, "That's what I want you to do."[81] Although both groups experienced prejudice, intolerance was mostly directed at effeminate men and not at more masculine men who engaged in same-sex activity. Thus one man talked of his feelings about his homoerotic experiences:

I think that many queens are born queer. Others acquire it. At many times I have felt to be able to make a pal of a queen, but on account of their likeness for men, I do not want a queen for a pal. I would be ashamed to be with them at a party and have to introduce them to a girl. I have never told a girl that I have browned or have been frenched. She would think that I was queer.[82]

Yet what is indeed most striking because it is so much less predictable than the homophobia is the extent of overlap and interaction between the heterosocial and homoerotic worlds as well as the amount of homoerotic practice that resulted. It was in reality difficult to differentiate a heterosexual and a homosexual world. A kind of tolerance therefore developed among the working class. Not merely were the two worlds physically close to one another, but often both kinds of activities were pursued in the same bars. At 18th and 125th streets in New York, for example, the New York Committee of Fourteen reported such a bar: "This place has two back rooms one of which is for males exclusively and another for mixed couples.

The section for males was vacant and the other contained three couples [and no one could] enter unless accompanied by women."[83]

The working class often in practice rejected simplistic definitions of who was homosexual/heterosexual. Kinsey commented on how many among his least-educated groups continued in both homosexual and heterosexual behaviors through major phases of their lives, resulting in greater tolerance of homosexuality.[84] The evidence from a study of Chicago homosexuals by Earl Bruce, a student of the qualitatitive sociologist Ernest Burgess, supports this conclusion. Bruce obtained a lengthy case history of a black man named Walt Lewis who moved between the two worlds. His enthusiasm for women was as great as that he felt for men. He saw little difference between his homosexual and heterosexual encounters:

> Some of them you cannot tell from a woman if they never have whiskers or mustash. They take in the ass, French you, like to be called girls' names and if they like you will give you money, let you stay with them like a man and wife.
>
> When they want to get married they go to a bull diggar's ball, a bulldiggars marries them put a mark on the fag, and they tells her next husband how many times she has been married.[85]

Lewis commented on how homosexuals often would date women: "You can pick about four out of ten that have women but they may not be fucking them now. In a place like this people turn if they never get any cunt or never talk to girls or go any place."[86]

Another young man remarked that "if I meet the right girl I will marry. I have found that both sexes satisfy me equally."[87] Still another young man moved between an affair with an older "temperamental" man while also conducting an affair with a woman.[88] Movie theaters were places where young men who "otherwise regarded themselves as heterosexual practiced for money."[89] A Bureau of Social Hygiene investigator asked one young man if he "ever run up against a fag?" "Plenty" he declared. "What do they do? Blow you?" (Ans) "That is all."[90] One young man confessed that he preferred homosexual activities because they entailed less risk of disease.[91] Further, a rather precocious young man named John W—— wrote extensively of his experiences with girls, women, boys, and men. At age fifteen, "I discovered by accident that I could receive a great thrill by having sexual intercourse with boys: an enema."[92] But he still insisted, "I really did not receive a thrill from this like I did if I had intercourse with a girl."[93] Further, while he sought out men largely to make money, he was sufficiently concerned about disease to write that he did not "intend to put on parties with any unless they look neat and clean."[94] None of this should be surprising to us, but it should serve as a warning of the dangers of categorizing working-class sexual behavior, even according to categories created by the working class itself.

Yet even for those who did not share these proclivities, the encounter with homosexuals made for greater tolerance. One young man described at great length and somewhat sympathetically his experience with homosexuals. He discussed how he first encountered homosexuals at a party and dance that was, apparently, heterosexual. "While I was dancing and enjoying myself at this party, I noticed there was one particular young fellow that always managed to give me a peculiar stare as though he wanted my friendship," he reported.[95] This man began discussing with him "how he was interested in art and literature."[96] But they both had girlfriends. Only after having walked home together did they begin homosexual activities. Although he, himself, enjoyed the experience, he was "unable to reciprocate."[97] Although he thought the man's advances were "silly," when the man threw himself on top of him, he "resented" it but nevertheless was keen to go with him on "an evening's entertainment which of course sounded very good to [him] as he felt he could protect himself from any harm he might inflict on me."[98] Because the lines between homosexuality and heterosexuality were not clearly drawn, an element of relative tolerance developed in this world alongside the homophobia, as men of different inclinations befriended one another. The pragmatic, uninhibited approach to sexuality clearly affected attitudes toward homoeroticism, too. Kinsey confirmed this by observing in the lowest social level a great amount of tolerance of homosexuality. "Sex," as he put it, "whether it be heterosexual or homosexual is more or less accepted as inevitable."[99] Indeed, attitudes toward homoeroticism have to be seen in the context of the larger attitude towards sexuality of the men of the dance-hall subculture. These men lacked restraint. They valued sensual experience for its own sake, especially orgasmic experience, and they cared little what gender the object of desire was. There were few controls to check the satisfaction of sexual urges around homoeroticism as there were few controls around heterosexuality.

Yet while the public, heterosocial, working-class leisure world operated as the very antithesis of the highest ideals of the Victorian middle class, in that it encouraged a single standard of sexual expression, attitudes toward women held by men still reflected the same dichotomy between "good" and "bad" women, except that they were not always divided along class lines. Middle-class standards of purity existed, too, in these working-class groups: one man at the Chicago Coast Guard station declared of his girl that he "would never of [sic] dreamed of any disrespectful behavior toward her. I thought too much of her. I had never touched her knee or even her ankle."[100] Men in the gang were also stimulated by a bizarre sense of chivalry:

> The boy who attempted to fight with a girl was punished by the other boys. A girl might slap a boy in the face and all he could honorably do was dodge the second blow, or, if he was very religious, as was seldom the case, he might turn his head around and ask to have the inequality rectified by a similar blow on the other side.[101]

And middle-class women were always by definition good women:

> In one case, considerable alarm was caused among women workers in a social settlement by the fact that gang boys followed them at night. The fear was alleviated, however when it was found that the interest of these boys was in protecting the women in accordance with the Irish idea of chivalry.[102]

Of Dreamland in Chicago it was said that "this ain't no place for a nice girl."[103] A young man declared that his "attitude towards girls at this time was the fact that some were respectable and would not indulge in parties of this kind and others were of the type that enjoyed only this kind of sport as they called it."[104]

It was important to determine whether a girl was decent or not. In William Foote Whyte's classic examination of the "Slum Sex Code," in which he focused on Italian-Americans in Boston in the mid-1930s, the dichotomy between the good and bad girl was most clearly discussed. There were first "good girls" who were the only ones fit to marry and who on no account could be defiled as the "corner-boy code strongly prohibits intercourse with a virgin" but who "may submit to a limited amount of kisses and caresses without compromising her reputation."[105] However, she must not "be a tease" or she automatically became a "bad girl" or a "lay."[106] These were fair game for anything and were divided into three groups—"one-man girls, the promiscuous, prostitutes."[107] What is striking here and most important is how dominant the double standard was in the working class as opposed to the middle class. Whyte emphasized further that the ideals of the boys, which they mouthed, had little to do with their real codes and attitudes. They had learned middle-class rhetoric and platitudes; the reality of their attitude was a double standard with a system of at best serial monogamy. If the working-class male had a concept of a "good," pure woman, he lacked the lofty concept of "purity" for himself that many of the middle class had, and a concept of romantic love. The trend was for the double standard to be waning somewhat in the working class, at least as regards attitudes to virginity. Fifty-nine and three-tenths percent of those with an eighth grade education or less aged 46+ wanted to marry a virgin, as compared to 40.9 percent of those adolescent to twenty-five at the time of the interview.[108] Nevertheless, the good woman/ bad woman dichotomy was still an important component of working-class male sexuality in the early twentieth century. And the likelihood was that in the dance halls of the early twentieth century, as more and more women asserted their autonomy, it became harder for men to draw the distinction between the two kinds of women, which caused confusion. For, despite the fact that the working class was used to women who had a certain amount of personal autonomy and therefore some control over sexual relations, men were confused about whether any given woman in the dance halls was a good or a bad one. This distinction remained important to them. Should they encounter a good girl, men determined to respect her: two Chicago interviewees declared that they "would run into the respectful girls who wanted men to always think high of them so we would not suggest any further doings."[109] Jane Addams touchingly described young men in dance halls as "standing about vainly hoping to make the acquaintance of nice girls."[110] Men devised makeshift codes to allay their confusion. One young fellow, Erickson, determined to establish "what kind of a girl [his girlfriend] was by talking dirty."[111] As one investigator noted, "Boys figure that any girl who allows a boy to feel her and tell her dirty jokes is not worthwhile taking as the 'best girl'."[112] Indeed, men continued to be confused by the often blurry distinctions between the good and the bad woman, a difference that was of paramount importance to them.

For if men remained structurally dominant, women were gaining greater controls over sexual exchanges. In a competitive game, women were often, in practice, abler to be more choosy or discriminating as to whom they dated now that they had greater economic independence and personal autonomy than in the nineteenth century. In the Roadhouse, according to one witness, "the girls two-thirds of the time come and leave alone. They do not want a date all night. Some good-looking little Sheik might ask [them] and they would have to refuse."[113] This could happen, too, if "some young man comes along that they like better," for men were subject to the same rules as the women.[114] The women reserved the right to reject men.

The culture of personality predominated in the heterosocial dance-hall world. Youth and good looks for men were at a premium. Paul Cressey noted that the presence of older men in the dance halls was seen as something of an oddity, and they were often resented by the younger crowd. Sociologist Daniel Russell, in *The Roadhouse*, observed an "old bald-headed, gray-haired man" dancing with a nineteen-year-old. Such a man, he noted, was often called "the cheater . . . because he is cheating youth out of its beauty and its rightful belongings."[115] Russell described this man as dancing "on the floor like a gay young boy of nineteen," trying "to make a few more classy steps than anybody else on the floor."[116] An interviewee of Cressey's insisted that, even though he was fifty-four years old, he still "had a lot of good stuff to [me] even yet." He felt he could offer something that flappers could not: "They appreciate a good steady man of mature years. Most of them have been married to some kid and found they weren't steady."[117] But the general flow and pace of the dance halls worked to the disadvantage of the older man.

Sex appeal, too, was acknowledged as an important key to success in this environment. A huge number of the patrons remarked on their muscle-building activities. They drew pleasure in being "built solid."[118] Members of the dance-hall subculture admired their bodies and gained pleasure in their strength. One man commented in Chicago that "wherever I go the girls all seem to fall for me. One thing is that they know I'm strong and that I can satisfy any of them."[119] In this world, young boys were proudly and overtly sexual both in attitude and behavior. Chicago sociologists Alinsky and Weinberger reported on "eight fellows," all steel workers in the same mill. "They go to White City every Saturday and Sunday to 'get a piece of tail.' They acted rather conceited and claim they get what they come for always."[120] One man loudly proclaimed to one of Bruce's investigators that "the queer people tell you you have a big prick. That gives me lots of satisfaction with the women because I know I will satisfy them."[121] Personality would attract women. One young man regularly presented what he called a "magnetic smile"—but what the investigator called a "silly grin"—at the better-looking of two girls.[122] One New Yorker noted to reformer Hutchins Hapgood that "a bloke ain't got no show wid a gal if he ain't good-lookin' wid good clothes, wid a fence [collar] round his neck."[123] A Filipino-American in Chicago, puzzled over his success with women, declared, "It isn't because I'm good-looking because there are better looking Filipinos that can't get anywhere with these girls. They turn them down flat." The only possible reason he could give for his success was that "I don't know what it is but I must have it."[124] Clothes might develop "it." A Bureau of Social Hygiene investigator noted, "They are standing in their best $22.50 suits, John Barrymore shirts, and $3 Snyder's Best Felt Hats. Black products of Tom McCannn cover their 'three pairs for $1 socks'."[125]

Men and women in the dance-hall subculture vied with one another for favors in a competitive game. There were some genuine skills to be learned. Men had to develop a "line" and cultivate their personalities if they wanted to be successful at dating. Thus, Daniel Russell reported that the men of the Roadhouse had a number of "lines" that were designed to accentuate their power with regard to women: one man might tell his partner whom he had never met before that he "is the Chief Purchasing agent for the Pullman company or Head Clerk in some bank downtown or the like."[126] Novelist George Ade, in a number of stories of working-class life in turn-of-the-century Chicago, featured several of his male heroes practicing their talent for the "line." Ade's hero, Artie, always makes sure he impresses his girlfriend by telling her "he's on the Board o' Trade."[127] Or he might be even more direct: "He walked up to her, brushed some imaginary dust from the bulge of her sleeve, and said: 'Hello girlerino. How's everything stackin?' " He brags proudly of how he "put up the tall talk, jollied her along, danced with her three times—well, of course, you couldn't blame her. I sprung them West Side Manners o' mine on her and I had her won."[128] Middle-class formalities were thrust aside at the Strand Cafeteria in New York, where the competitive game reached its apex: "Boys go right up to strange girls and are refused only if that dance is engaged. 'Can I have this dance?' or even 'Say kid, do you want to dance this one?' usually suffices for introduction."[129]

One group who were rejected were those who failed at the "line," who did not appreciate the need to "work slow and give them plenty of time," such as happened to one football player:

> He was all hot and was working hard to get a girl for a party that night. He went the rounds and tried each of them, and proposed a . . . party (for intercourse) but each of them backed out. One girl told me later that my friend was "pretty fast." He didn't know that you had to work slow and sure with these girls. He didn't seem to realize that they weren't regular streetwalkers and so couldn't be treated.[130]

As did not occur with prostitution, women associated with the dance-hall subculture endeavored to control the amount of thrills available to men.

Further, and most evidently, the date was an exchange: men spent money in order to secure companionship and sexual "favors" from women. Money limitations were a major problem for the working classes, as they were later to be for the middle classes. But it was the question of money that most reduced male power and that elicited the most complaints, as far as working-class men were concerned. This is extraordinary because men simply failed to grasp that their money was the very foundation of their power. We should never overestimate the extent to which working-class male involvement in this world was limited by low wages.[131] One of Cressey's male interviewees, an Italian, summed up the problem vividly when he proclaimed that when "you spend your money—you can't tell whether you're going to get anything."[132] Even in a taxi-dance hall, a man could not be sure what he would get for his tokens. A 30-year-old elaborated on this:

> Sometimes the girls make it difficult if not impossible for you to get anything. The trouble with taking out these girls is you never know whether you are going to get anything. Most of them are not regular prostitutes you know. If you strike them right you can get something but if you don't you just lose your time and your money.[133]

He went on to state that "whenever I want to dance I come up to a place like this but when I feel I want to get relief I go to a place where I can feel more sure of getting it."[134] It was always uncertain. An investigator noted, "But if any wise-guy tries to get a dance without a ticket, they get very sore, and urge the fellows to go and buy some more. They know their job very well. They fool around with a fellow so much that they get him half-crazy, and he is bound to go and buy some more tickets."[135] Further, a man commented to Hutchins Hapgood that "a bloke wat ain't got no money can't git a gal and if he does git her, den it's all up in de air wid de money wat he's got."[136]

To maintain a good line a man required money. A St. Louis man declared, "I don't trust these Chicago girls. All they want is a man's money. They will treat a person fine as long as they have tickets, but no longer. As soon as they find a man is through spending money on them they are through."[137] Another man in Chicago declared bluntly, "I don't have a girl. I don't want a girl. I don't want to be bothered by them or spend money on them."[138]

One interviewee for the Bureau of Social Hygiene explained what this meant quite vividly:

> Fellows do not only go up there for the matter of dancing, but because they like the way they dance. The fellow holds the girl very tightly, especially in closing her to him in the abdominal parts . . . this, of course, causes the emotions to be aroused, and by the time the boy thinks he is having a good time, his seven tickets are all gone, and he goes after more.[139]

Men trained in the disrespect for women that colored the male culture saw the exchange as entailing a right on their part to some kind of physical reward. The "gold-digger" was no mere figment of men's imagination as far as they were concerned. According to one woman,

> If a girl knows her stuff she can make just as much if she don't "put out" as if she does. I figure on working about four nights a week and playing the rest of the time. The first thing in being a successful gold-digger is to just choose the right fellow. He can be any age but they got to be ones who don't know too much.[140]

Men resented not only the blurring of distinctions between "good" and "bad" women but also women's greater control over the amount of "thrills" available to them in the dance-hall subculture.

All the same, men did not want to commit themselves. One of Whyte's interviewees declared that "if you go with a girl too long, even if she lays, you're bound to get to like her. That's human nature. I was going out with a girl, and I was banging her every date. After about four months, I saw I was really getting fond of the girl, so I dropped her just like that."[141] Relationships could be transient. One woman complained of her friend that "I go to the phone and give him a ring. An hour with him and I'm sitting on top of the world. But that's all he's good for. I know he doesn't mean it except for the moment."[142] One man proudly admitted to such behavior to a Committee of Fourteen investigator: "I said Grace must be sore at me, I dated her up some time ago for the following week and never showed up, I had to leave town, I asked her if I couldn't take her out and said I won't give her a stand-up."[143]

Various types entered the dance halls. Cressey referred to the "foot-loose globe-trotter" who would move from town to town, always making anonymous contacts.[144] Similarly, one of Cressey's interviewees proudly declared himself a "traveling man," "because I am not in Chicago much of the time. I have much of my social life out on the road where I know people."[145] One man declared to Cressey: "I'm through with girls for a while. All they seem to want to do is to get married."[146] The hobo was as "transient in his attitude to women as to their jobs." The hobo actively wanted "to avoid intimacies that complicate the free life to which they are by temperament and habit committed."[147] So he often embarked on homosexual relations as a conscious means of avoiding marriage, because he lived in a world that "attractive women" who lived "in social worlds infinitely remote from his" would not frequent.[148]

For another group, however, marriage remained an ultimate goal, albeit one that was cast aside for the present. A Filipino-American, after discussing his personal life at some length, including the seduction of a virgin, discussed his ambivalence with the investigator: "But what ought I do? I don't even know her enough to marry her. That's the trouble. We are entirely too intimate. We talk together just like a married couple."[149] The Filipino, even had he wanted to, would have feared trying to marry this girl because she was native born. He could only conclude that he was "a real danger to society" on account of his behavior.[150] Another man thought that even though it was "a lot better to be married . . . you have more excitement when you're single," hence his visits to the local halls.[151] However, many of the men regarded the adoption of this lifestyle as less a choice than a necessity. Cressey interviewed one man who declared that he was earning seven to eight dollars a day. Surely, declared Cressey, "That was enough to get married on." Apparently, he was wrong:

> I don't see how I can ever get married until I can get to making better money. The trouble with most of these girls is that they don't expect to do anything after getting married. If I can get a girl who is willing to work it won't be so bad, but unless I can get that I don't see if I can get married. But then, there's plenty of time, I'm only twenty-six.[152]

But another, at thirty-one, felt the desire much more strongly: "I could get better-looking girls around my own neighbourhood but they expect me to get married. I'd like to all right—I'm thirty-one you know—but I don't make enough money yet—so I come up here."[153]

Men in the dance-hall subculture behaved in essentially the same way as the men of the Victorian underworld from out of which the dance-hall subculture grew. As the early twentieth century New Woman appeared, men simply treated them as they had treated women who asserted their sexuality before. They lacked respect for such women. Men confirmed their masculinity by bragging about their conquests of women to other men. They regarded women as simply objects for their sexual gratification, and they celebrated acts of violence against them, treating rape as an ordinary part of life. Men also continued to be transient and rejected marriage as involving excessive commitment. Further, men continued to define their identities, sharply, against those of the developing homosexual communities. Most importantly, men still believed in the "good" and "bad" woman, but they complained that it was becoming hard to tell the difference. Yet women's increasing autonomy and relative financial independence served to accelerate male resentment toward women. Men had less respect for them, associated with them in public places where they did not know them, did not have to know them to try to have sexual intercourse, and used money to buy sexual favors. Men used what financial power they had to buy sexual favors, but they resented the women for the exchange, accusing them of being "gold-diggers" when they did not get the favors from them that they expected. For, once exchanges began to include more than money, men were threatened. Men were confused and disturbed, for in this world they could be rejected. Here youth and good looks were at a premium for them as well as women. Further, this system of heterosociality involved the cultivation on men's part of the "line" and of a performance in order to attract women. Surely this reflects male disquiet at the growth of women's power. For women were hardly mere victims. They gained increasing sexual freedoms as well as growing economic ones. Whatever men's attitude was, they no longer regarded themselves as limited in role to "good" or "bad," and so became more fully human. Yet overall women had less money, and therefore ultimately were dependent on men for marriage. Further, the entry into the male world of the dating system could not really provide the supports against underworld primtiivism that families and kin had given before. Male dominance therefore remained structurally intact.

Yet this lewd, crude, rude, and sordid world was the one whose ethos of youth and sex appeal, violence and sex expression Macfadden and the youth culture writers celebrated. They perceived the dance hall as a sexually vibrant society, rightly understanding its primitivism as the antithesis of the Christian Gentleman of respectable society and as a perfect contrast to set against the "myth of Victorian repression." Such was indeed the world that cultural radicals celebrated with such gusto and relish. But given the real nature of the subculture they, with only limited validity, perceived as "working class," what dangerous games they were playing. Yet, still they helped spread the sexualized society of the underworld/dance-hall subculture to broader groups as this mass, youth-oriented culture gained ascendancy in the United States. As a cutting edge of the sexual revolution, this subculture boded badly for American society because it encouraged underworld primitivism at the expense of gentlemanliness as a model of manliness. It was in this context that a group of radicals attempted to redefine the social relations between the sexes along feminist lines.

The Failure of the Feminist Option: Men and the Feminist New Woman, Part I

The most articulate, sophisticated, advanced embodiment of the changes in women's roles that made up such a major part of the "revolution in morals" was the feminist New Woman. This New Woman was more than a flapper. She was also a feminist who differed from most suffragists or feminists of the nineteenth century in her insistence on her right to self-fulfillment in both public life and relations with men. Unlike previous feminists, she desired both marriage and career.[1] She proposed to solve the dilemma of how to combine her new-found right to a career with her insistence on her newly claimed right to personal fulfillment by dabbling in Freudianism. She believed that modern feminism's central aim was attainment of success in both love and career.[2] Many such women clustered around the National Woman's Party and the Greenwich Village organization Heterodoxy and, therefore, self-consciously, they represented the most articulate and advanced manifestation of the sexual revolution.

The question of the impact of the feminist New Woman on her husband is therefore an important one because the couple entered a marriage in which the questions raised by both feminism and the sexual revolution were center stage. For the New Woman's husband, this meant that he went against the expectations for men in early twentieth-century American culture in a number of ways. First, his wife was most probably a feminist activist (and he had to endure all the opprobrium involved in being identified as her husband). Second, his wife's quest for achievement meant not merely that he was no longer the sole breadwinner but also that he was not any more necessarily the center of his wife's life. Third, the feminist New Woman and her husband attempted to attain equality in their private lives, which implied intimacy, openness, and lack of domination by either party. They openly sought sexual fulfillment with one another too. This also could imply nonexclusivity—that either one or the other could have affairs with other people. They indulged the practices of polygamy or polyandry, common in the underworld—which they called "varietism." Many avidly read the works of Havelock Ellis, Edward Carpenter, and Ellen Key, all of which expounded the ideal of free love for the twentieth century, as well as the importance of sexual pleasure.[3]

Men involved in such self-conscious feminist experiments represented a most decisive break from Victorian mores. In their advocacy of equalitarianism and of sexual pleasure, they attempted to redefine the meaning of manliness in America and to expand the boundaries of appropriate sexual behavior with middle-class women. They tried to define and establish a New Man to replace the older model of the Christian Gentleman. In this way, they prefigured many of the changes that later affected American youth, and thus were part of a genuine erotic avant-garde. Yet despite their importance the studies we have of such relationships have been of Greenwich Village Bohemians.[4] These are valuable, but Bohemians were hardly typical of the rest of the population in the nonsexual aspects of their life. Studies of broader groups engaged in such feminist experimentations are desirable to show more convincingly that feminist relationships did have an impact on the rest of the population. In the meantime, while undoubtedly these couples were privileged and successful, and, thankfully, articulate, they appear as ordinary people; above all, the women struggled to combine marriage, work, and career, unlike most Bohemians. I have therefore elected to study nine feminist relationships among couples who, while elite, cannot be strictly defined as Bohemian.

Two distinct patterns emerged. Five marriages succeeded in attaining the feminist ideals adopted at their onset while four failed. To discuss why this was the case surely is to get to the heart of the problem of the New Man.[5]

First, what caused four marriages to be unsuccessful as feminist experiments? The couples under consideration here are Ruth Hale and Heywood Broun, Jane Grant and Harold Ross, Doris Stevens and Dudley Field Malone, and Marcet and Emmanuel Haldeman-Julius. Ruth Hale was one of the founders of the Lucy Stone League, which fought for women to keep their names after marriage. She was a journalist, like her husband, the celebrated newspaper columnist. Jane Grant, too, was a journalist and founder of the Lucy Stone League, and her husband, Harold Ross, cofounded the *New Yorker*. Doris Stevens was one of the leading activists in the National Woman's Party. Dudley Malone, her first husband, was Collector of the Port of New York in the Wilson administration, but he is best remembered as a divorce lawyer for the rich and famous in the Paris of the 1920s. Finally, Marcet Haldeman-Julius, an actress and suffragist, was the niece of Jane Addams, while her husband, Emmanuel Haldeman-Julius, became known as the "Henry Ford of Literature" on account of his cheap Little Blue Book editions of the classics.

All of these marriages started with clear and unequivocal commitments to modern feminist ideals. Dudley Field Malone and Doris Stevens married in 1921, when their relationship was already of five years duration. Malone was identified in the public eye as one of the leading male supporters of women's suffrage, and as probably the most colorful. His spirited defense of the White House suffrage pickets and his dramatic resignation from the Wilson administration had, rightly, given him this celebrity. Stevens, one of the White House pickets, was herself rapidly emerging as an exemplar of the modern feminist New Woman.[6]

Their friends, Ruth Hale and Heywood Broun, were explicit in their marriage contract about the feminist commitment of their marriage.[7] The two signed a contract that gave Hale the right to a career as well as to an independent private life. Further, either one or the other could attain immediate dissolution of the marriage upon request. Ruth Hale made certain that she had a job before entering marriage—on the Paris edition of the *Chicago Tribune*; though this was hardly to help her in the long term.

Emmanuel and Marcet Haldeman-Julius, who also had an unconventional relationship, hyphenated their names when they married. Marcet Haldeman-Julius wrote to her grandmother in March of 1916 that she and Emmanuel had decided on independence. Each was to pay half of all common expenses but was to have full autonomy over his or her individual finances.[8]

Jane Grant and Harold Ross, like Ruth Hale, Heywood Broun, Doris Stevens, and Dudley Malone, endeavored to keep their own names. Grant later wrote in her autobiography, *Ross, the New Yorker, and Me*, that she and Ross "also agreed to give each other complete independence. We were by no means as one in our tastes. I had no intention of giving up dancing just because Ross couldn't dance, and I knew he would like to have his evenings with the men."[9] This was a very radical step for the early twentieth century.

The men's interest in and support for feminism extended from the private into the public arena. Obviously, Dudley Field Malone gave up a lucrative and prestigious post in the Wilson administration. He insisted in one letter to Stevens that "I am so fearful that you may get into bad news conditions because I literally *feel* the suffering in jail of each of those women."[10] The Haldeman-Julius's took on each other's names. Even Harold Ross, sympathetic but cynical and not a feminist activist, accepted the challenge of having a wife with a different name. Such support should not be underestimated; as Jane Grant pointed out, "registering at hotels as 'John W. Doe and wife, Jane Brown,' was quite an oddity at first but we finally established the idea."[11] This was, in those days, rather a bold idea, and took some courage.

Heywood Broun, however, went even further; he became a member of the Lucy Stone League—that Grant and Ruth Hale sponsored—which advocated that women keep their names after marriage. And he made it clear that he accepted equalitarian marriage out of principle and not because he was a "browbeaten husband." Also, he insisted publicly that the "oldest masculine ploy in history was a man's claim that he had no aptitude for domestic chores."[12]

Yet, despite the professed feminism of these men, feminist goals lacked the urgency for them that they had for the women they married. Their support for feminism took second place to their involvement in other causes. In the classic column Broun wrote on the death of his ex-wife, he discussed where his priorities had lain:

> Out of a thousand debates I lost a thousand. Nobody ever defeated Miss Hale in an argument. The dispute was about feminism. We both agreed that in law and art and industry and anything else you can think of men and women should be equal. Ruth Hale felt that this could only be brought about by the organization of men and women along sex lines. I think that this equality will always be an inevitable part of any thoroughgoing economic upheaval. "Come on and be a radical," I used to say, but Miss Hale insisted on being a militant feminist—all that and nothing more and nothing less.[13]

In other words, for Broun, feminist concerns should be submerged as part of a broader Socialist goal. Questions of class always consumed him more than questions of gender.

Still, one area did intrigue him: fatherhood. He insisted that "I believe in at least a rough equality of parenthood."[14] "As a matter of fact," he wrote, "even if men in general were as awkward as they pretend to be at home, there would still be small reason for their shirking the task of carrying a baby. Except for right side up is best, there is not much else to learn."[15] Broun wrote in his autobiographical novel *The Boy Grew Older* of walking his boy in a baby carriage, an unusual thing for a man to do in those days—"he felt a little conspicuous when he started for the park!"[16] And he wrote movingly of his exclusion from the birth of his son. The sister, on this occasion, told him, "I'm going to bundle you off. There really isn't anything around here for a father to do."[17] Poor Broun wished there was something he could do. But, to say the least, this was not the kind of thing men usually wrote about in the 1920s.

There is a further point, however. Broun had all the right rhetoric but his biographer wondered whether he merely just "liked the sensation of battling for freedom without much chance of getting hurt."[18] Revered though he was by his profession, he was a spectator who was not so very keen to work out the implications of his beliefs for himself. Those qualities that made him a good journalist did not necessarily make him a good feminist. Feminism, personified by Hale, helped, in part, to fulfill Broun's need for an authority by which to live: as Mildred Gilman put it, Hale was "his greatest authority."[19]

Haldeman-Julius's concern for feminist goals was also part and parcel of his desire to "debunk."[20] All forms of bias and superstition must be wiped out. Only by such debunking could progress be made. For Haldeman-Julius, all that was necessary was education, and all else, including women's rights, would follow. Feminism was purely incidental to his broader plan. Gender questions were not the priority for him that they were for his wife.

Harold Ross gave feminism a rather lower priority. Indeed, as both Jane Grant and Heywood Broun reported, it was Ross's boredom with feminist talk that led directly to the formation of the Lucy Stone League. As the *New Yorker*'s great satirist, James Thurber put it, "When Harold Ross, not yet of the *New Yorker*, had growled at Ruth and his wife Jane Grant as they plotted feminist strategy in his hearing—'For God's sake, why don't you hire a hall?'—they went out and formed the Lucy Stone League."[21]

Ross saw feminism as dull. Thus, very rapidly fundamental incompatibilities developed in the marriage. Ross wrote, "We have different tastes, different interests, different instincts, different ideas. We are distinctly two entities, two personalities. We differ in everything."[22] Ross wanted a woman who could look after him, not one who led an independent life, albeit one that—too noisily for the busy Ross—gravitated around their home. Grant dominated Ross—or tried to—and this made Ross feel uncomfortable. Jane Grant remembered a factor in their final divorce was that he had told "his poker cronies that he was afraid of women, and that he allowed me to dominate him." She admitted herself that this was the case. Of her second husband she said, "It turns out that I dominate him, too." But "he has liked it."[23] Not so Ross.

Dudley Field Malone, for whatever reason, seems to have tired of the women's movement soon after his suffrage activity was over. In December 1925, Stevens wrote to Malone:

> You have always been the one person since I have known you with whom I have wanted to share a joy. You have not always wanted to share a joy. You will remember countless times when my enthusiasms have bored you. But I think you will be the first to say that I have never turned a cold ear to whatever enthusiasm or cause you brought to me as mate. I have a so [sic] wanted to share a great many more things with you than you have wanted to share with me. Obscure you think my world sometimes. But whatever it was it was yours too.[24]

Men and women had different things at stake in the establishment of equality. The case of Dudley Field Malone suggests a further reason why men failed in this regard. Malone's support of feminism/suffrage must be seen in the context of his lifelong romantic attraction to unpopular causes. Malone saw himself as a stalwart for justice, freedom, and democracy wherever they were threatened. Hence his support of Irish nationalism and his celebrated involvement on the Darrow side of the Scopes trial. His support for feminism never went deeper than this; he never did understand that, for Stevens, feminism had personal implications. Further, his vigorous, spirited support for women's suffrage must be seen in the context of his infatuation for his wife. This is shown by the patronizing tone he adopted in their early love letters. On one occasion he declared that he was "so proud and thrilled at your wonderful speech and drawing-room meeting, you genius girl of mine."[25] After all, did she not "make stirring speeches about how women should-must stand *by-for-with*-one another."[26] He exclaimed, "You have a more marvelous mind than any human being I have ever known and you and Bertrand Russell are my favorite writers."[27] It is not that Malone did not believe his support for feminism to be genuine, but rather that it was, for him, just one of many causes that embodied his passionate belief in "justice." He failed to differentiate his involvement with the women's movement from his passion for Stevens.

Once the passion declined, however, so did Malone's commitment to feminism. He would deliberately use Stevens's feminist principles to justify his involvement with other women. Stevens wrote,

> You see I tried always not to blame the girls for their conduct because he told them all he had an extraordinary wife who represented a new era or some such tosh as that and they all thought it was true. It was a convenient legend for Dudley which he had erected for his own cinvenience [sic].[28]

She wrote him that this was a blatant misuse of her feminist beliefs: she "was the poor apostle of freedom. You were the communicant who profited by my doctrine."[29] On one occasion, when Malone and his latest lover came around late into the night, Stevens would be told that she was "nothing but an old-fashioned woman and not modern," which was "his favorite appellation whenever he wanted to take liberty." She was constantly being told to "act like a modern woman and not a dependent wife," as Malone brought floozies to their home.[30] For Stevens such an attitude to feminism was a betrayal of the high ideals of the original marriage. For Malone it was a fulfillment of those ideals.

The final cut was in his insistence in the press release following their divorce that the reason for the breakup was "the impossibility of two people of equally strong minds living together."[31] Whatever the reason for Malone's outburst, and however justified he may have been in making it, this public humiliation of Stevens, the very public feminist, serves to confirm that Malone's feminism was shallow. And since it was personal, when the marriage broke down, his support for feminism collapsed. In this case, the high ideals proved unworkable.

It was, however, in the area of their wives' need to work that this failure to grasp the equalitarian implications of feminism manifested itself most strongly. In the marriages examined here, only Malone felt threatened by his wife's career, but this was complicated by the fact that she wanted to work with him at one stage in the relationship. However, what is most interesting is the way in which some of these marriages failed as feminist experiments because the men, having greater access to the male-dominated public world, found it relatively easy to advance their own careers and, in terms of success, soon overshadowed their wives. These marriages, which started off with promises of genuine equality, soon deteriorated as broader societal factors that favored the advancement of men manifested themselves. Elite and privileged though they were, the couples could not transcend the fact that women's access to male-dominated professions was not increasing significantly at this time.[32] This applied especially in the cases of Ross, Broun, and Haldeman-Julius. In the cases of Haldeman-Julius and Malone, another factor entered in: they were able to control their wives' access to money because of the greater ease they had in obtaining it. In this way, inequalities manifested themselves, and the hope of a companionship of equals further faded.

Only recently has Jane Grant been recognized as cofounder of the *New Yorker* even though her role in the establishment of the magazine was considerable. According to both Jane Grant and Ross himself, Grant convinced Raoul Fleischman to invest in the magazine.[33] It was apparently Grant's idea to ask Janet Flanner to write the letter from Paris that became one of the magazine's most celebrated features. Undoubtedly, Ross was the genius who built on the magazine's foundations, but the fact that Grant got so little credit for her role serves to illustrate the facility with which Ross, as a man, could gain recognition. Further, while Grant's role was submerged, this must be seen in the context of Ross's lack of toleration for other successful women: he was "famous for his old conviction that women do not belong in offices."[34] This mellowed after he met competent women in World War I, including Jane Grant, the first truly independent woman reporter on the *New York Times*; but the deeply held convictions of his youth did not disappear so easily, and he always remained a little dubious about women in the workplace. Nevertheless, he supported his own female staff. When a young girl interviewed for a job and told Ross she understood she would be expected to perform sexual favors for the male staff, Ross called a meeting and told the men they were "giving [the] magazine a bad name around town."[35] Clearly, Ross disapproved of sexual harassment.

In the Broun/Hale and Haldeman-Julius households, the consequences of the husband's ease at advancing his work as opposed to his wife's were more serious for the women. Both Ruth Hale and Marcet Haldeman-Julius were significantly talented (and they were major influences on their husbands' successes), yet they were both bitterly frustrated in their desires for careers. As Haldeman-Julius began to develop his magazines, he and Marcet had a genuine partnership. They wrote a novel entitled *Dust* together, and she regularly wrote articles for his magazines. But ill health and care of children, in combination with Emmanuel's increasing conservatism about role experimentation, undermined her career. Much like Stevens to Malone, she wrote to her husband on June 30, 1925, that she wanted "so to work *with* you, Emmanuel in every way. Not pull against you."[36] By this time the marriage was in trouble. As Haldeman-Julius himself wrote in his *Thoughts on My Thirty-Sixth Birthday*, he would marry Marcet Haldeman-Julius over again because she was "so everlastingly ready to forget herself for the children and their father." He went on to declare that it was "great to have such a woman."[37] Undoubtedly, it was for Emmanuel, but Marcet was brought to a level of apathy that increasingly demoralized her and may have contributed to her early death. The Haldeman-Juliuses endeavored to keep their wealth separate. But with the outlay on the "Little Blue Books," their finances became intertwined. The sheer size of the Emmanuel-led Haldeman-Julius venture had overwhelmed their financial independence, which, in practice, meant that Marcet rather than her husband was the loser. As the marriage deteriorated, Marcet—once wealthy in her own right—was given precious little money by her millionaire husband. "Perhaps this really is generous," she pleaded on one occasion. "Anyway if you really feel it is, I shall try to feel so, too." There would "be no overdraft however hard the sledding."[38] For the next several years, there was endless squabbling about money—especially when the depression massively reduced the business. Quite simply, Emmanuel's greater access to money enabled him to keep his wife in thrall.

The case of Ruth Hale and Heywood Broun is even more tragic. On marrying, they were relatively equal. Both were successful journalists. But as Broun rapidly became one of the country's top sports writers, Ruth Hale fell behind him. Yet his development as a social critic owed much to her. Commentators have noted how Hale facilitated Broun's talent by injecting his intuitive flare with logic. Broun himself attested to her importance in the development of his work: he noted, "I suppose that for seventeen years practically every word I wrote was set down with the feeling that Ruth Hale was looking over my shoulder."[39] But as his career blossomed—thanks in part to her—her own career became increasingly difficult to sustain. She was not as talented as her husband, to be sure: "It must have galled her to watch Broun toss off a column or an article in less than an hour while she sweated for days over a similar composition."[40]

Their son, Heywood Hale Broun, noted that "I heard of many employers—although never by name—who turned her down for jobs because Heywood's wife didn't need a job."[41] Mildred Gilman, a fellow journalist and mutual friend, commented, "It was impossible because he became increasingly famous and she became somebody that—she couldn't make it in her own right, and this was really heartbreaking to her, because she was a brilliant, brilliant woman."[42] In one 1925 short piece, "The Wife of Lot," for example, he wrote that "it is not easy for any woman to lose her identity in the shadow of a great man and it is worse when she has to play supporting role to a husband of distinctiy minor quality," as though understanding and empathizing with his wife's dilemma.[43] Though Broun well understood that his wife's problem was "the inevitable bitterness of the person who projects herself through another, even if that one is close," it was not he who made the most telling comment.[44] Conservative journalist Westbrook Pegler noted the irony of Ruth Hale's destiny. He reveled in her fate as support for his own antifeminism by writing that "the great feminist was no less submerged, if that word will do, than the conventional wives of the neighbourhood, who called themselves 'Mrs.' and thought nothing of it."[45] As a man, Broun's greater ease in achieving success as a journalist caused him rapidly to overshadow his wife—something they had not anticipated when they embarked on their marriage. Eventually, they agreed on a divorce explicitly to help her career—to avoid her being overshadowed by him. But as Mildred Gilman indicated, it did not have the desired effect, for "when she left him she was the ex–Mrs. Heywood Broun, and she couldn't get away from this."[46] Poor Ruth Hale was caught in a bind from which there was no way out. She continued to make little impact as a journalist and this contributed to her death six months later: "Because she ultimately stopped eating. She died of—it has a psychological name, this kind of suicide. She wouldn't eat at all, and he [Heywood] would try so hard to have her see friends or doctors or psychiatrists, and she wouldn't, and so she just died."[47] Yet when she died so did a part of him. Mildred Gilman explained, "I think when she died something went out of him. I really do."[48]

Dudley Field Malone's financial clout caused difficulty for Stevens. Disagreements about money were continuous in their relationship. Malone, according to Stevens, never put into practice his expressed beliefs about the sharing of money:

> Furthermore he knows that I am on record as standing for a proper division between husband and wife of family income. He himslef [sic] has publicly

stated the same belief before hundreds of people in New York. He nows [sic] also that it was a source of great disappointment and humiliation to me that he would never consent to put my and his [publicly expressed] beliefs into practice in our menage. If I had recieved [sic] a proper share during our marriage, I would not now be without money. . . . That has been one of the great difficulties in our marriage. I was compelled to live at a standard equivalent to a domestic, while his expenses were unlimited, expenses for his own pleasure.[49]

Malone was always in charge of the money, even at the height of their relationship. In terms of the divorce settlement, Malone agreed to pay back the money he owed her, but in the Doris Stevens papers there are several letters from later years in which Stevens pleaded with him to give her the money that was her due. Once again, the man's greater access to power and money helped thwart the feminist ideals of the marriage, whatever the original intention of either party.

Feminist ideals proved no less viable in the area of sexuality. Although there were historical precedents for efforts between men and women to establish egalitarian relationships, attempts in twentieth-century marriages differed from similar nineteenth-century efforts because, for the first time, sexuality became a public feminist issue.[50] The feminist New Woman rejected the Victorian ideology of "passionlessness" and demanded the right to enjoy sex with men in a relationship of "modern love." This entailed intimacy, openness, and, above all, equality. It also, in the case of all these marriages, included the right for both parties to experiment with others in similar feminist relationships.

But "modern love" also meant the abandonment of the double standard in favor of a single standard of sexual pleasure for men and women. This was a far cry from the Victorian world, where the dominant concept of "character" for men was often understood as demanding sexual repression, and where, at best, the expression of sexuality with middle-class women was rigorously controlled, both before and within marriage, both publicly and privately. Obviously, marriage to a feminist New Woman challenged male identity at its very core. By emphasizing the importance of mutual sexual pleasure for its own sake as a continuing and ongoing aspect of marriage, as well as nonmonogamy, early twentieth-century feminist marriage blurred the distinction between a "good" and a "bad" woman. Was it really appropriate for a "good" woman to be so openly sexually demanding? Further, the feminist New Woman defied stereotypes, for she wished to be fully human in that she emphasized her right to sexual satisfaction on equal terms with men; as such, she stressed erotic as much as romantic fulfillment. Here was a more active rather than a passive female sexuality.

In response, and in support, these men rejected "character" and the Christian Gentleman as ideals. They believed the structures that were built around social relations to be inhibiting of sexual expression, and they accepted the "myth of Victorian repression." They thus feared above all that they be sexually repressed and unable to perform satisfactorily to the greater expectations of modern love. The men found, however, that, despite their professed radicalism, they remained recalcitrant Victorians, who, at heart, regarded a structured and controlled sexuality with middle-class women as for the best. They were more comfortable in a more familiar world of female passivity and male control.

At the one extreme, there is evidence that Dudley Field Malone and Doris Stevens did not always have a satisfactory sexual life. Malone saw a psychiatrist who told him that "Doris is really and truly your wife and you must make her quickly happy in the complete possession of you."[51] Stevens asked her lover Jonathan Mitchell in 1923 about Malone's sex problem: "Can it be that Mr. Tebrick [i.e., Malone] has imposed his feeling of guilt about sex-love on me? Or is it simply that he's a very busy divorce lawyer?"[52] Not only this, but Malone also feared impotence—that the demands of modern love were too great for him; he had "a devouring fear of impotency."[53] In particular, Malone's letters to Stevens during their courtship reveal his attraction towards her as a dominant, even maternal figure. In letters he wrote to her while on a hunting trip in 1916, he referred to his need for a "great, wonderful, lasting and controlling love," as well as to the "big love" that he had attained from Stevens.[54] He wanted "to be just filled inside and hugged outside in the power of your love."[55] Stevens fulfilled certain needs for Malone. But evidence suggests that Stevens was not as sexually attractive to Malone as his ideal. Malone maintained an ambivalence about Stevens's personal appearance. At one point he told Stevens she "was strange-looking. [She] looked like a man. [She] had a peculiar mouth. [Her] eyes were badly set. . . . [She] was an Amazon."[56] Though this was, admittedly, some years later when his marriage was troubled, it could well have reflected the expression of long-term frustrations. Malone, essentially a Victorian, could only see women in terms of good or bad. He understood the bad woman as sexual, the good as pure; Stevens fitted neither stereotype. Faced with involvement with a feminist New Woman, these simplistic definitions became blurred and uncertainty was the order of the day; he balked. While they were prepared to accept women's right to sexual expression, sexual satisfaction with a New Woman was a different matter.

In the other marriages, there is evidence that the men's Victorianism continued. Sources suggest that Broun, too, did not see Hale as his sexual ideal. She held his attention, "not with feminine wiles and a sexual magnetism, but with the quality of her mind." Theirs was an "intellectual comradeship" that, for a while, in its early stages, nearly did not survive Broun's affair with the dancer Lydia Lopokova.[57] Thus, in his novel *The Boy Grew Older*, Broun's character, Peter, despite his marriage to the feminist Vonnie (based on Hale), saw his earlier liaison with Maria (Lydia Lopokova) as more daring and romantic. He "took a definite pride in the fact once his heart had been broken." Under Vonnie, life "had become comfortable but safe."[58]

According to his son, Broun, "in everything except his social views about the world was timid. Physically, sexually, and intellectually."[59] The move away from monogamy was especially difficult for him. Broun's biographer noted that he was basically a moralist who had "doubts that so much abandon was really for the best."[60] He also suggests that Ruth Hale had practically to force him out on dates, to practice their ethos of sex freedom that demanded that they have other friends. Broun's marriage to a New Woman did not therefore change his deeply rooted Victorianism.

Jane Grant has remarked of Harold Ross that "in the presence of women he was especially Puritanical and I always found him excessively modest."[61] James Thurber confirms this. He described a celebrated incident in which, as a reporter on the Salt Lake City *Tribune*, Ross began an interview with the madam of a house of prostitution with the question, "How many fallen women do you have?"[62] Thurber went on:

> Sex, in or near the office, in any guise or context, frightened Ross. Sex was, to him, an ominous and omnibus word that could mean anything from the first meeting of a man and a woman, through marriage and the rearing of children, to extra-marital relations, divorce and alimony. When he swore, as he often did, that he was going to "keep sex, by God, out of this office," and then added, "Sex is an incident," he meant handholding, goo-goo eyes, fornication, adultery, the consummation of marriage, and legal sexual intercourse.... Sex, normal and abnormal, legal and illicit, paid little attention to Ross and his imperious commands. It hid from him and went on about its affairs as it had been doing for thousands of years.[63]

Thurber's account does have to be treated with caution. *New Yorker* writers E. B. White and Katherine Angell White, among many, disagreed with Thurber's portrayal of Ross.[64] This was probably because it seems to imply that Ross had some kind of sexual difficulty. There is no reason that this should have been so. Ross was merely reflecting his Victorian upbringing in Aspen, Colorado, where sex was kept firmly in its place and in perspective. Unlike Thurber—who made much money out of satirizing changing sexual mores—Ross had an instinctive distaste for the growing public obsession with sex that was not necessarily a result of his own squeamishness. He worried about the artists' "overemphasis [on sex]. 'Sex is not a career,' " he used to say, perhaps wisely.[65] And Jane Grant herself noted that he felt too much material on sex would lower the quality of the magazine by encouraging sloppy writing.[66] Ross's first biographer made the same point eleven years before Thurber, so Thurber was not alone in observing Ross's peccadilloes on the sex question.[67] But what is important here is that Ross remained a Victorian because he preferred sex to be in the background rather than because he was himself repressed. Either way, he remained a conventional man of his time.

Paradoxically, one suspects that Haldeman-Julius's own avowed anti-Victorianism and antiprudery, as obsessive as it was, may have reflected persisting Victorian tendencies. When someone needs to talk about and write about sex constantly, as Haldeman-Julius did, one suspects that he has not quite resolved his own discomfort with the subject, or at least that he is trying to prove to himself something of which he is not convinced— that he has resolved his difficulties. And Haldeman-Julius's anti-Victorianism was certainly carried to excess. He talked about having a "naturalistic view of sex."[68] He admitted that he "suffered some limitations in the number of young women friends I had as a result of this forthright policy," but he added that "prudery and sex ignorance [were] being attacked from many sides and that the work would not be in vain."[69] Evidence of his sexual life has not survived, but the sheer gusto with which Haldeman-Julius, a friend of Henry Miller, determined that the conspiracy of silence should be not merely breached but smashed makes us at least wonder about whether he really remained at heart a Victorian.

Men who married feminist New Women in general were men who were made aware of their feminine side by their marriages. Victorian men were expected to display tenderness towards women from a position of dominance. But their new roles demanded equalitarianism. For, like William Allen White and David Graham Phillips, whom historians Joe Dubbert and James McGovern, respectively, have studied, Malone, too, would make an excellent case study of the masculinity crisis of the Progressive era in his assertion of rugged machismo in the face of fears of effeminization.[70] There is evidence that Malone did not feel comfortable in the rough-and-ready male world. While on a hunting trip in the West in 1916, he wrote to Stevens how "wonderful to hear the voice and see again the gentle loveliness and magnetism of my beautiful love after having been in constant touch with very rugged vulgarity of thought."[71] Like a Victorian, he looked to Stevens for a haven from all this, at the same time that, like a little boy, he assured Stevens of his ability as a hunter. When he bagged a deer, he bragged that "the antlers . . . are the biggest that anyone has gotten in this country so far."[72] Two days earlier, he wrote to her of how he was "getting to look as tough and rough as the peasantry" and that "you have not seen how well I can ride. Yesterday, I spent all afternoon rounding up the eighteen horses and I felt like a real cowboy."[73]

But what was more significant was that this masculinity crisis led to decidedly ungentlemanly behavior. On several occasions he attempted to assert his masculinity in the rawest, crudest manner: the fact is that Dudley Field Malone, husband of arguably the leading feminist advocate of the between-the-wars period, beat his wife. Some of the abuse was merely verbal. On June 12, 1927, Stevens confided to her diary of an "evening telephone call from Dudley asking to see me—then [sic] I said no good would come of it he cursed over the telephone was obscene and threatened my life."[74] In a history of their relationship written for the divorce, Stevens expanded on the development of more violent incidents:

> He [Dudley] would return often drunk, from three to five in the morning and twice went out all night. On several such occassions [sic] he returned very violent and began to pull all the bed covers off me and throw me about. . . . When I tried to leave he yelled lowder [sic] so I sat down again. I got him out an [sic] home somehow and he continued to attack me first with words and when I tried to protect myself agaisnt [sic] hearing he attacked me physically. It was a devastating experience.[75]

Her diary accounts reveal even more vividly how "devastating" these experiences could be:

> When developed it was his party and he hadn't even invited me—he became violent. I ate something—left table—went home in rain, alone—determined to leave. T [Malone] came in—continued scene—smashed my hat—thumped me, choked me down on the bed, kicked me black and blue on legs so was scarred for days, kept saying, "I'll smash your jaw in"—I tried to pack to leave. He brandished cane. Threatening strike.[76]

Malone's crisis of masculinity was so intense that it led to an assertion of his primitive dominance in the crudest way; so great was the breakdown in his relationship with Stevens that their liaison moved from egalitarianism to this most sordid assertion of physical dominance.

Harold Ross admitted fear of the feminine in himself, too. He wore old-fashioned, high-heeled shoes, because he thought easterners were all "dudes," and that dressing as a westerner would differentiate him from them.[77] Any hint of effeminacy was suspicious. It was a long time before he could accept tuxedo suits as anything but the indication of "goddam sissies and dudes."[78] He "who secretly enjoyed being thought of as raconteur and man about town, was scared to death of being mistaken for a connoisseur, or an aesthete, or a scholar."[79] Indeed, he was nicknamed "hobo" so boastful was he of his youthful prowess as a tramp, and so proud was he of his identification with the lower orders.[80] His Rule 19 for the magazine was that "homosexuality is definitely out as humor and dubious in any case."[81] Ross was indeed what we would call homophobic:

> If Ross was unreliable in his opinions about heterosexual relations, when it came to homosexual ones he was all bluff and harsh-tongued male arrogance. He thought of homosexuals as being effeminate—nances, pansies, fairies. (He died before "faggot" became a popular form of derogation; he would have used it with pleasure.) He saw them as failed women, and his estimate of women was far from high. He would not have believed that his stereotype of the homosexual population as a limp-wristed lah-de-dah is but a small minority of the homosexual population as a whole; he would have scorned the notion that the majority of homosexuals are undetectable by mannerisms of dress, speech, or bodily movement and that many homosexuals are to be found playing the roughest and bloodiest of body-contact sports.[82]

Yet Ross needed a certain kind of homosexual, "whom he thought of as the only kind."[83] Somewhat bizarrely, he seems to have actively employed homosexuals who were meekly subservient to him, that is, "quiet and orderly nest builders, they took pleasure at being roared at and bullied and pushed to their limits."[84]

Like many Victorian males, Ross preferred the company of masculine men to that of women. In fact he even moved into an apartment with an actor known as the "singing policeman."[85] To him this was plainly more normal. Male homosexuals and the independent women of New York clearly made him feel uncomfortable. Ross and Malone indeed remained very conventional men of their time, unchanged by their marriages to New Women.

Although in all these marriages, sexual freedom had been agreed on, in practice this often enabled the men to date more conventionally feminine women, whom they felt they could control. Challenged by the New Woman to embark on a "feminist relationship," these men preferred to establish liaisons or relationships with women who did not expect as much of them as their wives did. The "varietism" that was such an important part of modern love was meant to include idealistic, intense, ethereal, passionate affairs such as Stevens's with an Italian cavalry officer, not promiscuous cavortings with dance-hall flappers. In effect, their attempts to adjust their sexuality to feminist expectations floundered. So they gave up. The greater temptations of the sexual revolution won out. The promise of instant gratification proved irresistible, and the men indulged in liaisons with the flappers of the dance-hall subculture. Here they felt comfortable. Here was a world with which they felt familiar. Like Victorian men, they could find a woman to satisfy them sexually, without commitment—only now they did not have to pay, or they could pay and control.

Dudley Field Malone surrounded himself with "geisha girls" and was a constant frequenter of nightclubs and various salons. In her unpublished autobiographical fiction, *Primer*, Doris Stevens noted how his interpretation of freedom in the marriage enabled him to continue to separate sexuality from love; she indicated that "there was something wrong with that party which she was slow to comprehend. One didn't mix wives with geisha girls. It wasn't done and she being superior should have known this."[86] For Malone, as many Victorian men had done, divided women into bad women and wives. As he tired of Stevens, he created for himself a new version of the Victorian world in which he had been reared. For him, the sexual promise of the double standard ultimately overcame any aspirations towards new forms of relationships.

Harold Ross had much the same attitude, if James Thurber is to be believed:

> Ross, as I have said, divided women into good and bad, but there was a subdivision of the bad, which, while not exactly good, was somehow privileged. These were the women of great talent, especially in the theater, whose deviations from convention and morality in their private lives were, by the very nature and demands of talent, excusable—"I guess" he might have added.[87]

Ross remained a conventional believer in the double standard. Although there is no evidence that he dated "bad" women during the marriage, he certainly did so after the marriage was over. Like Malone and Broun, he took advantage of the allure of the flappers of the dance halls of New York. After the marriage ended,

> As one of the town's more eligible bachelors, he was turning into something of a gay dog. Among his residences during the early years of his new bachelorhood were, fittingly, the Ritz and a Park Avenue apartment. He allowed his hair to grow longer and it more or less lay on his head.[88]

He and his friends would make inept advances at debutantes. Thurber recalled an incident in a nightclub when the "charm of one of the ladies had caught Ross's fancy and he made a gallant, though misguided, effort to bend over and kiss the back of her hand. The kiss ended up on the nape of her neck. Chairs were pushed back and the two men at the table stood up."[89] Ross and his friends were asked to leave—" 'I thought it was gay,' he said dejectedly," reported Thurber.[90]

Haldeman-Julius behaved in a similar way. For him, too, there were good and bad women, wives and mistresses. In her "What the Editor's Wife Is Thinking About," Marcet Haldeman-Julius wrote of her husband that "women are invariably drawn to him . . . and their interest . . . is as invariably reciprocated. That is if they are pretty or charming. . . . His attention is never held long by any one person."[91] This caused Marcet some considerable distress. His second wife, Sue Haldeman-Julius, noted that "he was known around the area for being a playboy. His extra-marital affairs sparked gossip over a backyard fence."[92]

One of Broun's biographers has noted that "he liked to squire pretty girls to speakeasies and night-clubs. In that day of considerable sex emancipation—and totally unrestrained talk about it—he went to some pains to establish a reputation as a Casanova."[93] Mildred Gilman remarked, "He was like a little boy, because he saw himself as the great gay lover."[94] Broun, too, in the face of the New Woman, merely adjusted his sexuality to the modern sexual culture. He adapted but did not change. There was his wife. And there were dance-hall flappers with whom he could have fun, but whom he could take less seriously, just as in Victorian America, there had been wives and prostitutes. When the divorces from their wives came through, Ross, Broun, and Malone remarried women who were very definitely not feminist New Women, but rather were women willing to be supportive of them and partners in marriages that resembled in many ways traditional styles of marriage. These women were not as demanding as their first wives had been. The feminist element in the marriages was in this way greatly reduced: significantly, the women took their husbands' names. Edna Johnson, third wife of Dudley Field Malone, was decidedly not a feminist. She was in fact a showgirl. Mildred Gilman wrote of her as cooing that "she hasn't any feministic leanings. But believes in women's having their rights whatever they may be," while Malone, memorably, declared in the same interview that he now believed in women having their rights "within the rules."[95] Neither Connie Broun, second wife of Heywood Broun, nor Edna Johnson continued their careers as dancers. Nor did Ross's second or third wife pursue a career. Haldeman-Julius found succor in his second wife, Sue, who was a traditional woman, that "dizzy-blonde" as Marcet referred to her.[96]

Heywood Hale Broun wrote of his stepmother that "it would take too long to catalogue all the differences between Ruth and Connie, but perhaps they are best summed up in the fact Ruth thought 'live and let live' was the motto of the damned and Connie thought it was the golden rule."[97] Quite simply, "if Ruth had set out to improve Heywood, Connie set out to make him happy."[98] Friends noted a "resemblance to Lydia Lopokova ... she was the physical type that attracted him, small, dark, lively."[99] In middle age, Heywood Broun no longer wished to confront the exhausting challenges of modern love:

> Praise is very hard to win in the world of perfectionist assessment, and for Heywood the cheerful, uncomplicated admiration he got as part of his second marriage was particularly welcome as the creaks of middle age became the voices of his phobias.[100]

And indeed, apparently, Connie called Broun "Commander," which no doubt suited his intrinsic Victorianism to a tee; clearly, she provided "the wifely touch lacking in his first marriage."[101] Broun, like Ross and Malone, divorced from their feminist New Women wives, chose very different women for their second marriages, and embarked on a more traditional kind of marriage.

Intriguingly, in the case of Marcet and Emmanuel Haldeman-Julius, the transfer between feminist marriage and more traditional marriage occurred within the same relationship, and very consciously so. They saw the change as entailing a move toward Judge Lindsey's then-celebrated concept of companionate marriage, or trial marriage, an attempt to adapt traditional marriage to the less rigid role dichotomies of the early twentieth century.

It was a change that Marcet Haldeman-Julius herself supported; she wrote a long article in the *Haldeman-Julius Monthly* about it. Companionate marriage involved "a legal marriage entered into by two people with the deliberate intention of having no children for an indefinite period of time." But should a child be born, then automatically the marriage would become "family marriage," and the husband would be responsible for the child and wife.[102] The Haldeman-Juliuses' adopted daughter symbolically married her first husband in a wedding that was billed as "the first companionate marriage."[103] However, both Haldeman-Juliuses renewed their vows according to the new idea. Their marriage in this way gave up all pretensions to be a feminist marriage, as the husband was now ultimately in charge. This reflected the entire pattern of their relationship.

Whoever was right or wrong in these relationships, what comes out most strongly here is the grappling and struggling and uncertainty that the men faced. There was no model for appropriate behavior for a New Man to accompany the New Woman. And these men received little guidance from their New Woman wives, who themselves were struggling similarly with their new identities. How were men reared as Victorians able to enter a relationship that demanded equality with sexual expression? Their wives could not answer this question either; indeed, convinced as Hale and Stevens were of the rightness of their own position, they failed to explore the theme of companionship. Men, like the women they married, were not ready for a feminist relationship, and had little grasp of what a lifelong commitment to one entailed. Where, after all, were the precedents? True, they accepted, if shallowly, their wives' feminism. But feminism was one of many interests for them, not the major interest. And they did not really understand what was required of them; nor did their wives. They accepted, too, women's right and need to work. But they found it easier to forge ahead with their careers, leaving their wives high and dry. Women also had a right to a sexuality. But they found the sexual demands of the New Woman bewildering. At their onset, the marriages promised much, especially as all the couples encouraged outside relationships, involvement in what was called at the time "varietism." This proved a major stumbling point. These men found that erotic interest was greater outside the marriage, where less complicated liaisons could be found. It was easier and socially acceptable for them, as men, to seek these out. This contributed to the failure of the marriages as feminist experiments, after which the men fled to more traditional relationships. The attempt to establish a new model for the social relations between the sexes—a "feminist relationship"—had failed. The men, in trying to break away from what they imagined were Victorian norms, found that they remained fundamentally Victorians at core who believed in a structured sexuality where the rules were clear. Pure and passive good women made wives while more sexual "bad" women made good mistresses. Such a system was easier for them. The attraction and novelty of an independent woman soon wore off for the men as their preference for control and dislike of being dominated rose to the fore, and as they found relief in primitive fantasies. The upshot was that the four marriages ended in divorces—two of them, the Haldeman-Juliuses' and Malone/Stevens's being extremely acrimonious. Ruth Hale and Heywood Broun and Jane Grant and Harold Ross, however, remained best friends. Yet, unquestionably, the attempt to redefine the meaning of masculinity and the sexual boundaries with middle-class women failed. So serious was this failure that it suggests that the whole effort was intrinsically misconceived. It seems to warn us of the dangers of the politicization of personal relationships. Yet the failure of these feminist experiments should not signal that such experiments were/are doomed to failure. There were other models.

The Success of the Feminist Option: Men and the Feminist New Woman, Part II

The marriages between Harold Ross and Jane Grant, Ruth Hale and Heywood Broun, Doris Stevens and Dudley Field Malone, and Marcet and Emmanuel Haldeman-Julius ultimately failed to attain the feminist expectations with which they had started. Most of the existing literature on feminist marriages in the early twentieth century confirms that such experiments were often unsuccessful.[1] Yet this material has not taken into account the success of several egalitarian marriages. Such experimental relationships were hardly without difficulties. But some marriages worked as feminist experiments because, even though the men in the partnership displayed symptoms of the early—twentieth-century masculinity crisis, they could still achieve love, intimacy, and companionship with their wives in a relationship of equals. The women's feminist aspirations in both public and private life were therefore realized—in a way that suited their husbands, too.

I focus here on the marriages of Fola LaFollette and George Middleton, Doris Stevens and Jonathan Mitchell, Inez Haynes Irwin and Will Irwin, Freda Kirchwey and Evans Clark, and Miriam Allen DeFord and Maynard Shipley. Fola LaFollette was the actress daughter of celebrated Progressive

Robert LaFollette and married an up-and-coming Greenwich Village play-wright, George Middleton, in 1913. Both were very involved in suffrage activities. Jonathan Mitchell was Stevens's second husband (they became lovers in 1923 and married in 1935). He was (and remained) a minor jour-nalist, though, by the 1950s, through his friendship with William F. Buck-ley, Jr., he contributed frequently to the *National Review*. Inez Irwin was a celebrated novelist, member of the National Woman's Party, and author of *Angels and Amazons*, a study of the suffrage struggle. Will Irwin, her second husband, was a prolific journalist who made his name in a series of articles from the scene of the devastation of the 1906 San Francisco earthquake. Freda Kirchwey was the editor of the *Nation* from 1935 to 1955, but was a lifelong feminist. At Barnard, she led a fight to remove sororities from the college, yet was still voted "the best looking, the girl who has done the most for Barnard, the most popular, the most famous in the future and the most militant."[2] In 1915, she married, by contract, Evans Clark, with whom she endured some difficulties, elaborated on at length in letters between them. Yet they nevertheless managed to maintain a marriage that, ultimately, was a successful one. Miriam DeFord Shipley and Maynard Shipley divorced their respective spouses in order to marry in 1921; their relationship lasted until Shipley died in 1934. Shipley was a Socialist, phys-icist, and pamphlet writer, while DeFord was a suffragist and writer as well as a sometime actress who played bit parts in Cecil B. DeMille movies.

These men supported their wives by active involvement in the suffrage movement and even by the sharing of household duties, and they showed an ongoing interest in their wives' work that was much less superficial than in the previous marriages. The Irwins, for example, shared in one another's writing. Inez Haynes Irwin wrote that they "read each other's manuscripts, accepted each other's suggestions amicably, or indulged in battles royal, as the case might be."[3] George Middleton gave active support and encouragement to Fola La Follette in her work as an actress. This we would expect in any successful marriage. But Middleton understood that his private efforts demanded public and political affirmation. With Will Irwin he got up at a suffrage meeting in New York City and spoke on "What Feminism Means to Me." He expanded on the significance of women's work. This could free women from the shackles of dependence on a man. He wrote that "the important thing about this whole matter of money in marriage is the potential power which lies in a woman's economic independence." For men this was a good thing, as it freed them from the demands of dominance. As he noted, "Any husband with such a wife can bear witness as to how it tempers his attitude toward her. It's splendid for any husband just to know that his wife can go out and earn a living. It curbs his inherent sense of possession."[4] In a manner that uncannily recalls the earlier failed relationships, he noted the importance of women's financial independence for the success of the marriage:

> Money matters wreck more marriages than outsiders. Financial independence is the best safety valve I know of out of some anti-feminist argument that this will take away men's incentive and sense of responsibility. My answer is that if love cannot supply both, then the marriage is a lie.[5]

Middleton believed that a husband should support his wife while she was pregnant and while their child was very young, but that, otherwise, she should be financially independent.

Maynard Shipley published in Calverton and Schmalhausen's feminist work, *Women's Coming of Age*, and shared intimately, if somewhat mystically, with his wife in her feminism and her pacifism. This added purpose to their relationship. He referred to their "real mission—nothing happens by accident—there are no accidents—we cannot fail. We shall yet do the work that was assigned to us because we were fit instruments for the work to be done. Be of good cheer."[6] Intriguingly, within the home Shipley and DeFord actually reversed their roles; as explained in *Uphill All the Way*, after Shipley's illness in the 1930s, Miriam DeFord "had to learn to wash and iron, to sweep and clean windows and scrub floors and carry coal and ashes and dig in the garden—all the things that for so long Maynard had done"—an unusual thing in the 1920s.[7] This was something about which he seems to have had no qualms. After all, he and DeFord could not afford servants.

Kirchwey and Clark also, apparently, shared domestic duties, though this was made all the more easy since they always had servants. He was delighted that an ill servant was to return to the household; he would not have to work so hard.[8] Clark gave Kirchwey active support in her every effort. In his diary, apparently, he commented on his wife's work. When she returned to the *Nation*, he helped ensure that, on account of her health, she would not have to put in too many hours.

Mitchell gave solid support to Stevens in her work. In a long analysis of their relationship, he wrote to her of his concern that "Tebrick" (Malone) had undermined her writing:

Everything you have written is pure gold. The curious thing about it is this. Some of it is straight article stuff—*Forum, Nation,* Pankhurst and the two newspaper stories—they are shining work, but you took on none of them, and needed to take, more than a few days. Say they account for a month out of more than two years. The rest are writing, as able, exciting, arousing writing as has been done.[9]

But for him the best of this work came when she had been away from "Tebrick." Mitchell also wanted to get involved in the movement: "I want to do feminist propaganda," he wrote at one point.[10] However, his support of Stevens's work could sometimes sound like Malone's hero worship. "You know all this," he wrote, "and you have already begun to find these answers and your work in my opinion is the most exciting thing that's happening in the modern world and the most revolutionary."[11] And when she participated in one particularly daring militant action, he wrote her, "Oh it was stunning dear, stunning, perfect, just everything. World opinion is rallied to you. Read the stories. They tell how you only wanted ten minutes. . . . O I'm glad you did it, it would have been rotten without this."[12] On another occasion he declared, "You're swell. You're glorious. You're a shining leader. You're a great person. I worship you again and again."[13]

But unlike Malone, he had a markedly sophisticated grasp of feminism—albeit one rather close to Stevens's. In 1927, they had an exchange on the origins of women's inferior position, following a heated argument that Stevens had had with Max Eastman at a friend's party. Like Stevens, Mitchell suggested that "physical inferiority" was not the reason for women's position but rather "sex fear" on the part of men—because "weakness was not a handicap among primitive people. Exceptional abilities, such as those possessed by Kings, priests and women, were terrible handicaps."[14] Fear of the power of women was responsible for their inferior position. To admit that men are often afraid of women's power is remarkable and shows great understanding. Because it implied that women do have power that men do not have, it was a much less safe feminist position for a man to take than Eastman's view that men oppress women on account of women's physical inferiority.

Mitchell was indeed not afraid to discuss feminism frankly with Stevens. He declared at one point that "the sticker for me has always been—intellectually not emotionally—how to account for women's acceptance of an inferior status."[15] Women could do everything that men could do:

That's why I've always had an unspoken cheer in my insides when Dinsche [Stevens] says, "I'll bet some women went in the boats and walked in running water, etc." Of course I've always known there was some fault with this male superiority argument; but I never knew what it was.[16]

All the same he concluded that women have been their own worst enemies, and often colluded in their own oppression: "Well, ma'am. I'll betcher one million trillion dollars you can find that women have been most down-trodden at the precise time that they have themselves been most convinced of their own inferiority."[17] Mitchell was unfrightened of intellectual honesty, and was refreshingly frank with Stevens.

Will Irwin's love for Inez Haynes Irwin also inspired him to support her feminist (in this case her suffrage) activity to the point where she remarked, "although I did not have to convince him to support equal suffrage, I made a complete feminist of him."[18] Will Irwin stumped for suffrage and put up with all the abuse that male women's suffragists received. Most appealingly, the Irwins recorded a humorous recognition of one another's faults. This came across notably in Will Irwin's mock *Interview with His Wife*, which Inez Irwin included affectionately in her papers:

(My husband had just flitted to the U.S. from the peace conference and was prepared to flit back again. He was going to take me with him again.)
"I notice your use of the verb 'take' Mrs. Irwin, said I. "Do you not consider such an expression in such a sense as anti-feministic?"
"Oh I suppose even an advanced woman has to follow her husband in some things," she purred.
"Would you mind putting that in writing for future reference?" I muttered.[19]

Their mutual tolerance and understanding and humor showed readily. They did not take themselves very seriously. To illustrate this, when the interviewer leaves early, Mrs. Irwin proceeds to discuss with her husband why he wanted to leave so soon. Could it be he wanted male company?

"If I may take the liberty of inquiring into your own personal affairs . . . I will ask why this sudden departure, and where are you going from here?"
"Since you have been so frank in asking me," I responded, "I will be equally frank in reply. To the club, Kelly-pool begins. Don't keep dinner warm more than half an hour."[20]

They could even make fun of Irwin's retreat from the home to the male world: a move that often symbolized male disgruntlement with women—but not here.

George Middleton expressed a view of feminism as humanism that was shared by many men at this time. Middleton developed his argument about work into a larger argument about feminism. He worked out a case for feminism as humanism that had received most articulate expression in the work of John Stuart Mill: "Basically men and women are human and from that standpoint, we face feminism. . . . It [feminism] asks primarily that men and women be considered as human beings."[21] Therefore, here was a movement that could "benefit men too," because it was categorically "not an assault on trousers." Middleton insisted that marriage be "a link not a handcuff," one that could enhance the relations between men and women and be mutually beneficial to them.[22] Each sex must "step with the other, in time and not in conflict. . . . [so] that each sex separately may be able to give to the other more comradeship, more freedom, more self-realization, more honesty, more beauty and, I believe, more justice."[23] Middleton confirmed his high expectations. Men who supported women were latter-day representatives of a kind of man who had always existed. According to him, "the man who believes in women's suffrage is not a New Man. He has always been with us. He has always welcomed any advance which women have wished to make."[24]

Evans Clark took an active interest in his wife's feminism; her book, *Our Changing Morality*, he was going to make required reading of himself a couple of times a year. Again and again in their letters to one another Clark asked to see Kirchwey's stories. And certainly he was prepared to support Kirchwey despite the pain this caused him: "I felt all the while as if they were stripping and lashing me," he said of his family's concerns about his involvement with an unconventional woman.[25] For his part, Clark went out of his way to defend his seemingly unconventional wife to his family when some members expressed their concern at Kirchwey's pursuit of a career in journalism. As he wrote of this to Kirchwey during their courtship,

> There was quite a fight over the wisdom of young girls reporting for *Morning Telegraphs* [as was Kirchwey]—there seemed to be an awful lot of dangers. But Ethelwyn, Uncle Howard Page and I backed you to the last ditch—and further than I should have in this particular instance under ordinary circumstances. The opposition was finally downed by someone calling for your "three prayers" to show what you really *could* do—and my reading

it with my heart in mouth and the fiery glows running riot in me. It was a poor session for me, dear, but I'm glad it happened for it'll open their eyes and hearts a little to the feminist adventure.[26]

Further, Clark was unafraid to discuss his wife's feminism, even with his journalist friends. Memorably, he would discuss "feminism with a bit of salad on the side."[27] Like the other men examined here, he grasped support for feminism as an important prerequisite of a modern marriage. His only comment, however, about what brand of feminism he might have supported was that he felt his wife's was "in the future, rather than here and now."[28] Kirchwey's feminism was strictly humanist. Her biographer has noted,

> By the elimination of barriers to women, she saw the specific search for women's rights as a stage toward the attainment of human rights. The struggle to obtain equality of opportunity for women would, hoped Kirchwey, bring forth a society of co-equal persons.[29]

Kirchwey's feminism was part of her long-term goal of human improvement. Clark shared in this aspiration. His feminist position was probably, therefore, vaguely humanist like his wife's—and like Middleton's. The fact that he never wrote on the subject or was active in the movement suggests that he simply stayed on the sidelines—implicitly supporting Kirchwey's feminism through his quiet support of her work, but never really getting involved.

These relationships attained the high ideals of companionship, too. George Middleton wrote to Fola LaFollette that he did not "know what all these days will bring me but I want you to know that you will be with me always sharing with me in the things I know you love also."[30] Later, he could write to LaFollette of his satisfaction at their marriage; he wrote, "Few people have had richer experience than I have had—through the people I have known and loved."[31] The Irwins made a point of sharing their common interests:

> We had many interests in common: authorship, books, theatre, movies, radio, animals, prize fights, athletic meets, dinner-going, and dinner-giving, hospitality of all kinds; motoring, walking, visiting historic spots, art exhibitions, art museums, art impulses, literature, history, isms and ologies, always and forever Shakespeare.[32]

In a sense, this may have contributed to their relaxed attitude to one area of contemporary feminism: Inez Irwin took her husband's name. She remarked that this saved her from the inconveniences that poor Ruth Hale had suffered, though, apparently, the Lucy Stone League had held her up as a "hideous example" on account of this.[33] Her lack of zeal in this area may well have helped focus her energy on less symbolic but, perhaps, more important concerns.

As already indicated, Shipley and DeFord shared everything, so did Mitchell and Stevens:

> In our case, we came to find that a passive, but elevated, venture, a visit to a museum, a concert or viewing scenery, followed by dinner, followed by play, the companionship of friends, the theater or, most often, games at home led to a warm and relaxed feeling between us.[34]

Like Middleton and the Irwins, Mitchell and Stevens fully shared in the companionship that was so intrinsic to a modern "feminist relationship."

All of the five men examined here enjoyed sex with their wives and proclaimed this enjoyment in their letters with the openness of discourse that developed with the sexual revolution. George Middleton's letters to Fola LaFollette were often blatantly erotic:

> The only thing that has entered portals is the fever stick. A cold unresponsive thing which nonetheless registers a reaction. If it would only go down. How damn proud it is.... But I dont [sic] mind confessing I'd like a little red moments—wet with sharp reaches that in their touch symbolize the immersion of life.[35]

Likewise, Evans Clark's letters to Freda Kirchwey are, if not exactly erotic, then certainly sensual:

> Last night I felt as if I was sleeping in a whirlpool. I didn't get to sleep for a long while and had a broken night—O how I yearned for you and your life-giving touch, my precious one. My insides are fierce—I'm wondering when they'll start working again on their own.[36]

There is evidence that for Evans Clark, sex had been a problem early in the marriage. Like Malone and Ross, he was essentially a Victorian. Kirchwey worried about his "conscious objection to 'intense' or 'overwhelming feelings'."[37] In a letter sent on February 1, 1930, she analyzed their early difficulties in some detail. Clark lacked the experience of Kirchwey:

> At first I was probably more mature sexually than you. I was just as inexperienced, but more awakened, more expectant, less afraid. My maturity was not quite real or wholehearted, probably, because of a part in which independence and pugnacity combined to make me more inwardly unyielding. I needed experience and sureness and art—on your side—to complete my growth—But you were not sure or fearless—and you had had no experience. So we groped along together and found a lot of joy and some disappointment.[38]

There is evidence, too, that Clark "liked feminine women."[39] Kirchwey herself remarked rather defensively that it was fortunate that she was "such a feminine creature—in spite of large doubts on that point? Knowing that, I may risk being a little more masculine."[40] This suggests that Clark, like Malone, while he loved his wife, had initial difficulty adjusting to a woman who broke away from conventional expectations of femininity. But eventually Clark solved these difficulties through psychiatry. As Kirchwey wrote, "Then you were analyzed and gradually you found yourself."[41]

Maynard Shipley, who authored sex manuals for Emmanuel Haldeman-Julius, wrote letters that were full of self-conscious sexual explicitness:

> We are still in the flesh—and the flesh has its purposes, too. The body is not a mistake. I draw your body and soul terribly close to me now as I kiss you a passionate goodnight. I hold your lips against mine, long and long! I drink of the nectar of life! I repeat over and over again, "Miriam, I love you, I love you. . . . To 'ell with celibacy, sacerdotal or pathological. Yea, or sentimental. Me for the exquisite thrill of the opposite sex contact."[42]

Jonathan Mitchell could be similarly sensual in his writings to Doris Stevens:

> I love your hair and eyes and lips—and the defect—and your neck, there are so many and so sweet spots by Dreka's throat, and white arms and hands. I've always loved, and Dreka's [crossed out] narrow heels and legs, "O small white reindeer. I love your effortless, hard-driving mind, your eloquence of voice and gesture."[43]

On Thursday, March 3, 1927 he teased,

> You are altogether glorious E-yow-ah, like a sea-lion, I love you. And come to think of it, I do feel a lot like the sea lion in the Battery Park Aquarium, swimming restlessly back and forth in his little tank, and barking. Only this sea-lion very presently is going to hop out of his cage. I guess

maybe a sea lion is too magnificent—well, I feel like a plain seal, and ar-r-r-up, ar-r-r-r-up I want Dinsche.[44]

It is reasonable to assume that one reason for the sexual success of these marriages was that they did not take sex as seriously, nor regard it in quite as political a way as in the failed relationships; and where there were problems, Freda Kirchwey was sympathetic to Evans Clark.

Another major reason for the sexual success of these marriages was a very conscious rejection of polygamy, of "varietism." This reflects further the relative lack of seriousness with which the couples took sexuality. George Middleton remarked how he resisted temptation many times. He wrote to LaFollette of his social meetings with women that "I'll wager I'll be the first one to take her away *still* a virgin."[45] Similarly, DeFord remarked of Shipley's early life that "the girls had practically to offer themselves and twice when he found the girl was a virgin she went home the way she had come."[46] While Shipley was probably shy, this is a sharp contrast in behavior to the men in failed marriages. For the men examined here, the choice of monogamy over "varietism" was a key to the marriage's success as a modern enterprise. While the new sexual openness was acceptable, after much wrestling they stopped at tolerating extramarital affairs. The Irwins stuck resolutely to one another through their years of marriage. George Middleton railed against polygamists. He told his wife that he loved her; then he asked, "Am I too damn good? At least I don't make a virtue of vice. I think, as I told you, that is merely inverted Puritanism."[47]

For Miriam DeFord and Maynard Shipley, as for Kirchwey and Clark, there were more complex questions involved. In her biography of her husband, *Uphill All the Way*, DeFord wrote that both she and her husband were "essential monogamists."[48] Apparently, he wrote to a friend at one point that "I have no more use for enforced monogamy than you have . . . I guess I'm just naturally that way; perhaps many years of casual temporary affairs taught me to appreciate a real attraction when I found it."[49] However, the realization that he and she were "essential monogamists" was a lengthy and painful one. They mused and debated over this issue ad nauseam. When they met, DeFord was married to anarchist John ("Armistead") Collier, a notorious polygamist. She expected Shipley to respect his relation to her, indeed to share her and proclaim his admiration for the dubious Collier:

> How dear and beautiful you are. Commend to me to your noble and enviable husband. What a truly great soul he is! May the full powers of the

unseen aid and comfort him in his work. I feel deeply honored to have his confidence and yours. Be assured, dear and rare Miriam, that what you hold high and noble shall be held sacred by me.[50]

On another occasion he referred to his rival as "dear, kind, generous, noble Armistead."[51] Shipley grappled with the question of monogamy in his letters to DeFord, trying hard to embrace her conviction:

> Monogomy [sic] is doomed. It is contrary to human nature when at its best, and we may as well be brave and honest enough to meet life and its problems as they are encountered. I am in perfect sympathy with you. Still, I believe if we were all brought up right, from adolescence onward, to look at things as they actually are, we would all be better prepared to enjoy ourselves under conditions as they really exist. I have suffered unspeakably because I approached life's problems from the wrong point of view. You have taught me, from A, a very great deal on this subject. I believe I shall yet end up a varietist.[52]

But as he continued, his ambivalence about polygamy came through:

> I realize that I have still more to learn (I believe I shall yet end up a varietist). As you say it is one thing to understand a thing philosophically and another to meet a practical condition in the right spirit of unselfishness.[53]

Later, once the divorce with Collier was over, he claimed that he was not "uncomfortable sexually," but asked her why she did not arrange to leave him a "shock absorber" (their euphemism for a casual affair).[54] Later he was tempted to have a "shock absorber."[55] Despite this frank discussion and his assurance that it was "possible for you to be non-monandrous, or polyandrous, and be wholly 'true,' in the best sense of that much-abused word, to all concerned," he did not really like nonmonogamy.[56] His heart was not in it. Even his casual references to affairs suggest that both in fact took them seriously. In 1919, he wrote to DeFord, "Don't be alarmed, there is no immediate danger of any one's wanting to shock-absorb me!"[57] Monogamy contributed to the success of their marriage. Theirs was indeed a rather bizarre situation. Shipley, to please DeFord, reluctantly tried to accept polygamy, a position DeFord herself held only half-heartedly, having learned it from her first husband. But they did not practice it. Instead, once Collier's influence waned, their relationship settled into a comfortable pattern. To an extent, therefore, Shipley remained Victorian. But he was modern in his adjustment to a New Woman.

There was a similar pattern between Jonathan Mitchell and Doris Stevens. The continuation of Stevens's marriage to Dudley Field Malone was a cause of great consternation for Mitchell, who was profoundly and deeply jealous:

> I did not like Mr. Malone and, until the last few days, I had never thought about the nature of his relations to Doris. Besides the obvious reason, my dislike came from my having been brought up in Maine at a time when Irishmen were regarded as Negroes are in Mississippi.[58]

How traumatic this must have been for him is further illustrated by his insistence that "whenever I knew they were together, I sweated blood. For years I dreamed of meeting Mr. Malone on the street and hitting him in the eye."[59] Later, after Stevens's death, he explained why:

> By this time, I had begun to wonder whether I was not unfit to marry Doris, whether, if I really loved her, I ought not to marry her. In that mood, naturally enough, I no longer felt she belonged to me, and, if she didn't, other men had potential rights. . . . While I was not sure of my own claim to her, the notion of other men's claims filled me with desperation.[60]

Indeed, it made him doubt his own potency: he said that he "felt impotent once or twice. I've felt impotent when I haven't been able to see you."[61] He tried to find ways of coping with this jealousy, and he was apparently successful, especially when he declared that he thought he had "discovered the cure. You get very close to the beloved, and love her very much, and when—as will happen unless something is very wrong—love is returned, you feel bursting with power and strength, and forget about jealousy."[62] But, ultimately, like Shipley and DeFord, the couple decided on monogamy. Mitchell indeed later claimed that "with a single hardly avoidable and wholly unimportant exception, Doris had been utterly faithful to me from the day we met, and was to be, conceivably with one or two equally unimportant exceptions, throughout our lives together."[63] This idea of "unimportant exceptions" is fascinating, but, whomever they were with, the couple proved successful, in part because they decided on monogamy.

Freda Kirchwey and Evans Clark also came to similar conclusions. Although the tenets of equalitarian marriage often did imply that both sides had the freedom to date others, there is only limited evidence that these affairs were ever sexual. Their son, Michael Clark, has insisted that "his parents, despite their new-fangled theories and modern behavior," essentially were "models of bourgeois virtue and morality."[64] He was right. This certainly was true after the crisis in their relationship at the time of the death of their son Jeff in 1930. But it was a hard-won lesson. There is some evidence of extramarital liaisons before this date. These were not necessarily consummated; they may well have been merely emotional. In the letter to Clark during Jeff's illness in 1930, Kirchwey discussed the issue of extramarital liaisons before this date, writing that "if you and I had more wholly fulfilled ourselves ... we would have wanted outside emotional excitement much less."[65] They had "gone out emotionally to other people."[66] Yet their marriage survived. Clark and Kirchwey, too, preferred monogamy, and had the sense to realize it before it was too late, like Shipley and DeFord. Clark, like the other men happily married to feminist New Women, by determining on monogamy saved himself from the problems that confronted those who tried polygamy: the sexual success of these marriages, in part, depended on this decision.

Ultimately, it was in his fearless rejection of Victorian primitive male roles that Mitchell was most interesting. These men were not frightened to abandon the strictures of these roles. If they went through a crisis of masculine identity, they soon overcame any attraction that early–twen-tieth-century primitivism had for them. Thus, Mitchell noted that "[he] began to struggle with a book review that I had promised for Thursday. It was a review of *The Drifting Cowboy* and full of nauseating male legend, about lean, bronzed wiry men."[67] He, too, had some credentials as a fem-inist and was deeply wounded when, after he asked her to marry him, Stevens declared that "men, in general, were difficult and that, instead of being an exception, I was behaving like all other men."[68] This must have stung him because he saw an element of truth in the accusations—"I must have thought there was something integrated and virile about being high-hat and saying 'here I am'."[69] As a man who regarded himself as a feminist, it must have disturbed him if he, too, was implicated in men's oppression of women by his lover. He must have felt terrible guilty.

Further, his homophobia was of a different kind from, for example, Harold Ross's. It did not emerge out of any fear of possible homoerotic tendencies on his own part but rather seems typical of the curiosity that characterized discourse about homosexuality among those leaders of the sexual revolution aware of Freud's writing on the subject:

> As I went down to find a place at table on the Majestic, a tall and semi-distinguished old duck suggested that we eat together. I didn't care much at

that time whether we sank together, and agreed. The next day at lunch he opened up on his sex-life in London and Munich and I discovered that my table-mate was Titana [sic], the Queen of the Fairies. Here, I thought, is a chance to be worldly and continental, so I asked him all the questions I could think of. He was very dull, however, and told the same story with few variations: there is a Turkish bath on New Oxford Street where you can pick up a young man. All I found out was rendezvous and prices so I became insulted, and had the old boy exiled to a seat by himself.[70]

At worst, Mitchell was curious but not frightened. He went on that he was "still in the market for info about the horrid business; there may be pure and noble passions but I doubt it. Senator Walsh represents the only type I have ever seen and what a nice feller he is."[71]

A similar kind of homophobia is evident in Irwin's autobiography, *The Making of a Reporter*. Here, he refers to how he used to regard basketball as only a " 'sissy' imitation of football."[72] Yet he did not fear taunts of "sissy" or "nance" directed at him as a male supporter of women's suffrage.[73] He dismissed such attacks in his autobiography quite simply as "uninspired," referring to "one original spirit [who] broke through the police lines and marched for some time beside me, asking in a piercing falsetto, 'O Lizzie, do you wear lace on your drawers?' "[74] Irwin, like Mitchell, was sufficiently unconcerned not to be bothered by such taunts. Why should he be? His reporting showed him to be a man of courage and conviction.

Historian Kay Trimberger has remarked on the importance of "psychic openness" as opposed to "personal distance and autonomy" in a man who successfully adjusted to the demands of a New Woman.[75] These men categorically were able to discuss their relationship with their wives honestly and openly and frankly. They were able to respond to problems in their relationships as part of the cultivation of a deep intimacy with their wives, which contrasted sharply with the five marriages discussed earlier.

This applied to Shipley and DeFord. There were constant references in their relationship to what they called "soul-love," which to Shipley was an elaborately defined mystical experience. He wrote, for example, that he pressed his "feverish life to yours. I take firm hold of your body—drawing you very close to my heart—very close, so that the corporeal is almost as one with the spiritual, we cling very hard and also together—rapturously."[76] They were able to develop their physical and spiritual unity by frank, open, and honest discussion of their problems.

Eventually Kirchwey and Clark were able to attain this psychic openness with one another too. Kirchwey wrote to Clark that she had always shrunk from "analyzing too much the problems of our own relationship—just as you always have."[77] But the series of letters they exchanged at the time of the illness and death of their son Jeffrey in 1930 broke the ice decisively. And Clark's psychoanalysis helped too. Here was a couple who had to work hard at their relationship—to ultimate good effect.

A similar pattern is discernible in Jonathan Mitchell. His "To D.C.S. Journal" at the Schlesinger Library is a lengthy discussion of his relations with Doris Stevens. Here, he emphasized and put into practice complete openness and honesty. He wrote that "I can heap up instances of deliberate dishonesty in word and action of which I have been guilty in our relationship." But, as he indicated, "I think that is ended."[78] The future was going to be different:

> Henceforth I am going to decide when anything happens whether it is important or trivial. If I think it is important I am going to try to do something about it. If it is trivial, I am going to forget it. Reversed—I am not going to make light again of anything which I suspect is serious, nor struggle and fuss over things that don't matter. This is a resolution.[79]

Mitchell thought "that by henceforth doing them—all simply to improve myself—I shall be a better reporter, better feminist, more warming and definitely gayer. I shall be most of all a better mate."[80] He was, however, realistic about his chances of improvement, declaring that "I don't expect to become a better person or lover abracadabra, presto all at once. I was filled as a Spring tide fills an inlet, with a new will to be a better lover when I knew you had gone. But I know sudden regenerations aren't so good."[81] Ultimately, his openness and honesty led him to grasp the way toward greater equalitarianism. Psychiatric help enabled him to reach this higher level of understanding:

> But as Parker talked, it became very clear. The important thing is not who belonged to whom, or who is preferred to whom. That is not important now. The important thing is for us to be secure and gracious people, and I think the rest can and will be worked out. The important thing is for me to be a calm and fervent lover of Dreka [Stevens] and titles and crises don't matter.[82]

As Mitchell wrote much later, in the 1960s (after Stevens died), they were able to develop an extraordinary psychic rapport with one another (indeed rather like Shipley and DeFord). Mitchell wrote that "one or the other of

us would have a sudden wish to visit a museum, without conscious recognition of what he or she was wishing."[83]

A similar psychic openness can be seen in George Middleton and Fola
LaFollette's relationship. He wrote her from London on June 24, 1942,
that he needed to determine what should be his "best attitude towards you
and [your] inner life." He needed to "readjust if [they] were to go on in
full comradeship."[84] Openness could be positively mystical. The Irwins
obtained psychic openness too. In *The Making of a Reporter*, Will Irwin
described a "recurring nightmare" that he had of being trapped in Germany
during the war.[85] Inez Haynes Irwin apparently had the same dream too.
Thus, these marriages attained a sexuality that was equalitarian in a context
of companionability and openness, yet also erotic.

But, nevertheless, to be fair, it is necessary to qualify the success of
these marriages as feminist experiments. Even after they had long been
married, the men examined here still displayed a very human failure to
attain the ideals of modern feminist love. Further, some of their characteristics raise serious questions about what men had to give up in order
to attain success in love with a feminist New Woman.

The New Man could, for example, be violent. There is evidence that
Shipley could behave very badly with DeFord when drunk. He was in fact
an alcoholic, though DeFord insisted that "he never became surly or quar-
relsome. Alcohol can only bring out what is in a man and Maynard's
sweetness of nature was as much his when he was drunk as when he was
sober."[86] But later on in her biography of Shipley, DeFord admitted that
"every indiscretion with alcohol was followed by dreadful remorse."[87]
Though there is no specific evidence of actual physical violence, this sounds
like Dudley Field Malone.

In his autobiography, Middleton commented on his own instinctive
feelings at having his wife support him on a summer lecture tour:

> We were hard up. To carry me without further borrowing, she went on this
> grueling Summer trip, under chautauqua tents where the temperature was
> often a hundred. I had had the usual male reactions about being "kept," and
> so, for the first time, grasped how many women have also felt. But, being a
> feminist, what could I do? In fact, I got a little play out of my own conflict.[88]

Middleton's amusing and witty insight into the strains of being a profem-
inist man endears him to us.

Finally, Jonathan Mitchell at times comes across as so indecisive that
we do not empathize with him. His patience is staggering. Why did he

wait so long to marry Stevens? Why did he not act more decisively towards Malone? His long note to Stevens (D.C.S. Journal) reads as if it were the culmination of years of frustration. He wrote that he was "trying to set down a charter for a union between a woman and a man which will be more complete than ever a union has been. I want desperately to know why I have not been a good mate for you."[89] He harped extensively on his own failures:

> I have done my job—sometimes well but often sloppily—and I think I am a more competent and workmanlike reporter. Beyond that I've written three Sunday pieces for the *Post-Dispatch* and a story on Marcus Garvey which was refused by the *New Republic*. This record is simply shameful.[90]

Finally, he wrote to Stevens that he wanted "to talk to you about ourselves. Once we played a game called 'finding defects.' So darling a defect Dreka [Stevens] has."[91] And then he at last proceeded to discuss her relationship with Malone.

The issue Mitchell's passivity raises is an important one: did he and Stevens attain a genuine relationship of equals, or rather one in which Stevens really called the shots? Certainly the general equality that seems to have been achieved between Shipley and DeFord, the Irwins, and Middleton and LaFollette suggests that equality of sorts between the sexes was and is possible. But the fact that the man who was most close to this feminist ideal was so deferent and weak in many ways raises the question of whether or not it was possible for a man to attain complete equality with women according to the feminist ideal. One could, on the one hand, argue that Mitchell and Stevens had redressed the power imbalance between men and women; but, on the other hand, one does rather get the impression that Stevens simply told Mitchell what to do. At the very least it suggests how precarious a thing it is to maintain any equality: when, for example, does the magic moment arrive when a couple can say they have attained this nirvana, one wonders? What did feminists mean by equality? As good Americans, they wanted happiness and success in all areas of their lives. But the ideal of equality with men in personal life remained vaguely defined.

This, then, was the New Man, who was not so very different from the Christian Gentleman. For one way in which the men supported women was, indeed, by behaving according to the tenets of the Christian Gentleman. When Mitchell discovered that Malone battered Doris Stevens he declared that "my obvious duty was to protect my girl."[92] On one occasion, he felt it necessary to protect another woman friend of his when she got in a row with a taxi starter; he hit the man. Maynard Shipley could be chivalrous too. On one occasion he said that "I shall again be near to love and comfort you—yes, and to protect you if need be."[93] Like the Christian Gentleman, he firmly rejected primitive behavior. He succeeded, above all, because he did not try to shift his role too radically from Victorian expectations.

Yet this similarity only went so far. He was modern in that he endeavored to enjoy his sexuality to the full as a central part of the relationship. Above all, perhaps, he was able to adopt a single standard of sexual pleasure that he and his wife reached through mutual accommodation and common sense, but that, perhaps, fell short of the very highest expectations of the four marriages discussed in chapter 6—and that was, perhaps, more reminiscent of the Victorian experience than, early on in the relationship, he would have liked. He was able to transcend the impact of the good woman/ bad woman dichotomy that so troubled the four men examined earlier. And he was not plagued by the need the other men had to prove themselves in extramarital affairs: monogamy was simpler for the New Man, who combined erotic fulfillment with an open, equalitarian persona. For the New Man was thus both companionable and democratic. He abandoned once and for all the baggage of patriarchal dominance that the Christian Gentleman had carried, and, in doing so, helped redefine the role of the American man.

This begs the question of what caused some of the marriages to succeed as feminist experiments while others failed? Certainly, it was important that inequalities did not emerge in the couples' engagement in the public sphere. The failure of Ruth Hale and Heywood Broun's marriage contrasted with Clark and Kirchwey's successful balancing of their public personae. But also some mutual agreement about and engagement in feminist goals was crucial. This was certainly helped if the women did not espouse an ideological feminism—however noble in rhetoric—that placed narrow women's concerns over larger human goals that sought to benefit both men and women. Thus, the feminism of the National Woman's Party and the Lucy Stone League, of Hale, Stevens, and Grant proved less amenable to men than the less militant feminism of DeFord and Kirchwey and LaFollette and Inez Irwin (though Mitchell, as noted above, represents an interesting exception). Those relationships that were most successful in attaining feminist goals were, paradoxically, those that took the political aims of the original marriage less seriously. So, far from proving by their success the viability of the politicization of personal life, these five marriages prove the contrary. What was needed for success, as, surely, with any successful marriage in any time period, however socially constructed, was pragmatism and compromise, as well as the mysteries of rapport and sex attraction; and both parties having a nonideological position on the personal certainly helped, especially in the area of sexuality, where the problems—of Kirchwey and Clark in particular—demanded openness and imagination and intelligence—all exhausting things. Sexuality was thus not quite as overwhelmingly important in these marriages. It was more integrated as a mere part of the relationship and not as demanding for the men. This same pragmatism applied in the rejection of polygamy, which the successful couples had the good sense to abandon. The expectations, then, were toned down somewhat. Yet the success of these marriages, with all the reservations I have indicated, does still suggest that, with a little trial and error, the original feminist goals of the marriage were not necessarily misconceived.

Modern American Male Heterosexuality: The 1920s

In early twentieth-century America, men faced increasing expectations that they be young and sexually attractive, that primitivism be empha-sized over gentlemanliness, that sexual expression be stressed over repression. This ideology gained ascendancy in mainstream American cul-ture, drawing inspiration from working-class sexuality as manifested in the dance-hall subculture in the cities. Not only was a sexual revolution in the air, but also a relative leveling of gender roles occurred among elite groups that reflected the diffusion of feminist ideas. To what extent, how-ever, did these influences actually affect mainstream American middle-class men?

The recent work on early twentieth-century sexuality has emphasized the importance of the development of an incipient youth culture by the 1920s. Influenced by sociologist David Riesman's classic conception of a shift in this time from an inner-directed to an outer-directed personality as a dominant goal of socialization, historians have observed the emergence of peer-led sexual mores among college youth in the 1920s: the peer group defined what was appropriate sexual behavior.[1] This analysis has recently been refined by the observation that the emerging practice of dating differed from the nineteenth-century practice of calling, most fundamentally in that in the former, young people, rather than parents or older people, guided one another; "sex became the central public symbol of youth culture, a fundamental part of the definition that separated youth from age."[2] But, most importantly, what these writers have not fully appreciated is the precariousness, fragility, and faddishness of peer-led mores, especially as manifested among the young. The dating system, far from developing in a consistent way over the period of the 1920s, was constantly in flux precisely because, as the creation of young people themselves, it ultimately placed the onus of responsibility onto the individual daters. To break peer-group sanctions was far less serious than to break the sanctions of the church or of parents. Therefore, the dating system moved from fad to fad, from "rating and dating" to "going steady" to a myriad of other approaches that individual men and women learned from one another. In this environ, a variety of different and always changing moralities replaced the hard and fast rules of chaperonage.

The vagaries and fancies of individual peer and family environment, therefore, defined courtship habits. But this applied far more to men than to women. The change from the system of calling, of chaperonage, to the dating system entailed a move from a woman-controlled courtship that involved men's entrance into a private women's world to a system where women entered the men's public world. This gave men a great deal of power that they were thoroughly ill prepared to use. For if the early twentieth century was marked by growing sexual choice as new alternatives developed and older taboos declined, it was also characterized by greater complexity and uncertainty around sexuality for men even more than for women. An individual man had to choose and to learn the sexual boundaries that worked best for him through trial and error, in response to peer pressure, in an environment in which the artifacts of the culture of personality increasingly set the pace. YMCA writer Sherwood Eddy analyzed the problem perceptively: "Whatever its abuses, young people today cannot be forced back under the former conventional restraints but must find safeguards in their own inward control."[3]

How did men reared as Christian Gentlemen respond to the more sexually demanding New Woman? Faced with a sexual culture that was ever more complex, men experienced confusion, uncertainty, and anxiety as to what was appropriate behavior. On encountering the institutionalization of a homoerotic subculture, they balked. Dating stressed "performance" and the learning of skills. Men wondered how to perform, for they had not lost power, merely the guidelines on how to use it. In the peer-led youth culture, young men were exposed to a multiplicity of codes that left many of them wondering how far it was appropriate to go with women. Faced with this confusing moral crisis, many men were left to their own worst behavior. They proceeded to treat middle-class women much as they had been socialized to treat prostitutes. They used lewd language to describe middle-class women; they paid for "dates" and expected "thrills" in return. When thrills were not forthcoming, they protested. Increasingly, men, frustrated in dealing with the New Woman, rejected the commitment to marriage that was expected of them. Further, as marriage became more sexually demanding, it also became more egalitarian, if hardly feminist; men fled, too, from the responsibilities that marriage entailed. It was in this way that by the 1920s, both marriage and dating among the population in general took on some of the dilemmas that the men of the working-class dance-hall subculture and elite men married to feminist New Women were then facing and had faced in the previous two decades.[4]

By the 1920s, sexuality was becoming more demanding and complex for men not merely in terms of the cultural ideal of manliness that I have discussed already, but also as regards actual behavior. According to Kinsey, among women born before 1900, only 14 percent experienced premarital sex, while among those born after 1900, 36 percent had such experience.[5] These figures set the pace for the changes in male sexuality. Put simply, the figures suggest that men were having sexual intercourse more often with women of their own class rather than with prostitutes. Writing in 1948, Kinsey observed that the average frequencies of intercourse with prostitutes were down to "two thirds or even half" as often among his younger generation than among the older generation.[6] The middle-class male experience of sexuality was therefore altered in these years in favor of an expansion of the sexual boundaries with middle-class women. An expert on adolescence, J. L. Richmond, observed that "the normal youth in a good environment visits such houses [of prostitution] far less frequently than formerly."[7] Figures from Terman's large study of 2,484 California married people in the middle 1930s further serve to confirm Kinsey. According to Terman, of women born before 1890, 8.7 percent had sexual intercourse with their spouses before marriage, but of those born after 1910, 45 percent had premarital sexual intercourse with their husbands.[8] Among those who had sexual intercourse with others as well as their future spouse, the figures almost exactly correspond with Kinsey: 5.8 percent of those born 1890–1899 had premarital sex with more than one partner, while among those born in the decade after 1900, 14.0 percent did.[9] Figures from Terman also show that among those born before 1890, 50.6 percent of men were virgins at marriage, while among those born between 1900 and 1909, 32.6 percent were (among those few born after 1910, the figure is even lower—13.6 percent).[10] Historian John Modell has recently used the Kinsey figures to establish that among the men born before 1890, 66.3 percent had sex with their fiancées and others, as compared to 76.5 percent of those born between 1910 and 1919 (among those born after 1925, 80.1 percent had sexual intercourse with fiancées and others).[11] Men in general were, then, having more sexual intercourse, whether with prostitutes or middle-class women.

More options, choices, and alternatives around sexual behavior developed for men on the path to marriage. If young men and women were not necessarily prepared to go all the way, they now more often went part of the way with one another. Of those women born before 1900, four in five had some kind of experience of petting with a man before marriage, while for those born 1910–1929, the figure was ninety-nine out of a hundred. Among those women born before 1900, 26 percent had petted to orgasm. Among the 1900–1909 group, the figure was 44 percent; and it was 53 percent of those born in the following decade.[12] Sex surveys conducted in the 1920s do not reveal the more esoteric practices of premarital cunnilingus

TABLE 8.1
Percentages of Total Petting Experience

Age	Older Generation	Younger Generation
12	3.7%	6.1%
15	36.5%	48.9%
20	75.7%	92.7%

SOURCE: Kinsey, *Sexual Behavior in the Human Male*, 406. Reprinted by permission of The Kinsey Institute for Research in Sex, Gender, and Reproduction, Inc.

TABLE 8.2
Percentage of Petting to Climax

Age	Older Generation	Younger Generation
12	0.7%	0.2%
15	6.9%	8.4%
20	37.2%	48.5%

SOURCE: Kinsey, *Sexual Behavior in the Human Male*, 406. Reprinted by permission of The Kinsey Institute for Research in Sex, Gender, and Reproduction, Inc.

or fellatio to be particularly widespread, but Kinsey's 1954 study of women's sexuality does support the contention that there was some variance of sexual practices among men with women of their own class: in those educated up to the age of seventeen and over born between 1900 and 1909 who had coital experience less than twenty-five times before marriage, 14 percent of women had experienced cunnilingus, while 26 percent of those born after 1910 had.[13] Among those who had engaged in coitus over twenty-five times, the figures for cunnilingus remained fairly stable. As regards fellatio, instances tripled among the group that had coitus less than twenty-five times, from 7 percent to 23 percent, while among those who had had sexual intercourse over twenty-five times before marriage, the instance was stable.[14] This suggests that during the 1910s, cunnilingus and fellatio became genuine petting options. This was widely suspected at the time. Psychologist Lorine Pruette noted how "many have developed techniques of mutual stimulation which do not carry the danger of impregnation," while commentator Theodore Newcomb observed the "ample confirmation of the general trend toward increased tolerance of formerly disapproved behaviors in the area of sex."[15] Psychologists Blanchard and Manasses declared that "even oral manipulations, may all come into sexual play activities."[16] Thus not only did the whole path to marriage become more sexualized and eroticized in this period, but Americans engaged in a greater variety of sexual behaviors.

Intriguingly, Kinsey reveals, too, that men began their sexual lives at a younger age. As tables 8.4 and 8.5 show, men petted to climax earlier. The increase in total petting experience shown in table 8.4 seems particularly consistent—and significant. It seems to confirm that the concerns of moralists in the 1920s were based on real changes in behavior. While these figures may be due in part to dietary/biological changes, it is still fascinating to note that they do suggest that the greater freedoms given to youth were reflected in actual changes in sexual behavior.

Evidence of a greater variety of sexual behavior extended beyond heterosexual practices. Evidence suggests that men increasingly regarded formerly tabooed behaviors, masturbation and homosexuality, as sexual options, which further serves to illustrate the extent to which sexuality became more complex at this time. If ideology about these sexual options was subtly changing, my qualitative evidence of attitudes towards masturbation and homosexuality among youth confirms that, at this time, the cultural ideal was indeed altering towards making both homosexuality and masturbation more guilt free, if hardly yet valued, alternatives.

Certainly men still worried about masturbation. Several young men confided to self-appointed mentor of youth Judge Lindsey, for example, the extent to which masturbation was a concern for them. One young man who lived at the National Co-Operative Association in 1925 wrote that on account of past masturbation habits, he was "ashamed to look a girl in the face."[17] Another young man desperately implored that he "would rather be a eunuch than continue this way. Oh, please help me!"[18] Almost as pathetically, a young man wrote on December 20, 1926, that "ever since I was about ten years old, I have 'abused' myself—masturbation I think it's called. And many times I have tried to stop—by jumping under a cold shower."[19] Yet others did not share such guilt feelings. One man wrote to Lindsey on December 12, 1926, that the "practice is not harmful when practiced with restraint":

> I know from twenty-five years experience. I married; we have one son, who is now away at college. I advise him to practise it when the appetite troubles him. I know that it does not weaken the enjoyment of intercourse with a woman and does not debase in any way. All the supposed experts who advise to the contrary are liars, parasites who are exploiting the young people.[20]

Several of the early sex surveys sifted out attitudes towards masturbation. They suggest further the accuracy of these conclusions from the Lindsey letters. These sources illustrate the sheer terror that men felt if they practiced this "solitary vice." In Paul Strong Achilles' 1923 study of the effects of social hygiene literature, masturbation was far and away the biggest worry, even more so than fear of disease.[21] In Peck and Wells's mid-1920s study of college men, only 7 percent indicated that they felt positive remorse over masturbation, although 19 percent admitted moral guilt. Only 25 percent felt no remorse at all, although for 50 percent, the physical effects of masturbation were a worry of some kind.[22] In W. L. Hughes's study of seven hundred urban and rural boys in North Carolina, 74 percent said that they believed that the effects of masturbation were "bad."[23] Gilbert Hamilton asked his one hundred married men whether masturbation had ever caused physical or mental injury. Twenty-two percent indicated that they felt it was "not injurious"; but 54 percent thought it was "mentally injurious."[24] As these studies seem fairly consistent with one another, they confirm my conclusions from the Lindsey sample that masturbation was a worry for a large percentage of men, but many men were not bothered by it. This cannot be interpreted as indicating that a liberalizing of actual attitudes was occurring because comparisons with Victorian attitudes and practices are not available. Presumably even in the nineteenth century there were men who were not affected by the rigid prescriptions of ideology, but the later material indicates that the impact of the strong antimasturbation ideology was never so great as to be all-pervasive; and it is plausible that more moderate attitudes towards masturbation were gaining ascendancy among the middle class as they were doing in ideological artifacts.

Further, that this was the trend is illustrated by the intriguing evidence provided by women journalists Dorothy Bromley and F. L. Britten's study of college men in the middle 1930s. Bromley and Britten did not provide statistics on this subject, but they did feature men who commented on the perceived prevalence of masturbation in order to put across the general attitude towards it. While "one man, apparently under the 'delusion that masturbation was a perversion and that it might drive him crazy,' made extreme statements which left some question as to their credibility," several male interviewees referred to their own experiences without embarrassment.[25] Bromley and Britten emphasized their observations that the old hysteria over autoeroticism was dying by ending their analysis with the statement that "modern medical thought is fairly well agreed that whatever bad effects may result are largely due to the individual's sense of guilt."[26] Evidence from the 1930s indeed suggests the direction in which attitudes towards masturbation in the 1920s were headed. Masturbation, of course, had always been a choice, but it was becoming more guilt free, a more viable alternative behavior for American men.

Evidence of attitudes towards homoeroticism are less tentative. This is an important subject for discussion because, as has been discussed already, the pressure to be heterosexual was part of the increasing sexual demands on men. What kind of an impact did this attempt to redefine sexual boundaries have? Bromley and Britten argued that homoeroticism became a more widely discussed subject about ten years before their study was published—that is, about 1928. I have suggested earlier that discussion of homoeroticism was widely diffused among the American middle classes as the Freudian popularizers and the Haldeman-Julius sex manuals gained broad popularity. At present, there is little evidence beyond the anecdotal of actual attitudes towards homoeroticism outside of working-class groups. Gilbert Hamilton did ask his one hundred married men about their attitudes towards homoeroticism in the late 1920s. He wrote that "the majority of American adult males probably fear their own homosexual impulsions more greatly than they fear all the other tabooed components of the human reactive equipment taken together," for Hamilton had clearly seen a tremendous amount of what we today would call homophobia.[27] But his conclusions belie a simplistic analysis. The prevalence of homoerotic activity among his respondents prefigured Kinsey. Fifty-six percent of the men he interviewed had experienced some kind of homoerotic activity during their lives, while 17 percent had practiced after the age of eighteen. Yet this did not stop 75 percent of the men from stating that they unequivocally, even if they threw "aside all considerations of conscience" and "fear of public opinion," did not believe that any person of their own sex would "appeal . . . sexually." Further, 47 percent of the men stated that it made them "uncomfortable to have a person of their own sex put his arm about [him] or make other physical demonstrations." Others were more tolerant, however, in their views: 89 percent indicated that "to no extent" did "fear of perversion prevent [them] from getting close to men." Further, 37 percent indicated that they were not bothered by physical demonstrations of affection.[28] These figures have to be treated with a great deal of caution, especially as the Hamilton sample is loaded towards theater people and as the sample was made up of couples whom Hamilton had been seeing at his psychiatric practice. Presumably such a group had had more opportunity to encounter homosexuals than other groups. Hence the extent—somewhat significant— to which they were not bothered may reflect this, since they are not an accurate sample of the broader population. However, as this survey is all we have, it suggests that in at least a kind of vanguard group there was reflected both accelerated homophobia as well as the incipient liberalism of the cultural ideal discussed earlier.

The only comparison that can be made to suggest the direction of the trend in attitudes towards homoeroticism comes again from the Bromley and Britten survey conducted in the mid-1930s. They noted that "over half of the men condemned the practice, some more severely than others." Some were horribly trenchant, one declaring "they should be hung," another that he would not even speak to "queers, pansies and fruits." But the rest were "variously tolerant," and "an enlightened ten percent considered homosexuality a matter of psychological adjustment." How "enlightened" this particular group was is debatable, but Bromley and Britten regarded their sample as "an object lesson in social change with thinking . . . clearly influenced by the new psychiatric humanitarianism stimulated by Freud."

Freud may indeed have actually liberalized attitudes towards homoeroticism, according to Bromley and Britten. These students' attitude was "live and let live." But not one of these men was prepared to admit that he had ever indulged in homoerotic practices. "For God's sake NO," one said, and "Hell NO" and "What do you take us for?" were other responses. However, Bromley and Britten praised these men for not sitting in judgment. They quoted some of the men's opinions. "Purely personal matter for those concerned. . . . Don't approve for myself, but don't object to others." Some men, according to Bromley and Britten, had probably had their intolerance tempered by Freud: "Too bad for the guys. . . . An unfortunate social and family background is the cause." Some men indicated much stronger tolerance than mere psychologizing. One young man who was widely promiscuous with women even said that it was "perfectly OK." Another young man declared that he was "disgusted impulsively by it, but have been able to rationalize myself to a tolerant attitude."[29]

Though this study was completed later than 1930, it was only a mere six or seven years after the Hamilton study and does confirm his findings. Intolerance still predominated. The "discovery" of homosexuality really did create anxieties among middle-class heterosexual men. But equally as interesting was an incipient liberalism embedded in this qualitative material, reminiscent of working-class tolerance and even suggesting homosexuality as an option for some men: Kinsey, of course, found that in his sample, 37 percent of men had had a homosexual experience to orgasm after puberty. This should not surprise us, but it should warn us of the need for wariness regarding attitudes towards homosexuality as having been simplistic in the years before there was a "gay" movement.[30] Taboos in general were less great for men after 1920. Although it was taboos regarding heterosexual practices rather than homosexual ones that lessened first, the roots of homosexuality and masturbation as more tolerated choices for men were probably laid in the 1920s. But we should be wary as to what this toleration and liberalism actually entailed (and indeed still entails), especially as it was so reminiscent of patterns in the dance-hall subculture. Certainly, in part, it reflected for many men a liberated recognition of the possibility of a healthful sexuality, whatever the object of desire. But it also reflected the uncritical attitude of the men of the dance-hall subculture that any means to orgasm was acceptable, whether in fact psychologically healthful or not. That these behaviors grew as options is anyway part of the developing, and recognizably modern, complexity and uncertainty that developed around sexuality at this time.

The decline of Victorian structures and guidelines about sexuality and the concomitant growing complexity and uncertainty in personal relationships was perhaps best illustrated in the emerging heterosocial "dating system," one of the most important legacies of the early twentieth-century sexual revolution. The culture of personality stressed and valued "the performing self."[31]

Above all else, therefore, the dating system, which by the 1920s had become the dominant form of courtship in America, stressed "performance." The most valuable analysis of this system at this time remains that of Willard Waller, who in his classic 1937 article, "The Rating and Dating Complex," described the form that dating took among young people in the 1920s and 1930s as very different from the Victorian practice of calling.[32] Because dating was not immediately regarded as a first step on the route to marriage, it demanded very different skills of men than had nineteenth-century courtship. In many ways, calling demanded "character" of men, while dating demanded "personality." Waller's description of what constituted male success under this system is worth quoting in its entirety:

> Young men are desirable dates according to their rating on the scale of campus values. In order to have class A rating they must belong to one of the better fraternities, be prominent in activities, have a copious supply of spending money, be well-dressed, smooth in manners and appearance, have a "good line," dance well, and have access to an automobile.[33]

Waller has come under significant criticism in recent years. One scholar has argued that "going steady" was as prominent among girls and boys in the 1930s as was "rating and dating."[34] In other words, young men and women took each other more seriously than Waller admitted. No doubt that was the case, too, in the 1920s. The fact is, however, that despite these caveats, Waller was right about the values involved in the youth culture. The initiation of any relationship increasingly turned on the superficialities of the culture of "personality," which influenced personal relations. "Performance" was of the essence.

Waller expanded, too, on the nature of the "performance" that was required of young men. Dating was a competitive game in an even more accentuated and accelerated way than Victorian courtship had been. To meet the criterion for a valued male, according to Waller, one had to cultivate a "line." This "line" was a "conventional attempt on the part of the young man to convince the young woman that he has already at this early stage fallen seriously in love with her ... a sort of exaggeration, sometimes a burlesque of coquetry."[35] Not only was the "line" crucial in starting the relationship, but it also was of importance to its continuation. It was vital to "invite the other to rapid sentiment formation—each encourages the other to fall in love by pretending that he has not already done so." The purpose of the game was to cause one or the other to "rise to the bait," that is, actually to fall in love.[36] Waller famously emphasized the "principle of least interest," according to which he or she who was less interested in the continuation of the affair controlled the relationship.[37] Continued use of the "line" could ensure for men that they got the upper hand. Further, "the line" guaranteed that the performance would continue throughout the relationship and, indeed, even into marriage.

No wonder young men, who lacked guidance from other sources besides peer pressure, turned to the artifacts of the culture of personality for inspiration, most notably to the movies and to personal advice columnists. The evidence for this is diverse and widespread. Most revealing is material on the impact of the movies gathered in the late 1920s and early 1930s by Ohio State University professor W. W. Charters and his associates. These studies offer astounding empirical evidence of the extent to which the movies influenced social relations in the United States. Their impact is an example of what Coughlin has called "artificial social relations," that is, the identification with a person one has never met, such as a movie star, which in the age of mass media becomes an important part of a person's social experience.[38] "Performance" involved literally performing as movie stars. Several young men in the study insisted that they took their cues from stars such as Rudolph Valentino and Douglas Fairbanks, Sr. One young man, a Jewish college student aged twenty, freely admitted that he wanted "to be Douglas Fairbanks Sr. or Tom Mix or William S. Hart this afternoon."[39] A 17-year-old black high school student declared that "Douglas Fairbanks . . . seemed so carefree and light that he won nearly everyone with his personality." However, when he endeavored to "try some of my 'Doug's stuff' on one of my girlfriends," he knew he was awkward, and it proved "more or less a flop."[40] Similarly, a 22-year-old white college junior looked to Valentino:

> I studied his style. I realized that nature had done much less for me in the way of equipment than she had for the gorgeous Rodolfo, but I felt that he had a certain technique that it would behoove me to emulate. I practiced with little success. My nostrils refused to dilate—some muscular incompetency that I couldn't remedy. My eyes were incapable of shooting sparks of fiery passion that would render the fair sex helpless. I made only one concrete trial. The young lady who was trial-horse for the attempt is still dubious

about my mental stability. Worse yet, she made a report of the affairs [sic] to her friends. The comments that came drifting back to me left no doubt in my mind about the futility of carrying on any longer. I gave up.[41]

Such evidence suggests that the dating system caused men anxieties because, aware of the need to acquire skills and to "perform," they were uncertain as to how to do so.

That this was the case is confirmed by the popularity of personal advice columnists such as Doris Blake in New York and Martha Carr in St. Louis. The new system promised success to a kind of man who would not have been respectable under the Victorian system. Many men who might have been successful in the nineteenth century now found themselves left out in the cold. One such young man, Jay, "not good-looking" but "somewhat athletic in appearance and called neat with a conservative taste for good clothes," could not find a date. He wrote that "I suppose I am overly civilized and with strong inhibitions, but there you are. In five years I have not met as many girls with whom I could develop a friendship."[42] Another young man wrote in that "I can't get myself a girl. I am not much for parties and do not fancy dancing. What's the trouble?"[43]

Success at dating required the learning of skills, and many young men just were not adept at acquiring them. One young man wrote in that he liked a "certain girl and would like to know how I would ask her for a date."[44] Another feared that, on account of shyness, he "never had much to do with girls."[45] The first date was a difficult time for a young man. "Anxious" wrote in that he was "going to take a young lady out for the first time in [his] life. What [should he] do to show her a good time?"[46] Another man asked Miss Blake, "On what subject should I talk when I take a girl out for the evening?"[47] Some men had difficulty even getting this far; men wrote in explaining how they were "afraid to ask them to go out."[48] For those who were unafraid, the new emphasis on looks as central to the "performance" caused embarrassment. "Heck" wrote in that he was "tall and considered good-looking. I have a lady friend who keeps raving about my looks. It embarrasses me. Should I correct her?"[49] No wonder Miss Blake commented that "male beauty becomes an out and out handicap" for young men such as "Heck" who were uncomfortable with their looks.[50] Male anxieties about how to get a date set the tone for the larger implications for men of the emergent dating system. Characteristically, Waller believed the system involved mutual exploitation for the attainment of "thrills" rather than any long-term commitment. Waller has been justly criticized for being too "cynical" about dating.[51] The emphasis on "thrills," for example, did not preclude the possibility of long-term commitment, as he suggests; and long-term commitment, was probably an ultimate goal even if only in the back of the daters' minds. However, the stress on "thrills," by helping to eroticize the path to marriage, injected into premarital relationships a heavy responsibility on men. But what kind of "thrills" were acceptable under the new system?

The movies were especially influential in informing doubting young men exactly how to "perform" on a date. The movies helped establish "kissing" as an essential "thrill." A 22-year-old white college junior insisted frankly that "in this matter of the technique of love-making I have been more influenced by the movies than by any other factor."[52] Revealingly, this young man considered that "without it [the movies' influence] . . . I would have been an unbearable prude; with it I was encouraged into indiscretions which I have later come to regret. On the whole, I think it was an evil but as with most evils it was not unmixed with elements of good."[53] The movies were indeed a clear catalyst in accelerating the erotic pace and helping to define boundaries. One young man declared that "I found that I, the pure virgin, actually conceived of the idea of kissing a girl, and actually enjoying it, too."[54] Such men freely admitted that "ideas about kissing definitely came from the movies."[55] Thus, a white Jewish sophomore confessed that the movies caused him to "want to kiss and fondle any young lady that happens to be with me" and that his technique was so good that on leaving the cinemas after seeing his heroes he was often "successful in attentions that at other times would have been taboo."[56] Noted expert on adolescence J. L. Richmond observed how the movies "inflamed the boy's imagination."[57] Just as they altered and defined what constituted an attractive man in the culture of personality, the movies also set the pace for the new emphasis on performance in dating. They helped to eroticize leisure by expanding boundaries for the social relations between the sexes. The movies were a central resource for the mores of the peer-led youth culture. They could determine that at least kissing was an acceptable "thrill" on a date. Indeed, they helped establish it as an essential part of performance.

Petting, however, was another matter. The question of how to pet, when to pet, even "why they pet" was one that was constantly discussed in the 1920s: this reflected the deep concerns the issue aroused at the time.[58] One of the characteristics of the "flapper" that was oft-quoted was her willingness to pet. Yet the flapper who petted represented a departure in clouding the distinction between a "good" and a "bad" woman; she was prepared to go some of the way, but not perhaps all of the way. Or perhaps she was? The question of how far it was appropriate to go was one that became central for men in the 1920s. What should be the nature of the performance? Dating, as an institution, did not incorporate a means for a "good" woman to have sexual intercourse because of its emphasis on sexual expressiveness rather than on "romantic love." As women were encouraged to be more sexually expressive under the dating system, for men the distinction between a "good" and a "bad" woman became more and more blurred as young people claimed time for one another even in the early stages of courtship, long before a relationship could be firmly established. When was it right to become sexually expressive? And how far was it appropriate to go? Was it all right for a "good" woman to pet? What were the sexual boundaries in the world of dating? They were no longer as clear-cut as they had been in Victorian society. To be sure, sex among engaged couples represented less of a contrast from Victorian mores and therefore less of a problem, but even this caused doubt because the lines between what constituted a "dating" relationship, "going steady," or "engagement" were not clearly drawn as the private world of nineteenth-century courtship was replaced by the public, twentieth-century dating system.

This change entailed several kinds of difficulties for men. Once the dating system took hold, it became harder for men to be "good"—that is, to conform to the single standard of the Christian Gentleman, the "athlete of continence."[59] For, unlike in the dance-hall subculture, in the middle class there were many men, who, like Victorians, were quite clear that chastity was an ideal. For these men, petting was unacceptable. Young men constantly wrote to Lindsey and the personal advice columnists like Doris Blake and Martha Carr of the *New York Daily News* and the *St. Louis Post-Dispatch*, respectively, lamenting how hard it was to be pure. If the men and the feminist New Women tried with differing degrees of success to overcome a socialization that demanded purity, evidence suggests that middle-class youths not only felt the demand for purity and for a single standard but accepted it readily. In this guise, Victorianism lived on among youth. A young man wrote to Lindsey of his father's advice to him that he should "never indulge in sex relations until [he] married" and how glad he was that he had not.[60] Another young man declared that "the thought of sex intimacy except as an expression of love . . . is obnoxious to me, not taking into account the dangers of vital venereal disease."[61] A fellow who wrote from New York to Marie Stopes in London asking for advice about contraception insisted that he and his fiancée "have never had any sexual relations and absolutely will not until after we are married, a few months hence. I mention this for fear that you might refrain from replying for fear that we might abuse your advice. Our intentions are nothing if not honorable."[62]

To such men as these, flappers elicited nothing but contempt:

> To me the purity of a girl's character is the most beautiful thing on earth. . . . My disgust knows no bounds. There are times when I would give anything for the privilege of walking up to some of those little lobby loungers, jerk the cigarettes from between their painted lips and slap their feigned sophistication from their dumb little faces.[63]

The made-up flapper conjured up images of prostitutes and evoked the corresponding moral revulsion from some men. A country boy coming to the city wrote in to Doris Blake saying that he had heard "many stories about the girls and women of big cities—stories that have made me fear the acquaintance of any city girl."[64] These stories actually prevented this young man from speaking to the women he worked with in his office for fear that they might be "bad" women. Another young man wrote in to Doris Blake of his efforts to maintain his high ideals despite the peer pressure that drove him to behave to the contrary. "Every one of my friends," he wrote in, "tells me I'm a sissy . . . but no one has ever convinced me to the extent of making me indulge in their so-called fun."[65] Men emphasized purity, too, in letters they wrote to Lindsey. Typical was one young man who prayed that "God will give me strength to resist the temptation of which so far I am master."[66]

The double standard was an affront to these men; one commented that "I don't need a girl who can gratify my passion and don't intend to find one until I can master it myself and be a fit subject to ask for it in the legal bonds of matrimony."[67] Another young man noted that he seemed to be "able to control my sexual desires better when I am alone until I see some shapely woman, who happens to appeal to me in a sexual way and then it is much harder for me."[68] This same fellow went on to declare that "this is especially so where the woman is scantily and gaudily dressed." One man chided Lindsey for "underestimating the extent to which people these days are over-sexed . . . they should think less about the subject."[69]

It was hard to maintain purity for those who were certain that they wanted to be celibate before marriage. And it was becoming harder as fewer and fewer people believed in chastity as an ideal. Confirming this observation, among Read Bain's sample of college men, only 3.3 percent in 1934 believed that sex was "dirty," while in 1928, 28.3 percent had believed it to be so.[70] Further, 33.4 percent of the older generation in the Kinsey sample said that they had lacked the opportunity for sex, while among the younger generation, 51.4 percent indicated that they had had opportunities.[71]

It was clearly becoming more difficult to be pure. The sexual demands that made it so hard to maintain purity steadily withered away men's actual need to be so. In the Kinsey sample, of those with some college education, 76.2 percent of those aged forty-six or more at the time of interview believed in purity before marriage, while of those aged from adolescence to twenty-five, only 62.5 percent believed in it.[72] Evidently, those who believed in purity were on the decline. All the same, the fact that they were in the majority does indicate the continuing strength of chastity as an ideal.

The dominant theme of the period remained uncertainty, because standards declined more slowly than practice. A variety of sources show the lack of clarity and the confusion at the time. Young men commented on the "many codes" available to them in the 1920s.[73] A YMCA pamphlet, *The Sex Life of Youth*, declared that "the question for all thoughtful youth . . . is what type and degree of physical-emotional intimacy, if any, is advisable before the more definite mutual commitment of one man and one woman to each other in engagement?"[74]

Multifarious social commentators observed the confusion over changing mores. Theodore Newcomb discussed these contradictions:

> "It is expected by both boys and girls that men should prefer virginity in girls, but don't insist"; "Boys do not expect nor particularly want the Victorian concept of purity in the girl they marry"; "it is right and decent to have intimate relations with the person you love, but you mustn't be promiscuous—that's cheap and vulgar."[75]

Indeed, writing in the mid-1930s, he concluded that all the codes were only united by an aversion "to marital infidelity and premarital promiscuity."[76] In Middletown, the Lynds noted in 1925 that "a heavy taboo, supported by law and by both religion and popular sanctions, rests on sexual relations between persons who are not married."[77] But, by 1937, they observed that "the range of sanctioned choices is wider, the definition of the one 'right way' less clear, causing confusion."[78] Ultimately, Newcomb wrote, "If there is a 'typical' attitude of college youth today, it is presumably one of conflict between codes which diverge in greater or lesser degree in respect to the point beyond which one may not go."[79] The evidence shows that Newcomb was right.

The options and choices around petting, especially, increasingly blurred the definitions of acceptable behavior for men. YMCA Director Clarence Robinson, with the insight of years of experience, marvelously captured the dilemma of young American men,

> The old advice used to be "Treat every girl as you would want some other man or boy to treat your mother or sister." And that was good advice. But translate it into a concrete situation. Five or six boys and girls are speeding along in a motor boat or an automobile, the night is splendid with glistening moon and tiny diamond like stars way up there in the blue sky. . . . A question of conduct arises in a boy's mind. . . . Someone is putting popcorn down his back just at the moment of decision and it is exceedingly difficult to deal with sticky popcorn, a pretty girl and an ethical problem all in a minute. Usually what happens is that the boy tends to the popcorn, also the girl, but the solution of the ethical problem goes a-glimmering.[80]

Robinson continued that "what he needs is a settled attitude toward all girls, sufficiently vital and chivalrous to grip him and direct his conduct in moments of wild hilarity or sudden desire."[81]

It was precisely this sense of structure that was lacking in the 1920s. Yet the evidence is strong that it was structure that men craved. With this in mind, sociologist Ira Wile called for "strong distinctions to be made in petting because erotic activity may or may not have coitus as a goal."[82] Any and every level of petting could present problems. One young man wrote in to Doris Blake that "one night I felt there was no harm in kissing a girl I know goodnight, which I did. The next morning she refused to speak to me."[83] But kissing and hugging could lead to further stages of petting and all too easily to the still usually tabooed intercourse:

> When we kissed and hugged a lot, I would become so aroused as to forget my restraint and my unselfish desire to help her and selfishly go as far as I could. Just before we got to the point of intercourse I again caught hold of myself and stopped seeing her so frequently and avoided intimacy.[84]

One young man wrote in from Clarendon, Texas, to Lindsey to ask advice as to whether, now that he had gained his girlfriend's confidence and love—

"Should we hug and kiss now? Or will it endanger our womanhood and manhood?"[85]

Defining the appropriate sexual boundaries was a matter of great importance for young men because the old double standard lived on: it was acceptable for many men to defile a "bad" woman but was unacceptable—indeed, a very affront to manliness—to defile a "good" woman. Promises to maintain purity were as nothing compared to the guilt that young men felt once they broke their promise. They feared they had committed a grave sin. One fellow declared that he "had been fighting all those years and was very proud of my record. I went with her, but I felt ashamed later, for I had broken a resolution."[86] Strongest was the fear of defiling a good woman: "Dear God. That I had to do this to her alone . . . she of all girls whom I cared for alone, she who had been so pure and sweet—blasted by my own damned uncontrollable passion."[87]

The question of how far the girl had gone before became a crucial one, because men again and again were clear that they still wanted to marry "good" girls. And the girl who had gone all the way before lost credentials as a future wife. One young man wrote in to Judge Lindsey that he was "looking for a nice girl that wants and will make a nice home, not any flirts."[88] "I know 'em" wrote to Martha Carr that he was certain that many of the flappers were really "all just nice girls who want, some day, to marry and settle down."[89] But not all men were as confident. According to the Kinsey survey of generational attitudes, the number of men who wanted to marry virgins actually increased from 41.6 percent of the forty-six or older group to 50.7 percent of those aged between adolescence and twenty-five at the time of interview.[90] Men were concerned as to whether their wives might not be virgins. In a mid-1930s study, 38 percent of college youth still insisted that sex before marriage was wrong. Thus, a young man wrote to Lindsey from New York that "in all this time I have not dared ask her as to her physical standing, and neither have I told her as to mine and all that, but I would like to know frankly just what is what."[91] This young man admitted that he at least expected chastity of himself, but that he could not expect the same necessarily from a future wife was something that was, for right or wrong, genuinely new and confusing for men.

Most men, though, still held to the double standard. Katz and Allport's 1930 study of student attitudes found that men were much more concerned about women's indiscretions than their own.[92] Seventy-one percent found that illicit sexual behavior placed a heavier moral response upon the woman. JN observed,

> Most codes are that a fellow will not if he knows it seduce a virgin, but any advances on their part will be accepted. But the sad part with most boys is, that if a good girl permits this, he thinks she has conducted herself the same as when this is not the case and they will not believe her.[93]

In other words, if a girl petted with a man, he would assume that she had done it, and more, with other men and was perhaps not really suitable marriage material. But still, as the "many codes" increasingly showed a trend towards greater liberalism, so too did the double standard seem to be waning. In a *Fortune* magazine survey in 1937, one-tenth of men interviewed considered premarital intercourse all right for men only and a quarter regarded it as all right for both men and women.[94] The 1930 Katz and Allport study of undergraduate adjustment found that half of the men and 69 percent of the women "believed in a single-standard."[95] But, revealingly, the study found men to have "a keener consciousness of moral propriety when contemplating the behavior of women than when judging themselves."[96] Yet males were still puzzled. For no clearly defined New Man emerged to accompany the New Woman. Men were not able to imagine a new way of behaving in the public heterosocial world.

Evidently, men in the early twentieth century were ill prepared for the revolution in morals. The breakdown of the rigid Victorian structures and therefore of the relative clarity as to what was right and wrong was a major problem for many of them. The greater choices available to men undermined older structures and resulted in confusion and uncertainty. But, perhaps most significant, the dating system gave free rein to every "cad," "Sheik," and "bounder," not to say "masher," who sought his way. The dating system suited men for whom gentlemanliness towards even a middle-class woman was unimportant, as it made it harder for men to be "good." For such men the underworld primitive ethos could now be given free rein with women of their own class. For them the extent to which the flapper would go—would this one "go all the way" or would she not?— became, as in the dance-hall subculture, a means of calibrating manliness. Men validated themselves by the number of their conquests—indeed, by counting orgasms. The dating system freed men to seek simple "thrills" with as many women of their own class as they fancied. One young lady wrote in that she had "been going with a young man who talks about nothing other than the girls with whom he goes out."[97] A girl complained to Doris Blake that her boyfriend was "always telling me he loves me, but when we go out together he is always talking about taking my girlfriend out."[98] Another woman complained that her boyfriend "has informed me that he has been going around with other girls, and wants one to do the same with other fellows, which I refuse to do."[99] Women wrote in to Martha Carr of male braggadocio on this subject; they feared that dates with such men as these involved merely chatter about their "cars, dates, good times," etc. For example, one girl wrote in of her boyfriend that he "talks constantly of his numerous girls and how the girls all fall for him. I just can't get him off the subject."[100] Even when a man and woman had a steady relationship, the man might still flirt with other girls. Men took full advantage of the power that the dating system gave them. One defeated young lady introduced her "girlfriend to my boyfriend and he liked her. He left me and went with her."[101]

Men had more choice than they could handle. One young man wrote in to say that he had met "two girls who are very close friends. They resemble each other in many ways. One of them is my friend's sister. I like both of them alike. Who should I go out with?"[102] For undoubtedly, the moving of courtship into the public sphere accentuated male power enormously. Men reveled in the opportunities for abuse of that power that the system gave them.

Nowhere is this more clear than in the use of language. Among the nineteenth-century middle classes, men talked of middle-class women with the utmost respect and deference.[103] It was simply not respectable to do otherwise. But as middle-class women began to become more sexually available, men began to speak of them in ways they previously talked only of working-class women or prostitutes. The journal *West Side Men*, written and published by the New York West Side YMCA, is a rich source for male braggadocio about dating and the extent to which success in dating gave a man value with other men. Here country boys were introduced to the wild ways of the city. Discussing an imminent dance, a writer declared,

Bring your favorite skirt with you ... wife, sweetie, friend, acquaintance, or the other bloke's girl. If you're a poor bum and you can't get a chicken, remember you're coming to a pilot's affair.[104]

In a questionnaire distributed in the once-sedate and moralistic YMCA, only four of a hundred men said there was any need for "more talk about drinking parties and experience with wild women," so ubiquitous was this kind of chat.[105] Men running the YMCA desperately tried to improve manners, but it was a losing battle. Left to their own devices, dorm writers described movie starlets to their friends as "beautiful but dumb."[106] They cheekily wrote of the "it" girl who had "wiles highly developed for a collegiate."[107]

Never before had such talk been so public. A girl (understandably) "worried" wrote in to Doris Blake complaining that her boyfriend "embarrasses me with smutty remarks."[108] In Percy Marks's descriptive *Plastic Age*, young college men gather together to discuss their motives for talking dirty, as they had been doing to their "dates." On being accused of being lewder than the others, one young man yells, "Go to hell. I'm no dirtier than anybody else. . . . I admit I chase around with rats but the rest of you do it on the sly. I'm no hypocrite."[109] The eminent Jungian psychologist Beatrice Hinkle observed that "when young men are gathered together in easy familiarity . . . sexuality still dominates the minds of men even though its expression is so largely confined to the jocose and the obscene."[110] Victorian middle-class men undoubtedly indulged in such banter, but what was different now was the greater respectability of talking in such a way to middle-class women, as well as the public nature of such discourse. This was widely commented on at the time. One young man admitted frankly to psychologist Lorine Pruette of "the rough sort of attitude you need to take to the girls of [this] hard-boiled generation."[111] Sociologist Ernest Burgess noted, too, how sex was now "an open subject and repartee for discussion among mixed groups."[112] Psychologists Stoke and West, in their examination of the "conversational interests" of college students, noted how sex was the "greatest interest."[113] Similarly, Walter Buck, in his study of differences in college student attitudes between 1923 and 1933, concluded that words with a "sex connotation" were less disapproved of generally, as was slang, by a significant factor.[114] While discussion of sex itself did not necessarily involve use of unclean language, seen in its context in the 1920s, especially as a heterosocial activity, it was daring indeed.

Men further accentuated their power. But the new freedom offered in the youth culture liberated them to abuse that power beyond mere use of language—in actual relations with women. What was to stop them? The reduction of the power of sanctions left men to their own vagaries and moods. As the barriers and controls around male sexuality broke down, so men behaved in more sexually expressive and impulsive ways. The dating system gave encouragement for them to behave so. Increasingly, as earlier among the lower classes, men came to expect that the money they spent on a date entitled them to a "thrill" in return. And they were affronted when women would not grant them their desires. "Frank" complained that he "gave a girl a good time but when I ask for a kiss she refuses. Don't I deserve at least one?"[115] It was becoming ever more difficult for women not to pet, if they would rather not. Doris Blake, in 1926, presented what she called a typical letter from a girl and her friend who declared, "We are non-petters. So far we have upheld our views but we are becoming desperate. Every young man we have met so far we have found to be inclined toward petting."[116] Another girl quoted by Blanchard and Manasses complained that she "was not popular" for she had "yet to find [a man] who does not want a girl to pet the first time he meets her."[117] Another girl asked Doris Blake why she could not get dates: "I never kiss a boy—is that why?"[118] If women were not prepared to indulge men's need for thrills, they had to suffer the consequences. One "Pat" confessed unashamedly that he had taken a girl out twice but that "the last time I was with her, I kissed her by force," even though he "esteemed her above any other girls."[119] One fellow wrote to Judge Lindsey of his experience with one girl: "I asked her to kiss me goodnight and she refused in such an unnecessary way that I tried to force her to. I'm afraid it was pretty vulgar for she tried to resist me."[120]

There can be no question that, by driving courtship into the male world, the dating system accelerated and accentuated male power. The Victorian system of morality was designed precisely to provide a rigid structure of mores that tried to prevent, however imperfectly, male sexual exploitation of women. The precarious, relatively fluid and free-floating strictures of peer mores that replaced this system by the 1920s looked to the "culture of personality" to set its pace, which meant much less control of sexuality in general and of male sexuality in particular. It was a field day for the least savory males, who now could indulge their shallow selves all the more easily with women of their own class, and it was confusing for everybody. Not merely did middle-class male behavior towards middle-class women become like that of the men of the working-class, heterosocial dance-hall subculture, but so did mores. As eminent surveyor of campus habits, Eleanor Wembridge, commented perceptively, if perhaps a trifle patronizingly, "The sex manners of the large majority of uncultivated and uncritical people have become the manners for all."[121]

As male confusion abounded, male resentment accelerated. Dating was expensive. "John" wrote in to Doris Blake that "a certain young lady who accepts my gifts has a habit of disappointing me on the night of a date. Should I continue to go with her?"[122] Martha Carr published a letter from one "I Hatem" who declared that "girls simply can't play fair. Their creed seems to be not 'Give and take' but 'Always take' never 'Give'."[123] This letter touched nerves, and a debate ensued. One young man wrote in a couple of weeks later that, with reference to "I Hatem's item in your column I agree with him precisely so far as city girls go. They are all gold-diggers and deceivers."[124] "Gold-digger" became a generic term for a woman who demanded a good time but gave nothing in return. Doris Blake frequently warned men that they were dating "gold-diggers" and to avoid them. The YMCA men constantly complained of them:

> 2m. surplus flappers
>   Both in and out of school
> Are turning fellows nappers
>   But through it all I'm cool.
> All through this year I'll ban 'em
>   And to overtures say no
> For a surplus Eve per annum
>   Needs more than surplus dough.[125]

As in the dance-hall subculture, men referred to women as "gold-diggers" when they could not get from them what they wanted. If some men regarded women as "gold-diggers" who were not prepared to offer them "thrills" as payment for the cost of a date, other men increasingly complained that they had been forced to abandon dating altogether because of the "too high cost of courting."[126] One young man who wisely chose to remain anonymous wrote in the *American* magazine in September 1924 that he had spent five thousand dollars on courting in the previous five years; in comparison, his parents had spent three hundred dollars on their entire courtship, marriage, and honeymoon. Yet, despite the expense, he had still "not met a girl who cared if I made much of myself or little." He went on: "There is a point at which any commodity—even such a delightful commodity as feminine companionship—costs more than it is worth. In my life, that point has been reached and PASSED."[127] This young man went on to declare a "one man buyer's strike" until the situation improved.[128] Several young men wrote in to Martha Carr or Doris Blake on the same theme, although no other had the pluck publicly to declare a "buyer's strike." Much like the author of the *American* article, one young man, "Iconoclast," wrote in to Miss Blake of the financial demands on men, declaring that "nowadays when a young man is in love it is necessary for him to shower his sweetie with gifts of candy, flowers, theater tickets, jewelry, taxi rides and the like."[129] It got worse once the engagement started, he continued; then the "spending orgy" really began.[130] Another young man wrote that his girlfriend had been used to "good times" when taken out by her other boyfriends. Rather desperately, he asked, "Do you think that she would enjoy herself with me if she went with me to less expensive places?"[131] Another fellow wrote in to Martha Carr that he "hadn't much money to spend, but I do manage to scrape up enough."[132] Yet the girl he was dating had a mother who preferred a richer man. Although having easier access to money was the foundation of male power, clearly this power did not come without its problems. A chagrined girl wrote in to Doris Blake that her boyfriend had been forced to abandon her after "he explained that it will be a year before he can take me to any place of amusement."[133] Men found that the demands made by the New Woman were not merely sexual, but financial as well.

Without dating, however, there could be no marriage. Men in the 1920s complained that they quite simply could no longer afford to get married. The wider abundance of consumer goods created greater material expectations. At the same time, the position of the middle class became ever more precarious as the clerical workers and bureaucrats of the "new middle class" replaced the self-employed entrepreneur of the Victorian middle class.[134] Material goods had great symbolic value for this class because they sensed they had less control over their destinies and thus were more afraid of losing class status than Victorians had been. The contemporary YMCA writers Grace Elliot and Harry Bone captured the dilemma of young couples very well:

> A stereotyped idea especially among young men is that a man should be able to take care of his wife in the manner she is used to. In a majority of cases this will require postponement of marriage. Unfortunately, there is a widespread feeling that it is somewhat disgraceful to live on a restrained budget or to start a new home without all the comforts and advantages which a well-established couple are able to afford.[135]

The New Woman or "modern girl" was simply too financially demanding for men. One man wrote in to an advice columnist to complain that his girlfriend insisted upon marrying him although "I cannot see my way clear on $15 a week."[136] One young lady hesitated to marry a young man because he could not "support a wife on $25 a week."[137] This attitude was not helped by the advice columnists, especially Doris Blake, who frequently insisted that young men in such a predicament should "advance

[your] career" or "raise [your] salary."[138] A college fellow, on being asked if he ever thought of marrying, insisted,

> Get married. Why I can't even afford to go with any of the sort of girls with whom I would wish to associate. . . . I can't afford to even see them. I am making only $40 a week. . . . If I took a girl to the theater she would have to sit in the gallery, and if we went to supper afterward, it would be at a soda counter and if we rode home it would be in the street cars.[139]

This could hardly have helped the poor man whose fiancée broke their engagement because he was "making only $20 a week." She would not "marry a man making less than $35."[140]

No wonder young men regularly used the term "gold-digger," not merely to refer to women who refused to offer them thrills on a date, but as a generic term for the perceived manipulativeness of the modern girl. Typical of this genre and attitude was a "young man" who wrote in to Martha Carr:

> I think the modern woman is too calculating. If she is a young girl with an eye to matrimony she coolly sits down and figures it out. What am I going to get? Where will I have to live? Can we afford a car? Will I have to cook? Does his mother have to live with us? Can we keep up to a certain set?[141]

So serious was the perceived problem that magazines held elaborate symposiums with titles like "Why Men Won't Marry the New Woman." Endemic were complaints that the New Woman was "only looking for a good thing." One man insisted that while he was prepared to be a "good provider," he was forced to wonder whether the "modern girl" would be a "partner or a parasite." There were too many women who wanted to "eat their cake and have it too." If "physically they are attractive," said a 34-year-old bachelor, "in all other ways I find them superficial, selfish, conceited or uninteresting." When women's expectations of marriage were so great, "no wonder we men hesitate," said another man. Few of the young men were as generous as the one who declared that the modern girl has "loads of common sense and I really do not doubt that she will gradually settle down and make a good wife." But, despite his optimism, he recognized that "the modern man isn't so sure."[142] If men reared as Christian Gentlemen did not know what to expect sexually from the New Woman, they, therefore, did not know what to expect in other areas either.

Male unwillingness to marry and resentment over the financial demands of the New Woman were reflected, too, in the 1920s cult of singleness. Marriage manuals appeared with titles such as *How to Be Happy Though Married.*[143] Bernarr Macfadden joined in the fray by publishing titles in *True Story* like "Under Sentence of Marriage."[144] Men openly declared that they preferred the company of other men; one said that "women have nothing to offer that he cannot obtain from a man."[145] William Johnson, in an article in *Collier's*, noted that "the general opinion seems to be that the young men of today do not wish to marry."[146] He interviewed a Greenwich Village playwright by the name of Avery Hopwood who proclaimed,

> Living conditions today are entirely favorable for the bachelor. He can be quite comfortable. If he possesses enough of this world's goods he can be just as comfortable as if he were married. The idea that a bachelor cannot get food and service is a myth. I have seen several friends whose houses were run much better before they were married than they have been since.[147]

A "Happy Bachelor" wrote to Martha Carr that the modern girl was simply "cheap."[148] Magazine articles reveled in the "joys of single blessedness" with renewed vigor.[149] If a young man remained free, he could "take a blonde to dinner in a Bohemian restaurant." He could dance "on a table with her" and he could "vamp three other women" all at the same time. On Saturday he could dance "with all the debutantes and young married women at the country-club."[150] Bachelordom freed men from the commitments of marriage and the demands of the New Woman: to assuage loneliness, one might get oneself "a female Mexican jumping jelly bean" (an abusive term for a "flapper"), declared Theodore Pratt in the *New Yorker.*[151] Men reacted against women's demands by rejecting marriage. Jungian analyst Beatrice Hinkle commented in *Harper's* in 1925 on this subject: she went on to say that "the disinclination of men toward marriage is not a recent development ... their former attitude was more of an egoistic unwillingness to give up the pleasures of bachelor freedom or to assume the responsibility and obligations of a family," whereas the situation now was different, being "frankly one of fear and uncertainty regarding women."[152] Ira Wile observed that "the men are afraid of marriage and fatherhood; all are afraid of the burden of a family and some fear the moral obligation of being faithful to one woman."[153] Thus in a more articulate, more refined way, men of the middle class responded to the New Woman much as men of the working class did; that is, by hesitating to commit to marriage because of the perceived unpredictability of her behavior.

The American experience of marriage also was in transition. Marital expectations were directly relevant to the path to marriage and informed that experience. The moral revolution that affected dating therefore also affected marriage, and married men were faced with confusion, uncertainties, and anxieties as the trend towards egalitarianism and the undermining of patriarchal structures continued and as the urge to sexual fulfillment came to play a much greater role in marriage. It was under these circumstances that, as the male role in marriage became more egalitarian and sexual, "performance" was demanded and the explorations of the men and the feminist New Women were diffused to a broader population—with similar uncertainties. For men reared as Christian Gentlemen such change demanded some adjustment.

One landmark was Lindsey's book, *The Companionate Marriage*, which, despite disclaimers to the contrary, advocated trial marriage, what he called "companionate marriage."[154] With the aid of birth control, the arrival of children could be delayed so that the married couple could determine their compatibility and, if necessary, obtain an easy divorce should they decide they were incompatible. This approach to marriage was not, for Lindsey, the same as "trial marriage." Lindsey insisted that "companionate marriage ... stoutly proposes to overcome ... the awareness that there is at least a possibility of failure ahead," which he insisted made companionate marriage different from trial marriage.[155] But Lindsey failed to appreciate that, without the rigid and rigorous codes that had existed before, trial marriage was all that companionate marriage amounted to.

Lindsey's concept of companionate marriage did not reflect either the ideology or the reality of marriage in the late 1920s; hence the controversy it stirred. But Lindsey's ideas are important because they represent, in their most accentuated form, the trend and direction of marriage in the period—towards easier divorce, a greater emphasis on sex, and more democratic roles for men and women. Lindsey well understood that marriage was simply becoming a less momentous event, while other advocates of companionate marriage such as the Chicago sociologists discussed the same trends but did not advocate trial marriage. In 1924, there was one divorce for every 6.9 marriages, as compared to one for every 17.1 marriages in 1890.[156] As the Lynds put it in *Middletown in Transition*, "Marriage need not be final since divorce is no longer a serious disgrace."[157]

The cultural demands for sex expression in marriage had impact. Kinsey's evidence does not suggest that men were having more sex in marriage; his figures for total intercourse among the generations reveal no statistically significant differences. But couples continued the more esoteric practices they had begun before marriage. Among Kinsey's generational sample of those aged over forty-six at the time of the interview, 41.4 percent of men practice cunnilingus, while among those aged twenty-six–forty-five at interview, 49.6 percent practiced it in marriage (13+ educational level).[158] As regards fellatio, among the group aged over forty-six, 36.3 percent had been fellated, while 45.5 percent of the twenty-six–forty-five age group had been fellated.[159] All the same, most sex surveys conducted in the 1920s do not reveal these practices to be widespread, but of Hamilton's men, 20 percent varied their practices with fellatio, while 22 percent practiced cunnilingus: this confirms that more esoteric sexual behaviors were not rare.[160]

Terman provided further intriguing evidence of the impact of the cultural demands for sex expression in marriage. He suggested that

> the fault of excessive modesty is rapidly disappearing among women of the populations sampled by our group. The proportion of husbands reporting the wife to be overmodest or prudish decreased from 21.9% for husbands born before 1890 to 12.3% for those born after 1909.[161]

Again, this offers confirmation of the actual realization of increasing sexual demands. Even more suggestive, though, is the fact that men actually spent longer in performing the sex act. The amount of time spent having sex itself increased by around 30 percent from those born before 1880 to those born after 1905.[162] This Terman himself equated with "the effects upon young people themselves of the widely popular literature dealing with sex technique."[163] So concerned was one man that he wrote from Chicago to Marie Stopes in London of his anxieties about satisfying his wife:

> She you would classify as "cold" or very exceedingly slow. I am the other extreme unfortunately and crassly stupid. And in my ignorance I ask her if there is some mode of caressing that might be happily preparatory and she told me the first time I inquire that if my instincts don't keep me at such a time then certainly she can't—and at another time she answers the same question this way. "No . . . if I could tell you would probably go through your lesson in a mechanical [?] way and all the element of surprise and pleasure would be lacking." Certainly an indictment of the modern business man.[164]

Further confirming this trend, Elaine Tyler May has found in her study of marriage and divorce in California that greater expectations of sexual felicity entered into people's conception of what made a successful marriage.[165]

Many commentators also noted how the male role in marriage became more democratic. Instead of the Victorian family, held together by the often tyrannical dominance of the patriarch, the family was merely a "unity of interacting personalities," according to sociologist Ernest Burgess. For men this meant abdication of some of the dominance they had traditionally enjoyed: "Why is it that the father who in the country was the center of all the activities of the family, economic and cultural, is seen in many city homes to be reduced to the negative role of saying no to the other members of the family?"[166] Further, what the Chicago sociologists called companionate marriage was also a stop on the way to a greater egalitarianism. Thus, for Burgess's student Ernest Mowrer, the trend of marriage was towards more careers for wives. In the future, he thought,

> The role of the wife will be characterized by a more widespread acceptance of the position realized in not a few experiences at the present time. She will find employment in some sort of vocation which is as interesting to her as her husband's is to him.[167]

This would lead to a marriage on a "more equal basis."[168] Pioneer marriage counselor Ernest Groves was even more unequivocal, writing that "the war changed the old idea that women's place is in the home. Today women's place is in the world side by side with the men."[169]

This trend away from patriarchy in marriage lay deep in the nineteenth century in the roots of the "new middle class." By 1912, a less patriarchal, more egalitarian form—"masculine domesticity"—was clearly visible in large sections of the population.[170] This entailed male involvement in, rather than aloofness from, their families as men became "more nurturing and companionable."[171] As sociologist Ernest Groves put it,

> In spite of the fact that the mother must ordinarily be chiefly concerned with the care of her infant, it is a mistake for the father not to take a serious interest in the new household program if he has any opportunity to share actively in caring for the infant.[172]

By the late 1920s, people other than the Greenwich Village Bohemians and the men married to feminist New Women experimented with sex roles. Companionate marriage was therefore only one step on the route to more feminist roles for men and women. Many articles appeared about role experimentation within marriage. Few men were as amenable to the changes as the "50/50 husband," writing in the *Women's Home Companion* in April 1928, who discussed his attempts to divide up household duties equally with his wife. "Yes," he wrote, "it seems to me that a 50/50 husband's great reward lies in being married to a woman who because she has found a satisfactory channel of self-expression is a well-balanced personality."[173] Yet even this man felt that he "could not allow her to pay a waiter when I am with her any more than I could allow her to open the door for me and let me pass out ahead." And he continued that sometimes he "wished all the while that a wife in a gingham apron was doing the job."[174]

In contrast, the writers of "We Both Had Jobs" abandoned the project altogether because, ultimately, the man saw housework as the woman's responsibility. As they put it, "Jerry, good progressive though he was, fell instinctively into the attitude by which the work of the world has been done to date—the attitude that it is of first importance." For Jerry, "the instinct was strong to be what his father had been—sole provider for the family."[175] Other articles commented and expanded on some of the problems of women's working. *Good Housekeeping* in 1926 ran an article on whether or not husbands should do housework: it compared the Jones family, "who were in order," and where only men worked, with the Brown family, in which women worked and whose home was therefore "in pure chaos." The article did, however, at least, conclude that men "SHOULD do housework."[176]

These symptomatic articles reflected the novelty of such experimentation. The order of the day was uncertainty and transition. In fact, in the 1920s there were several surveys that provide evidence of what the implications were for those men in the middle classes who followed the lead of the men and the feminist New Woman in abandoning more patriarchal roles. In Virginia McMakin Collier's study of one hundred couples involved in what were called "career marriages," in which both the husband and wife worked, eighty-six out of a hundred men were favorable to their wives' careers. Twenty-six of these men were enthusiastic. Fifty-six of the husbands would do one or many of the following chores: "help cook the dinner, set the table, wash dishes, give the baby his early morning bottle, start breakfast while the mother dresses the children ..." Not everyone was as lucky as one woman whose "boys are always shooing me out of the kitchen." Of the fourteen men left, only one was definitely opposed and two more were "indifferent."[177]

On the other hand, Lorine Pruette's study of three hundred men who applied at a commercial employment office (i.e., men of a much lower social scale) came to very different conclusions. Two hundred and four regarded it as desirable that married women should stay at home, while ninety-eight insisted that a married woman should work outside if she desired, "except when the care of young children demands her time." Of these, seven thought that "married women should all earn part of the family income, the husband assisting her with household duties and the care of the children." Only five thought that "housework should be put out. Women, like husband, to be used in outside work."[178] The contrast between the results of these two studies suggests that the practice of egalitarianism was first diffused through upper social groups, a pattern still discernible in the 1950s. It was still a rare thing, however. In 1920, 9 percent of married white women were in the labor force, and by 1930, that figure had only increased to 12 percent.[179] Taken together, these figures serve amply to confirm that the 1920s was a period of flux and transition. But the overwhelming direction of movement remains clear: marriage was becoming more egalitarian, even if only relatively so.

Periodical literature, perhaps inexorably, picked up on and emphasized the anxieties of the period. In the 1920s, the genre of the "neurotic husband" gained currency, replacing the image of the weak and ineffective husband of the turn of the century and of the teens: the "nervous husband" reflected, too, the period of transition. The perceptive critic, Alexander Black, against the grain, compared the American man unfavorably to the European:

> He blends traits that do not belong together. He violates ethnological grammar. He is absurdly docile, yet fearfully self-centered. Professionally, he has imagination. Domestically, his mind is blankly plastic. Publicly, he is a pusher. Privately, he does what he is told to do. He is submissive without gallantry. He never really worships. He only offers sacrifice. Even his brutality, when it happens, lacks the grand style that belongs with a technique ripened under classical conditions. No woman with a caveman complex can hope to do anything with him.[180]

In a similar vein, a writer in *Life*, in 1917, declared the "decline and fall of the American husband," who was "rapidly being forgotten."[181] In response to this issue, psychiatrist Abraham Myerson detected that a "nervousness, a kind of neurosis normally associated with housewives," was spreading to men, that this entailed "in both, the same fatigue, easily arising and hard to dispel—changes in mood, loss of desire for food, restlessness."[182] Significantly, Myerson equated the nervous husband with the "triumph of feminism," whose greatest victory was "the taming of men."[183] A similar article on this theme was Florence Woolston's "Delicatessen Husband," in which one man dreamed of days gone by when someone would cook for him: "Menu for May 10, dinner cream of Asparagus soup, roast stuffed veal, hashed brown potatoes, fresh string beans and old-fashioned strawberry shortcake and whipped cream." For the man in the sorry tale, Perry, now "lives from can to mouth."[184] His wife only gives him canned food.

A similarly torrid story was that of Maurice and Beatrice. Maurice "collapsed as Beatrice went out to become a hairdresser." Writer Smiley Blanton explained this phenomenon sensitively as part of the transitional period:

> In the meantime, while this modification of our culture is going on, man, with his unconscious feeling of superiority, his ignorance of women's subtle sex life, his repression and shame at the art of love, his insistence on domination by force or by infantile methods, is undergoing a severe emotional strain that is causing him to break down with an actual neurosis.[185]

Further, to this genre of publications that expressed concerns about the husband belonged the series of lurid, embarrassing confessions by husbands who had divorced or who were about to divorce their wives. One such confession appeared in the journal *Sunset*: "End of the trail by a bewildered husband": "This note of Jane's cuts me to the marrow and at the same time it makes me mad all over.... There is a feeling of wounded pride here in my breast, and it hurts as much as though I had been dealt a stiff blow."[186] Another man declared that he, compared to his wife's young lover, was "built along lines of the proverbial bean-pole, regret a sprinkling of gray over my ears, shall probably be nearly bald within six years and, as a movie star, would make an admirable bookkeeper or professor." He concluded that "the essential fact is plain. I have failed to provide that subtle and supreme something ... necessary in an ideally reciprocal relationship between men and women, which my wife feels it is her right to have from life."[187]

What is striking in the arena of public discussion is how few men, once married, genuinely critiqued their roles. Their silence is surely deafening if only because a few men did complain. When asked, ten of Hamilton's men complained about how "irksome" marriage was because of its "unfreedom, limiting duties."[188] "My Wife Won't Let Me Be a Gypsy," com-

plained Marcus Ravage in the *American Monthly* in 1927, while author
Joseph Hergesheimer asked in the *Pictorial Review* of 1926 whether or not
it was possible to be "married and free?"[189] The modern woman simply
would not allow a man to have the same freedom he had before:

> He has been made to face the most embarrassing and damnable queries. He
> has been giggled at and waved aside. Where once he had been in control,
> now he must explain to unsympathetic ears just why he supposes he is a
> Moses.[190]

Men rarely gave an honest critique of their role. It took a woman, Suzanne
LaFollette, to call, in a strikingly modern manner, for "a movement for
the emancipation of men."[191] But the rare man, if he did not quite suggest
forming a movement, did complain about his role. "Office Man" wrote in
to Martha Carr that "women in general have a pretty soft time of it," but
that was about the limit of his understanding.[192] A San Francisco "husband"
wrote to the *Nation* in 1927, with an extraordinary analysis of his dilemma,

> In youth and early manhood I took life seriously; now in midchannnel it
> rests on me more lightly. I am infected by the spirit that is in modern youth,
> but I am no longer young, and the conventions and duties of marriage do
> not permit one to behave too frivolously. For the first time, and far too late
> in life, I long to sow a (carefully selected) crop of wild oats. I should like
> to have one (or more) passionate love affairs. But every intimation of for-
> bidden romance must be regarded as a danger signal. I should like to embark
> upon some voyage of adventure to the South Seas.
>
> I am not arguing that life is harder on men than on women. I merely
> assert that from a masculine standpoint life is not necessarily that unending
> round of Sunday dinners without dishwashing, that ever verdant series of
> love affairs without responsibility, that continuing vaudeville of adventure
> and daring which literary ladies imply it to be.

"There is no salvation," he concluded, "in being born a man."[193]

But why did men not complain more? Ultimately, the key to why they
did not may be that they still benefited enormously from their role. While
male roles in marriage did become more democratic and more sexual, many
men were not aware of a fundamental challenge to their power. And it
may be that anyway men preferred the changes. Fifty-four percent of the
men in Hamilton's survey felt that they were "well-mated socially and
intellectually" with their wives.[194] There was much satisfaction as well as
dissatisfaction: the precise amount must ever remain uncertain, but the
extent of "crisis" should not be overestimated, especially as comparisons

with Victorian America are not available. And, besides, the loss of power on men's part should not be exaggerated, either: it was only relative.

Thus, by 1930, modern male sexuality was firmly in place among the mainstream middle class in the United States. Men gained power as courtship moved into the male world and lost it in the more democratic expectations of companionate marriage. Greater sexual choice worked to men's advantage while greater complexity and uncertainty worked against them. The new morality prevalent in the cultural ideal of masculinity had a real impact on male sexuality. Sexual mores for the middle class began to be more reminiscent of the working class: behavior that was not respectable in the Victorian middle class became the norm in the youth culture of the 1920s. Mainstream middle-class male behavior and attitudes had always been shared with the working class to some degree, at least as regards the masculine primitive ideal and the double standard, but the emphasis on petting and "performance" meant that middle-class men had to learn a whole new set of skills, reminiscent of turn-of-the-century working-class patterns, which they had not needed before. However, what all witnesses agreed on that was particularly new in the middle-class youth culture was that there was no real agreement on codes and mores appropriate for youth. Above all else, the central difficulty was that no model of a New Man arose to complement the New Woman.

There remains one further question of significance. If men were still expected to be more sexual in dating, as in marriage, they were expected to be dominant. The dating system did not foster egalitarianism. In some ways it increased male power; in other ways, it reduced it. Yet within marriage, male power was unequivocally lost, and the home was expected to be more of a democracy. Surely there is a contradiction here. A gulf grew between the expectations of the youth culture—that is, of the path to marriage—and the expectations of the husband's role. Dating therefore prepared men inadequately for marital responsibility. No wonder so many anxieties occurred, and articulate males floundered in attempting to express what a difference being married meant.

While the difficulties of the male role remained outside of the ability of middle-class men to analyze, what is also significant is that so few of the men who did analyze their situation had any awareness of personal guilt or blame for their collective dilemma or for the condition of their spouses or girlfriends. Surely the obverse of the general unwillingness of men to examine their situation in any deep or meaningful way was their inability to take the blame for where they had erred in their relations with women. Men lacked a sense of guilt.

New Moralities, New Masculinities

etween 1910 and 1930, Victorian definitions of manliness declined in favor of recognizably modern forms of manliness that developed as a concomitant of the heterosocial youth culture. The key to understanding the change in the cultural ideal of masculinity in these years is the shift from a culture of "character," in which men were expected to be good Christian Gentlemen and in which the keywords to describe manhood were "morals, manners, integrity, duty, work," to a culture of personality, in which men were expected to cultivate the "performing self."[1] The culture of personality placed greater sexual demands and expectations on men. Movie stars such as Douglas Fairbanks, Sr., and Rudolph Valentino set the pace with their gently erotic and athletic images. Advertisements encouraged men to develop youth and sex appeal in order to make themselves attractive to women. Men's clothing loosened up from staid and straitlaced Victorian styles. Bernarr Macfadden's sex confession magazine *True Story* and his muscle magazine *Physical Culture* spread and popularized lower-class and underworld conceptions of male attractiveness to a wide audience among the young. These images promised sexual success to young men: yet, paradoxically, sexual expectations on men grew because the new ideals differed so radically from the dominant Victorian image, the patriarch who had to worry far more about the substance of his "character," his integrity, and his success at work than about the cultivation of his appearance as part of his "personality."

The new ethos had a similar influence on the models of masculinity deemed appropriate for the youth culture as diffused in popular literature aimed at youth and in sex confession magazines. There were two styles: the male flapper and the tramp Bohemian. The first style, the male flapper, had something of the Christian Gentleman about him in that he was gentle and sensitive, attuned to women's needs. Yet there the resemblance ended, for he was opposed to the capitalist work ethic, even if he ultimately conformed to it. He was interested in sex and intellectual companionship with the same woman, though he could be a little promiscuous and was keen to have fun. In the long run, though, his was no more than a mild rebellion against commitment. For the Bohemian male flapper barely controlled his sexuality. Gently sexually expressive and more democratic and boyish than his Victorian predecessors, he was more of a watered-down underworld Masculine Primitive than he was a Christian Gentleman. And, further, he could use violence against women when this seemed appropriate to him. While he was the perfect foil to the flapper, he would have been considered a little unrespectable and a dubious character in the best Victorian circles.

The second ideal model of masculinity in the world of youth was the tramp Bohemian. This model came directly, and self-consciously, from an idealization of the Underworld Primitive style of masculinity, and therefore looked positively towards the body and the homosocial male culture of the underworld, as well as to black culture. It encouraged men actively to flee from commitment to women and, most disturbingly, encouraged an ethos of violence. The Macfadden publications spread this style to even broader groups. In this way, models that had not been deemed appropriate or respectable in Victorian times gained ascendancy in the youth culture, where the Victorian protections against male primitivism did not exist for the flapper.

Sexual demands and expectations for men also grew in the realm of sexual ideology. The open portrayal of sex that characterized the sexualized society brought underworld sexual expressiveness to a broader audience of middle-class youth. Bohemian writers and popularizers of Freud created "the myth of Victorian repression" in order to exaggerate what they called "Puritanism" and, effectively, to encourage underworld sexual expressiveness.[2] While they certainly did not emphasize the more extreme underworld mores at this time, and while they even placed a veneer of morality on their stories, the Macfadden publications did so well because they presented titillating, mildly erotic, thrilling stories to a wide middle- and working-class youth audience. Such stories would not have been respectable among the Victorian middle classes. Yet Macfadden's popularity suggests an unprecedented mainstream acceptance, whatever the efforts of moralists. Similarly, even stronger erotica was more widely and publicly available by the 1920s. This literature not only incited desire but encouraged men to celebrate their potency and fear their loss of virility in a way that Victorians certainly would have understood but would have tried to check by a rigorous emphasis on control.

Sexual expectations also accelerated in other areas of men's lives. More and more, men were supposed to conform to a heterosexual norm that was set against a homosexual other. This accentuated anxieties because of the artificial nature of such rigid dichotomies. Sex and marriage manuals compounded the further spread of the culture of personality by emphasizing male sexual expressiveness and sexual performance in a complex, tricky, and contradictory ideal that expected men to be aggressive, but gentle. Yet this therapeutic ethos failed to establish a viable new morality. It may have given guidance for the pursuit of pleasure but advice for the practical living of life for young men it failed to deliver. Instead, the literature clouded the earlier certainties and aggravated the anxieties it purported to cure/overcome. In this way, the underworld primitive ethos of the lower classes strongly influenced the sexual ideology of the emergent heterosocial youth culture.

So what of the reality of men's experience in these years? Did changes in the cultural ideal have any actual bearing on men's lives? How did men reared according to the Victorian system of morality respond to the new sexual system that the New Woman symbolized? These questions have been addressed here by examining men's experience in two groups that were on the cutting edge of the revolution, the men of the heterosocial, working-class, public dance-hall subculture and men married to feminist New Women who demanded sexual fulfillment as well as equality. The experience and dilemmas of men in these groups in the early twentieth century prefigured the later experiences of a broader middle-class youth by the 1920s.

The working-class, heterosocial, public dance-hall subculture of the early twentieth century, which so influenced the ideology of the youth

culture, remained essentially the same as its nineteenth-century precursor—
the Victorian underworld. Men enjoyed a rich and vital homosocial world
that defined itself in antagonism to women and homosexuals. Violence and
lewd language, as well as fly-by-night, quick-and-easy relationships were
the order of the day. An unrestrained and unchecked male sexuality ran
rampant. The ethic of the double standard predominated, and de facto
prostitution and promiscuity were the rule; any behavior was appropriate
with a "bad" woman, if "good" women were, of course, expected to remain
virgins. The tendency at this time was for a move towards an undermining
of the double standard in favor of a low single standard of sexual expressiveness for men and women; thus men adjusted to the emergence of the
Charity Girl in the growing world of city amusements and dance halls.
Here men experienced a division between "good" and "bad" women that
was much less clear than that to which they were accustomed. This led
to uncertainty and confusion for men who could not cope with a single
standard as the competitive dating game became the vogue. Yet, this world
remained unchanged in its essential lewdness as it became incorporated in
the public mass culture that steadily included more and more of middle-
class youth. Surely this was hardly a healthy model for a new sexual system?

The privileged and elite men who married feminist New Women under-
went a variety of similar experiences that resembled and yet differed from
those of less privileged men. The marriages that failed to attain feminist
goals essentially did so because, while the men empathized with their wives'
feminism and right to work, on a fundamental level they could not grasp
that more than token support was needed in a society where the dice were
firmly loaded against women's success in the public world. These marriages
failed also because of sexuality. As Victorians, the men had difficulty with
a woman who did not conform to the category of "good" or "bad." They
had trouble with the excessive sexual expectations of modern marriage.
Further, the practice of "varietism" created power imbalances that helped
the marriages to flounder. The men simply found more conventional
women to nurture and sustain them.

However, several of the marriages were successful, and, in being so,
they genuinely showed a way forward for men and women in the modern
world. The men married successfully to feminist New Women fully and
actively supported their wives' feminism and work, but they also were able
to resolve the sexual difficulties that the New Woman raised. The couples
did this by rejecting outside relationships; instead, they advocated monogamy. They were able in this way to fuse their socialization as Christian

Gentlemen with the demand for equality posed by the feminist New Woman. These relationships were, however, strikingly traditional, if non-patriarchal, but their success indicates the real possibility of fusing the sexual revolution with feminist aspirations for equality so long as monogamy, common sense, and mutual tolerance and respect were practiced. Significantly, the successful relationships were not as politicized as the unsuccessful marriages.

Yet, by the 1920s, many elements of the sexual attitudes and behavior of the vanguard had reached a larger middle-class group. Ultimately, men reared as Christian Gentlemen faced greater complexity in their relationships. Without clear moral guidance, men floundered in greater uncertainty in the precariousness, yet compulsiveness, of a peer-led moral system. Men showed that they needed Victorian structures and support as much of the ideology directed at youth began to have real effect. Sex surveys show quite consistently that men experienced increasing sexual demands in that the middle class was having more sexual intercourse before marriage and practicing more varied types of sex. Central to the changes was the emphasis on "performance" in the emerging dating system. Men came to think of interaction in dating between men and women as a "performance," as, lacking better moral guidance and the rigors of religion, they turned to the artifacts of the culture of personality for advice on how to perform. In doing so, they faced complexity as they were exposed to many different moral systems that replaced the dominant Victorian model. Attitudes towards masturbation and overt homosexuality also softened. Men reared as Christian Gentlemen complained about how hard it was to be pure. Others accepted the double standard but feared that they might be defiling a "good" woman. The great dilemma men faced was how far it was appropriate to go. It was in this many-layered scenario that no clear model of appropriate behavior for the New Man emerged to accompany the New Woman as men lost Victorian strictures and structures.

These confusions and uncertainties fueled male resentment. Evidence suggests that middle-class men publicly used less respectful language to describe flappers. Young men, too, celebrated bachelorhood, in many ways emphasizing satisfaction and independence and fleeing from commitment to marriage, at least in the rhetoric of periodical literature, much as the men of the dance-hall subculture did, but in more traditional terms. For it was not merely guidelines that were lost, but the controls that had protected women—and men—from men's worst excesses. This blurring of boundaries at the very least fostered miscommunication and overt competition and resentment on both sides.

Within marriage, the trend in the 1920s was towards more egalitarian relationships. Marriages where both partners sought careers more and more were entered into by nonelite groups. Men were not especially bothered by women who worked. Evidence also suggests that more lovemaking and more varied lovemaking was practiced within marriage, too. Further, it seems that many American men experienced both the successes and failures of the men married to feminist New Women. The earlier trends thus were reflected in more marriages by the 1920s. What is clear from all of this is that, by the 1920s—"modern times"—a recognizably modern American male sexuality had emerged in the United States.

To what extent did the change benefit men? Men certainly gained tremendously from the emergence of the modern construction of male sexuality. Young men and women were given greater autonomy and freedom to explore their sexuality together without the elaborate system of etiquette that pervaded Victorian culture and that had constricted and confined and limited both sexes. They were liberated more and more from the sanctions against the breaking of taboos and therefore from guilt. Far better surely that young men explore their sexuality with various girlfriends than with prostitutes. It was young men who gained most of all. Society, far from wishing to control them, geared itself to their every whim. If a man was young, muscular, and sexually attractive, an erotic jamboree could await him, with a little bit of luck, as, increasingly, more and more varied alternative practices lost their aura of forbiddenness. Nor were men merely freed to explore more esoteric heterosexual practices; they were also liberated to investigate their homoerotic proclivities. Put simply, the emergent sexual system meant more fun. For sexual liberalism involved, most worthily, an ultimate loosening of legal regulations concerning sexual morality. Marriage lay a long way in the future and many men balked at it with greater respectability and less risk of sanction.

Yet marriage, too, became a more attractive proposition, as its responsibilities were downplayed in favor of its pleasures. Companionate marriage also freed men from the strains of patriarchal dominance and enabled them to enter the domestic arena where they could share, for example, not merely household tasks but also the bringing up of children. Yet still male dominance remained intact. Further, should the marriage not work out, men could obtain a divorce without too much difficulty. Men, as ever, had it all their way. There can be no question, then, that the new sexual system benefited men.

Some qualification is nevertheless required. Surely, with the revolution in morals, Americans substituted a bad system of morality—the Victorian—

for one that was worse. The emerging sexual system emphasized only short-term gratification.[3] As the culture of personality encouraged men to go on an ever more frantic search for sexual pleasure and satisfaction, something very important was lost. As the veil of mystery that pervaded sex and sexuality among men and middle-class women in Victorian times was lifted, sex lost much of its transcendent importance as an "ultimate" experience. Sex became merely commonplace and relatively ordinary; as the celebrated critic Walter Lippmann astutely commented, "In a generally devaluated world they [the young] are eagerly endeavoring to get what they can in the pursuit of satisfactions which are sufficiently instinctive to retain inevitably a modicum of animal pleasure, but they cannot transmute that simple animal pleasure into anything else."[4] In this way, sex literally attained a wholly different meaning in American society as "modern times" began.

Further, the focus on youth, the sexualization of male images, the emphasis on sexual performance in sex and marriage manuals, the greater availability of erotica, the glorification of violence against women, dating as a competitive game, what Barbara Ehrenreich has called the "flight from commitment," the greater visibility of anxiety-causing homosexuality, the liberalization of attitudes towards masturbation—all really worked against men because they injected into the American middle class the rough, tough masculine ethos of the underworld and thus led to a brutalization of private life in mainstream American culture that has grown steadily more pernicious ever since.[5]

Central, of course, to these developments was the emergence of the New Woman who demanded greater sexual satisfaction in the context of a more democratic relationship. Many men perceived her as breaking age-old rules. She not only threatened to undermine their own "character," but they feared she herself also lacked "character." The blurring of guidelines and the ever-changing moral codes of the youth culture together with creeping permissiveness led to growing resentment on both sides that steadily aggravated suspicion between the sexes. At worst, this has led to a profound politicization of personal life as pressure groups have sought to give public credence and authority to new moralities to replace the old. For right or wrong, American men—and, indeed, women—have been unable to find their sexual system conducive to the happiness the experts insist is so important. For what was being offered to Americans was, indeed, a pseudoliberation.

Several solutions have been devised for these dilemmas. In the 1970s, feminists advocated the overthrow of the "patriarchy," a vaguely defined system of male dominance that allegedly oppressed women, both publicly and privately. Some feminists also identified male sexuality with a "rape culture." Specifically, the erect penis was the root cause of all women's oppression.[6] For these writers, the power of the phallus had held women in thrall and bondage over the centuries; in particular, for one celebrated author, pornography has been the means by which this has been accomplished.[7] Some of these positions are questionable at best. They only perpetrate a view of women's innocence and male evil that is uncompelling to sensible people, including most feminists, and that, anyway, stereotypes both "genders" by tainting all men—even non-Americans—with the excesses of a few Americans, and with peculiarities endemic to American society. It is to be hoped that such positions represent a tangent and diversion from the rich and honorable legacy of American feminism. All the same, they do express many women's rage at the consequences for them of the rise of underworld primitivism as a construction of American manliness.

Equally problematic—and indeed often ludicrous—has been the response of men. In the seventies and eighties, men divided up between "masculinists" and "feminists": the masculinists emphasized the perpetration of male culture as defense against women's criticisms; the "feminists" advocated acceptance of the demands of the women's movement, whatever they happened to be at any given time.[8] More satisfyingly, by the mid-1980s, the "Changing Men" appeared. They accepted the desirability of equality with women.[9] They actively tried to think out how to change in response to women's requests, but also utilized their own observations of what might work for men. The spirit of this movement can be seen in the theory of "masculinities"—that there are black, gay, and working-class men, all of whom have different experiences and needs as men, and all of whom have different positions in the patriarchy.[10] According to this view, the patriarchy is no longer monolithic. This position represents progress, but, less promisingly, the nineties have seen an attempt to rediscover men's primitive roots. We should be particularly wary of any efforts to sift out "the inner warrior" and the wild man within. Such a regression towards more primitivism surely is not a solution, but rather will accentuate the problem. No wonder this has enraged women.[11]

In the end, all these vogues that focus on the flaws of men or women as gendered surely are missing the point. They only skim the surface. This work suggests much more complex reasons for the malaise that afflicts the American social relations between the sexes, and gives more complex insight into the connection between gender and power.[12] The revolution in morals that grounded the present sexual system was the result of a subtle, and almost infinitely complex interaction between intellectuals, experts, advertisers, and journalists—of both sexes—with varying agendas, motivations, and intentions, and young men and women. What linked and drove the differing facets and elements of the early twentieth-century sexual revolution were the imperatives and urgencies of consumption. It was the manipulation of desire that was most central to this, not the dynamics of gender: in a sexualized society, consumers could be persuaded to purchase products more readily. With the population placated, ruling elites could maintain their power and hegemony. Society presented messages that made it harder and harder for men and women to maintain "character." Of course, each individual remained responsible for his or her actions and behavior. But what if people were not taught how to behave? Surely in a culture that encouraged the worst in people—that is, men to rape, to perform violence, to have transitory, shallow relations—and that stirred competition between the sexes, how could more be expected of the vulnerable and gullible young? In this environment, how could the masculinity of "character" that, for all its flaws, men understood and were familiar with, easily flourish? Such have been the pernicious consequences of the commercialization of sex.

Therefore, given that the dynamics of sex and gender alone cannot explain the construction of power in personal life, we should at least consider the possibility that the mere study of gender (even in the guise of "women, race, and class" that now dominates) may be a red herring in the search to improve human social relations. Worse, in that it has so helped, along with other factors, to set men and women against one another, it may help perpetuate the conditions in which elites can continue to dominate and thrive. For, above all else, the crisis between the sexes is a result and consequence of the dynamics and structures of the consumer culture, and of that fragmentation of daily life into competing consumption communities that has characterized modern and postmodern existence. This has undermined the civilized behavior that Victorians tried to encourage. For Victorians acknowledged that civilization had a price. Perhaps spoiled and pleasure-seeking young twentieth-century Americans are unwilling—or, worse, unable—to pay that price?

There are larger implications here. For ultimately, what has been missed by scholars is the American context of the social system that began with the revolution in morals. The same narrowness that caused Kinsey to call his study of American males a study of "human" males has permeated latter-day academia. The great American themes of violence and of the pursuit of pleasure, plenty, and consumption have produced the New American Man of the twentieth century.[13] He is the perfect dupe of the larger American hegemony. Sex-driven, preoccupied with personal life and inward looking—among other malaises that result from the culture of personality—the New Man is apathetic about the world beyond his own inner circle. He has lost his moral bearings. He has, in this way, lost, too, comprehension of the meaning of citizenship that the Christian Gentleman took as his birthright. Thus the personal becomes political. The sexual systems that began in the early twentieth-century sexual revolution cannot facilitate American democracy: nor do they bode well for the development of a genuine freedom or liberation—that is, a freedom with responsibilities. Without a doubt, this bodes badly for the United States, and for the rest of the world that looks to America for inspiration.

Notes

ONE : *Introduction*

1. This has been suggested in Frederick Lewis Allen's *Only Yesterday* (New York: Harper and Brothers, 1931), William Leuchtenberg's *The Perils of Prosperity, 1914–1932* (Chicago: University of Chicago Press, 1958), Henry May's *The End of American Innocence* (New York: Knopf, 1959), George Mowry's *The Urban Nation* (New York: Hill and Wang, 1965), and James McGovern's "The American Woman's Pre–World War One Freedom in Manners and Morals," *Journal of American History* 58 (September 1968): 315–33.

2. Quotèd in Frederick Hoffman, *The Nineteen Twenties: American Writing in the Postwar Decade* (New York: Viking, 1955), 19.

3. Two among several articles specifically discuss the problem of defining the "New Woman"; they are Carroll Smith-Rosenberg, "The New Woman as Androgyne," in *Disorderly Conduct: Visions of Gender in Victorian America* (New York: Knopf, 1985), and Estelle Freedman, "The New Woman: Changing Views of Women in the 1920s," *Journal of American History* 64 (March 1974): 398–411. An important earlier work remains Kenneth Yellis, "Prosperity's Child: Some Thoughts on the Flapper," *American Quarterly* 21 (Summer 1969): 44–64.

4. The question of men's part in the revolution in morals simply has not been addressed, except, perhaps by Michael Kimmel, "Pro-Feminist Men in Turn-of-the-Century America," *Gender and Society* 1 (September 1987): 261–83. There are

two surveys on the history of masculinity that cover the period: Peter Filene *Him/ Her/Self,* 2d. ed. (New York: Harcourt, Brace, Jovanovich, 1986), and Joe Dubbert, *A Man's Place: Masculinity in Transition* (Englewood Cliffs, N.J.: Prentice Hall, 1979). But these are speculative and show the need for further research, which, however, they have clearly helped to stimulate, especially Peter Stearns, *Be a Man: Males in Modern Society* (New York: Holmes and Meier, 1991; originally published in 1979); Mark Carnes and Clyde Griffen, eds., *Meanings for Manhood: Constructions of Masculinity in Victorian America* (Chicago: University of Chicago Press, 1991).

There are works that look at other aspects of the revolution in morals. There is some scholarship on American youth. John Modell's "Dating Becomes the Way of American Youth" (in David Levine, et al., eds., *Essays on the Family and Historical Change* [Austin: University of Texas Press, 1983], 91–127) does raise the question of what happened when the dating system started, and posits that, because the rules were made by women, there was a challenge to the double standard; as he states, "the boy who came to call had to pass . . . as a boy who would behave himself." While Modell has written on dating, Paula Fass has provided a very effective discussion of middle-class college youths in the 1920s (*The Damned and the Beautiful: American Youth in the 1920s* [New York: Oxford University Press, 1977]). Many of her insights are useful, but a difficulty with her book is that it is not her purpose to consider that men and women had different things at stake in the development of dating. There is work, too, on marriage. Christina Simmons, "Marriage in the Modern Manner: Sexual Radicalism and Reform in America, 1914–41" (Ph.D diss., Brown University, 1982) focuses primarily on the role of sexuality in the new "companionate marriage." The standard work on divorce remains William O'Neill's *Divorce in the Progressive Era* (New Haven, Conn.: Yale University Press, 1967), which, by stopping at 1920, does not fully concern itself with the revolution. But particularly useful for my purposes is Elaine Tyler May's excellent *Great Expectations: Marriage and Divorce in Post-Victorian America* (Chicago: University of Chicago Press, 1980), which compares the causes of divorce in the 1880s with those thirty years later.

5. Robert Wiebe, *The Search for Order* (New York: Hill and Wang, 1967) is the classic statement of this development. But Stuart Blumin has recently brilliantly traced the roots of this class in the growth of white collar groups such as clerks deep in the nineteenth century (*The Emergence of the Middle Class: Social Experience in the American City, 1770–1920*) [New York: Cambridge University Press, 1989]).

6. Nathan Hale, *Freud and the Americans: The Beginnings of Psychoanalysis in the United States, 1876–1917* (New York: Oxford University Press, 1971). I am really discussing here his concept of "civilized morality," but I prefer the more neutral term "system of morality." But see also Richard Wightman Fox and T. J. Jackson Lears, *The Culture of Consumption* (New York: Pantheon, 1983); Wiebe, *The Search for Order.*

7. Mowry, *The Urban Nation,* 3.

8. These terms, "Masculine Achiever," "Christian Gentleman," and "Masculine Primitive," are from Anthony Rotundo, "Learning about Manhood," in J. A. Mangan and James Walvin, eds., *Manliness and Morality: Middle-Class Morality in Britain and America, 1800–1940* (Manchester, UK: Manchester University Press, 1987), 35–48.

9. Irwin G. Wyllie, *The Self-Made Man in America: The Myth of Rags to Riches* (New York: Free Press, 1954), 71.

10. Rotundo, "Learning about Manhood," 37.

11. Ibid., 37.

12. David Reisman, *The Lonely Crowd* (Cambridge, Mass.: Harvard University Press, 1950), passim.

13. Alexis De Tocqueville, *Democracy in America* (New York: Knopf, 1945), 129.

14. Rotundo, "Learning about Manhood," 38.

15. Ibid.

16. Warren Susman, "Personality and the Development of Twentieth-Century Culture," in *Culture as History* (New York: Pantheon, 1984), 271–84; see also Stanley Coben, *Rebellion against Victorianism: The Impetus for Cultural Change in 1920s America* (New York: Oxford University Press, 1991); Bertram Wyatt Brown in *Southern Honor: Ethics and Behavior in the Old South* (New York: Oxford University Press, 1982) talks of the concept of honor in the southern states. This was much closer to respectable primitivism than to the northern concept of the Christian Gentleman.

17. Charles Rosenberg, "Sexuality, Class, and Role in Nineteenth-Century America," in Joseph H. Pleck and Elizabeth H. Pleck, *The American Man* (Englewood Cliffs, N.J.: Prentice Hall, 1980), 224.

18. I have borrowed Michael Gordon's term for the attitude towards sex in nineteenth-century marriage manuals; see Michael Gordon, "Sex in Marital Education Literature, 1830–1940," in James M. Henslin, ed., *Studies in the Sociology of Sex* (New York: Appleton, Century, Crofts, 1977).

19. Ben Barker-Benfield, *The Horrors of the Half-Known Life: Male Attitudes to Women and Sexuality in Nineteenth-Century America* (New York: Harper and Row, 1976).

20. Sylvester Graham, *A Lecture to Young Men* (Providence: Weeden and Cory, 1834), 17, 33; quoted in Dubbert, *A Man's Place* (see note 4 above), 42; Stephen Nissenbaum, *Sex, Diet, and Debility in Jacksonian America* (Westport, Conn.: Greenwood, 1980), 26.

21. Charles Rosenberg, "Sexuality, Class, and Social Role," 230.

22. As suggested in Nancy Cott, "Passionlessness: An Interpretation of Victorian Sexual Ideology," *Signs* (Autumn 1978): 219–36.

23. Sigmund Freud, *Civilization and Its Discontents* (London: Hogarth, 1929).

24. Neil Larry Shumsky, "Tacit Acceptance: Respectable Americans and Segregated Prostitution, 1870–1910," *Journal of Social History* 19 (Fall 1986): 664–79. On this theme see Peter Cominos, "Late Victorian Sexual Respectability and the Social System," *International Review of Social History* 8 (1963): 18–48. A similar argument to Shumsky, also using California evidence, was developed by Robert Griswold, *Family and Divorce in California, 1850–90: Victorian Illusions and Everyday Realities* (Albany: State University of New York Press, 1982).

25. Shumsky, "Tacit Acceptance," 672.

26. Mark Twain, "American Manners," in *Tramp Abroad* (New York: Harper and Row, 1977; originally published 1880).

27. Ibid.

28. Rosenberg, "Sexuality, Class, and Social Role," 224.

29. F. A. David, *Plain Talks on Avoided Subjects* (Philadelphia, 1899).

30. Captain Marryat, *A Diary in America*, Vol. 2 (London: Orme, Brown, Green, and Longman's, 1839), 244–47. Carl Degler has argued, rightly, that this was hardly typical ("What Ought to Be and What Was: Women's Sexuality in the Nineteenth Century," *American Historical Review* 79 [December 1974]: 1467–90). But it still represents the kind of extremes to which people would sometimes go.

31. Robert L. Dickinson and Lura Beam, *The Single Woman: A Medical Study in Sex Education* (Baltimore, Md.: Williams and Wilkins, 1934), 404; quoted in Simmons, "Marriage in the Modern Manner," Ph.D diss., Brown University, 1982, x.

32. Quoted in John C. Burnham, "The Progressive Era Revolution in American Attitudes towards Sex," *Journal of American History* 59 (March 1973): 885.

33. Reverend Phillip Moxon, *The White Cross Purity League* (New York: YMCA, 1888), passim.

34. Burnham, "Progressive Era Revolution," passim.

35. Henry Seidl Canby, "Sex and Marriage in the Nineties," *Harper's* 169 (June–November 1934): 427–36.

36. Walter Lippmann, *A Preface to Morals* (London: Allen and Unwin, 1931), 287.

37. Robert and Helen Lynd, *Middletown: A Study in American Culture* (New York: Harcourt, Brace, Jovanovich, 1929), 112.

38. James Thurber, *Alarms and Diversions* (New York: Harper and Brothers, 1957), 99.

39. Beth Bailey, *From Front Porch to Back Seat: Courtship in Twentieth-Century America* (Baltimore, Md.: Johns Hopkins University Press, 1988), 17.

40. Ellen K. Rothman, *Hands and Hearts: A History of Courtship in America* (New York: Basic, 1985); Karen Lystra, *Searching the Heart: Women, Men, and Romantic Love in Nineteenth-Century America* (New York: Oxford University Press, 1989); Steven Seidman, "The Power of Desire and the Danger of Pleasure: Victorian Sexuality Reconsidered," *Journal of Social History* 24 (Fall 1990): 47–67.

41. Lystra, *Searching the Heart*, 3–37.

42. Lewis Terman, *Psychological Factors in Marital Happiness* (New York: McGraw Hill, 1938), 321.

43. Ira Reiss, *Pre-Marital Sexual Standards in America* (Glencoe, Ill.: Free Press, 1960).

44. In Judge Ben B. Lindsey, *The Revolt of Modern Youth* (New York: Boni and Liveright, 1925), 56.

45. Lewis M. Terman, *Psychological Factors in Marital Happiness*, 321.

46. Kellow Chesney, *The Anti-Society: An Account of the Victorian Underworld* (Boston: Gambit, 1970); Steven Marcus, *The Other Victorians: a Study of Sexuality and Pornography in Mid–Nineteenth-Century England* (New York: Basic, 1966).

47. The Victorian underworld is discussed in Eliot Gorn, *The Manly Art: Bare-Knuckle Prize Fighting in America* (Ithaca, N.Y.: Cornell University Press, 1986); Benjamin Rader, *American Sports: From the Age of Folk Games to the Age of Spectators* (Englewood Cliffs, N.J.: Prentice Hall, 1986); Christopher Lasch, *The Culture of Narcissism: American Life in an Age of Diminishing Expectations* (New York: Norton, 1979), 198–99; John C. Burnham, *The Forces of Evil in American History*, chap. 7,

unpublished manuscript; Timothy Gilfoyle, "City of Eros: New York City, Prostitution, and the Commercialization of Sex, 1790–1920," Ph.D diss., Columbia University, 1987; Pamela Haag, "The 'Ill-Use of a Wife': Patterns of Working-Class Violence in Domestic and Public New York City, 1860–1880," *Journal of Social History* 25 (Spring 1992): 447–77.

48. E. Anthony Rotundo, "Romantic Friendship: Male Intimacy and Middle-Class Youth in the Northern United States, 1800–1900," *Journal of Social History* 23 (Fall 1989): 1–25.

49. David Brion Davis, *From Homicide to Slavery: Studies in American Culture* (New York: Oxford University Press, 1986), 42–43.

50. John F. Kasson, *Rudeness and Civility: Manners in Nineteenth-Century America* (New York: Hill and Wang, 1991), 78; Gilfoyle, "City of Eros," 245.

51. Kasson, *Rudeness and Civility*, 127.

52. The *Police Gazette* is discussed in Benjamin Rader, *American Sports: From the Age of Folk Games to the Age of Spectators* (Englewood Cliffs, N.J.: Prentice Hall, 1980), 79. On American primitivism see Jean Baudrillard, *America*, trans. Chris Turner (New York and London: Verso, 1988).

53. T. J. Jackson Lears, *No Place of Grace: Antimodernism and the Transformation of American Culture* (New York: Pantheon, 1981); Peter Gardella in his extraordinary *Innocent Ecstasy: How Christianity Gave America an Ethic of Sexual Pleasure* (New York: Oxford University Press, 1986) shows how religious writers increasingly encouraged orgasmic ecstasy by emphasizing spiritual ecstasy as a goal in marriage.

54. John Higham, "The Reorientation of American Culture in the 1890s," in John Higham, ed., *Writing American History* (Bloomington: Indiana University Press, 1970), 60–103; James McGovern, "David Graham Phillips and the Virility Impulse of the Progressive Era," *New England Quarterly* 39 (September 1966): 348; Joe Dubbert, "Progressivism and the Masculinity Crisis," in Pleck and Pleck, *The American Man* (see note 17 above), 383–420.

55. Harvey Green, *Fit for America: Health, Fitness, Sport, and American Society* (Baltimore, Md.: Johns Hopkins University Press, 1986), 214–15.

56. Rotundo, "Learning about Manhood" (see note 8 above), 41.

57. Ibid.

58. John Fraser, *America and the Patterns of Chivalry* (New York: Cambridge University Press, 1982), 27.

59. Mark Carnes, *Secret Rituals and Manhood in Victorian America* (New Haven, Conn.: Yale University Press, 1989).

60. Fraser, *America and the Patterns of Chivalry*, 125.

61. Benjamin Rader, *American Sports*, 141.

62. John Higham, "The Reorientation of American Culture"; Coben, *Rebellion against Victorianism* (see note 16 above), 76.

63. Henry Nash Smith, *Virgin Land: the West as Myth and Symbol* (New York: Oxford University Press), 1953. David Brion Davis comments in *From Homicide to Slavery* (p. 44) that the Western chivalric heroes were always more crude and "demonic" than their European counterparts, and were of a sort that had previously largely been confined to the lower orders.

64. Roderick Nash, *The Call of the Wild* (New York: Braziller, 1970); Edgar Rice Burroughs, *Tarzan, Lord of the Jungle* (New York: Grosset and Dunlap, 1928). See

discussion of literary primitivism in Oscar Cargill, *Intellectual America: Ideas on the March* (New York: Macmillan, 1968).

65. Theodore Roosevelt, *The Strenuous Life: Essays and Addresses* (New York, 1900).

66. Jack London, *The Call of the Wild* (New York: Macmillan, 1903), 131, 132, 119, 142.

67. Frank Norris, *McTeague: A Story of San Francisco* (New York: Norton, 1977). See also the scandal caused by Stephen Crane's *Maggie: A Girl of the Streets* and by Theodore Dreiser's *Sister Carrie*. Their sympathetic portrayal of fallen women broke with Victorian morality.

68. Agnes Repplier, "The Repeal of Reticence," *Atlantic* (March 1914): 297–304; "Sex O'Clock in America," *Current Opinion* 55 (August 1913): 113–14. The author was anonymous, but the phrase is from William Marion Reedy, editor of the St. Louis Mirror, quoted in John C. Burnham, "Progressive Era Revolution" (see note 32 above), 163.

69. T. J. Jackson Lears, "The Concept of Cultural Hegemony," *American Historical Review* 90 (1985): 567–93: Gramsci, *The Modern Prince*, in A. Gramsci, *Selections from Prison Notebooks*, trans. Q. Hoare and G. N. Smith (New York: Basic, 1983).

70. Frank Mott, *A History of American Magazines* (Cambridge, Mass.: Harvard University Press, 1938).

71. Lary May, *Screening Out the Past: The Birth of Mass Culture and the Motion Picture Industry* (New York: Oxford University Press, 1980); Lewis Erenberg, *Steppin' Out: New York Night-life and the Transformation of American Culture, 1890–1930* (Westport, Conn.: Greenwood, 1980); Kathy Peiss, *Cheap Amusements: Working Women and Leisure in Turn-of-the-Century New York* (Philadelphia: Temple University Press, 1986); John Kasson, *Amusing the Million: Coney Island at the Turn-of-the-Century* (New York: Hill and Wang, 1978).

72. G. Stanley Hall, *Adolescence* (New York: Appleton, 1904); Joseph Kett, *Rites of Passage: Adolescence in America, 1790 to the Present* (New York: Basic, 1977).

73. John Whitely Chambers, *The Tyranny of Change* (New York: St. Martin's, 1975), 94.

74. Peiss, *Cheap Amusements*, 110–13.

75. Bailey, *Courtship in Twentieth-Century America* (see note 39 above).

76. Kinsey, *Sexual Behavior in the Human Female* (New York: Saunders, 1954), 299.

T W O : *The Masculine Image*

1. Jo Paoletti, "Changes in the Masculine Image: A Content Analysis of Popular Humor about Dress, 1880–1910," Ph.D diss., University of Maryland, 1981; Lois Banner, *American Beauty* (New York: Knopf, 1984); Mary Ryan, "The Movie Moderns: The Projection of a New Womanhood in the 1920s," in Friedman and Shade, *Our American Sisters* (Lexington, Mass.: Heath, 1982), 500–518; John Kasson, *Rude-*

ness and Civility: Manners in Nineteenth-Century America (New York: Hill and Wang, 1991), 117–21.

2. James Whorton, *Crusaders for Fitness: The History of American Health Reformers* (Princeton, N.J.: Princeton University Press, 1982), 274; Harvey Green, *Fit for America: Health, Fitness, Sport, and American Society* (Baltimore, Md.: Johns Hopkins University Press, 1986), 201.

3. James Whorton, *Crusaders for Fitness*, 284.

4. Warren I. Susman, "Personality and the Development of Twentieth-Century Culture," in *New Trends in American Intellectual History*, John Higham, ed. (Baltimore, Md.: Johns Hopkins University Press, 1979), 271–85.

5. Gilman Ostrander argues that from the 1910s American society shifted from patriarchal dominance to "rule by youth." (*American Civilization in the First Machine Age* [New York: Harper and Row, 1970]). His sensitive analysis has had a major influence on my thinking on the period.

6. Paula Fass has spiritedly identified a mature subculture among college youth in the 1920s (*The Damned and the Beautiful: American Youth in the 1920s* [New York: Oxford University Press, 1977]). John Modell has recently confirmed that the subcultural patterns extended beyond college youth (*Into One's Own: From Youth to Adulthood in the United States, 1920–1975* [Berkeley and Los Angeles: University of California Press, 1989]).

7. Ben B. Lindsey and Wainwright Evans, *The Revolt of Modern Youth* (New York: Boni and Liveright, 1925), 14.

8. Ibid.

9. Warren Susman, in "Personality and the Making of Twentieth-Century Culture," uses Fairbanks as typical of the "culture of personality," too, but my illustrations are original ones and add to our understanding of this important figure in the twentieth-century social construction of masculinity. My discussion of Fairbanks is also indebted to Lary May, *Screening Out the Past: The Birth of Mass Culture and the Motion Picture Industry* (New York: Oxford University Press, 1980); quotation is from James Oppenheim, *How to Be Happy though Married* (Girard, Kans.: Haldeman-Julius, 1927), 8.

10. *Physical Culture*, November 1921, 21.

11. Ibid.

12. *Physical Culture*, February 1923, 27.

13. Gilbert Seldes, "Good Old Sex Appeal," *New Republic*, April 21, 1926, 275–76.

14. Raymond Williams, "Advertising: The Magic System," in *Problems in Materialism and Culture* (London: Verso, 1980), 173.

15. Daniel Pope, *The Making of Modern Advertising* (New York: Basic, 1983).

16. Raymond Williams, "The Magic System," 188.

17. American historians of advertising influenced by Williams have included Stewart Ewen, *Captains of Consciousness: Advertising and the Social Roots of the Consumer Culture* (New York: MacGraw Hill, 1976). See especially the studies by Roland Marchand, *Advertising the American Dream, 1920–40* (Berkeley and Los Angeles: University of California Press, 1985), and Jackson Lears, "Some Versions of Fantasy: Towards a Cultural History of American Advertising, 1880–1930," *Pros-*

pects 9 (1984): 349–405. The implications of advertising for sexuality are suggested but not fully realized in these works. However, John D'Emilio and Estelle Freedman have recently placed the emergence of advertising as a full-fledged industry in its own right in the 1920s in its context as helping provoke the roots of what they usefully call the modern "sexualized society" at this time (*History of Sexuality in America* [New York: Harper and Row, 1988]). Advertisers, by putting "sex on display," stimulated desire in the consumer, and also stirred up insecurities about sexual attractiveness (though D'Emilio and Freedman confine their analysis of this to women).

18. "Changelings," *Saturday Evening Post*, January 10, 1925, 17. On the exploitation of desire to sell products, see Judith Williamson, *Decoding Advertisements: Ideology and Meaning in Advertising* (London: Boyar, 1977). But Jackson Lears has marvelously shown that the motivation of advertisers in this period was complex. They had little idea of the impact they were having, or of the effect of their work. See Jackson Lears, "From Salvation to Self-Realization: Advertising and the Therapeutic Roots of the Consumer Culture, 1910–1930," in Lears and Fox, eds., *The Culture of Consumption* (New York: Pantheon, 1983), 3–38.

19. *Life*, June 25, 1925, 32.
20. *American*, August 1925, 141.
21. *New Yorker*, September 27, 1928, 89.
22. *New Yorker*, January 5, 1929, 91.
23. *Literary Digest*, April 24, 1926, 56.
24. Ibid., April 10, 1926, 59.
25. *Life*, June 15, 1922, 32.
26. Ibid., May 22, 1926.
27. *Life*, May 20, 1925, 29.
28. *American*, December 1925, 202.
29. *Collier's*, July 3, 1926, 38.
30. *Literary Digest*, April 10, 1926, 74.
31. Ibid.
32. *American*, September 1925, 80.
33. For example, *Saturday Evening Post*, July 12, 1919, 140.
34. Ibid.
35. *Association Men*, November 1926, 423.
36. *Physical Culture*, June 1927, 67.
37. For example, *Life*, October 16, 1931, 17.
38. *Collier's*, August 14, 1926, 33.
39. *Saturday Evening Post*, October 16, 1926, 98.
40. *American*, July 1925, 130.
41. Marchand, *Advertising the American Dream* (see note 17 above), 18.
42. *Delineator*, February 1924, 62.
43. *Life*, March 19, 1925, 31.
44. *Saturday Evening Post*, October 11, 1919, 86.
45. *Life*, April 23, 1925, 1.
46. *Saturday Evening Post*, October 2, 1926, 182.
47. *Vanity Fair*, June 1925, 79.

48. *Saturday Evening Post*, April 26, 1924, 19.

49. *American*, September 1925, 136.

50. *Delineator*, February 1924, 62.

51. *Delineator*, March 1924, 81.

52. *Saturday Evening Post*, April 19, 1924, 85.

53. *Life*, January 1, 1925, 28.

54. Ibid., 28.

55. *Vanity Fair*, May 1925, 117.

56. *Association Men*, December 1928, 327.

57. *Saturday Evening Post*, November 15, 1919, 108.

58. *Association Men*, December 1928, 327.

59. *Collier's*, July 3, 1926, 24–25.

60. *Physical Culture*, June 1925, 83.

61. *New Yorker*, September 15, 1928, 89.

62. *Vanity Fair*, April 1925, 21.

63. *Saturday Evening Post*, July 31, 1920, 16; August 6, 1919, 33.

64. Ibid., October 11, 1919, 14.

65. *Life*, September 4, 1924, 31.

66. *Saturday Evening Post*, October 23, 1926, 74.

67. Ibid., July 31, 1920, 16.

68. Ibid., January 10, 1925, 16.

69. Ibid., January 24, 1925, 3.

70. Ibid., November 1, 1919, 48.

71. Paul Nystrom, *The Economics of Fashion* (New York: Ronald, 1928), 21.

72. "Solomon's Sartorial Glory Rivalled by the Modern He-Man," *Literary Digest*, March 3, 1923, 56–57.

73. *Life*, May 17, 1929, 33.

74. For this information, I am indebted to Jo Paoletti, "Changes in the Masculine Image" (see note 1 above), passim.

75. *Saturday Evening Post*, July 5, 1920, 188.

76. Paoletti, "Changes in the Masculine Image," 72.

77. "Solomon's Sartorial Glory," 56.

78. Nystrom, *Economics of Fashion*, 345.

79. Robert and Helen Lynd, *Middletown: A Study in American Culture* (New York: Harcourt, Brace, Jovanovich, 1929), 181.

80. Quoted in Clifford Waugh, "Bernarr Macfadden: The Muscular Prophet," Ph.D. diss., SUNY Buffalo, 1979, 81.

81. Writing a true story became something of a joke among journalists in the 1920s. There were tales that the tormented flappers, supposedly the writers of the confessions, were in fact sedate old gentlemen. See the several exposés of Macfadden, especially Mary Macfadden and Emile Gavreau, *Dumbbells and Carrot-Strips: The Story of Bernarr Macfadden* (New York: Holt, 1953), a revealing and quite reliable exposé by his former wife; and Joseph Hershey's *Pulpwood Editor* (New York: Stokes, 1937). On Macfadden see also Harvey Green, *Fit for America* (see note 2 above) and Christina Simmons, "The Dream World of Confession Magazines, 1920–40" (Paper presented at the Fifth Berkshire Conference on the History of Women, June 1981).

These figures are from the Ayers Directory. *Physical Culture*'s readership was solidly middle class. Macfadden was an important cultural figure in the 1900s and even in the 1890s (though not so in the 1910s) largely through this journal, which has been identified as one aspect of the masculinity crisis of the Progressive era. Of course, Macfadden caused anxieties at this time but not necessarily about sex, because in the early years of the century he was not able to be as sexually explicit as he was in the looser atmosphere of the 1920s, when I am arguing that he gained renewed cultural importance—and certainly a wider readership—in the context of the success of *True Story* and of the more sexually demanding New Woman of the 1920s. *True Story* has rightly been associated with a strong readership among working-class women. However, in its early years, it was widely read by men too. Certainly, ads in the journal were aimed at men and ads appeared in *Physical Culture* for *True Story* (e.g., p. 81, April 1919). In one study of high school students in Columbus, Ohio, several of the students of both sexes placed *True Story* on a list of their favorite magazines, though several others were found to have crossed it out, probably on account of its low intellectual content and reputation (Reginald Stevens Kimball, "What Magazines Do High School Students Read?" *School and Society* 14 [October 16, 1920]: 486–88). In a study of workers in Milwaukee, it was found to be the most popular journal among boys and girls (see Gray and Munroe, *Reading Habits and Interests of Adults* [Macmillan, 1930]). I am arguing, too, that the readership crept up into the middle classes, as is suggested by its wide readership in Middletown.

82. *Physical Culture*, November 1925, 41; and December 1923, 35.

83. "His Fatal Beauty," *True Story*, vol. VII, no. 6; "When Memories Burn," vol. IX, no. 1, 79.

84. "The Price," *True Story*, vol. VIII, no. 4, 33.

85. "It Might Happen to Any Girl," *True Story*, vol. VIII, no. 1, 56–59.

86. "After the Eleventh Hour," *True Story*, vol. VIII, no. 3, 74.

87. *Physical Culture*, July 1920, 46.

88. Ibid., June 1918, 17, 80; November 1920, 111.

89. Ibid., November 1925, 129.

90. Ibid., September 1925, 17.

91. Ibid., January 1924, 66.

92. *Physical Culture*, May 1923, 36.

93. Ibid., January 1926, 115.

94. Ibid., November 1923, 38.

95. Ibid., November 1925, 41.

96. *Physical Culture*, June 1921, 95.

97. "For His Brother's Sins," *True Story*, vol. VIII, no. 3, 21.

98. "The Lady Bug," *True Story*, vol. VII, no. 2, 64.

99. "The Penalty He Paid," *True Story*, vol. II, no. 1, 17; "Rainbow's End: Life Is Sometimes What We Make It," vol. III, no. 3, 45.

100. "How I Lost My Husband," *True Story*, vol. III, no. 1, 65; "Lover or Husband?" ibid., vol. VIII, no. 5, 3.

101. "Lover or Husband?" Ibid., vol. VIII, no. 5, 33.

102. "Just a Showgirl," *True Story*, vol. VII, no. 4, 23; "Can a Woman Come Back?" ibid., vol. X, no. 4, 73.

103. *True Story*, "The Husbandless Wife," vol. VIII, no. 3, 25.

104. "A Life for a Love," *True Story*, vol. IX, no. 3, 59; *Physical Culture*, November 1926, 113.

105. *Physical Culture*, January 1924, 117.

106. Ibid., July 1920, 21.

107. "Bullets and Oysters," *True Story*, vol. II, no. 1, 34.

108. *Physical Culture*, January 1926, 30.

109. Waugh, "Macfadden" (see note 80 above), 60–61.

110. Ibid.

111. Ibid., 175.

112. Ibid., 221.

113. *Physical Culture*, February 1919, 15.

114. "What Really Killed Valentino," *Physical Culture*, October 1926, 27.

115. *Physical Culture*, November 1918, 36.

116. Ibid.

117. *Physical Culture*, November 1923, 26.

118. Ibid., January 1922, 135.

119. Ibid., March 1926, 103.

120. Ibid., June 1924, 17.

121. Ibid., October 1923, 23.

122. Ibid., January 1926, 87.

123. Ibid., March 1926, 103.

124. Bernarr Macfadden, *Manhood and Marriage* (New York: Macfadden, 1916), 10.

125. *Physical Culture*, November 1923, 92.

126. Concept discussed in introduction. But see the works of Eliot Gorn, *The Manly Art* (Ithaca, N.Y.: Cornell University Press, 1986); and Benjamin Rader, *American Sports: From the Age of Folk Games to the Age of Spectators* (Englewood Cliffs, N.J.: Prentice Hall, 1923).

127. See John C. Burnham, "The Progressive Era Revolution in American Attitudes towards Sex," *Journal of American History* 59 (March 1973): 885–908.

128. "Her Morning After," *True Story*, vol. VI, no. 5, 19.

129. "A Greased Pig and My Romance," *True Story*, vol. II, no. 3, 62.

130. "Love's Turmoil," *True Story*, vol. XIII, no. 3, 44–45.

131. *Physical Culture*, June 1918, 71.

132. Ibid.

133. *Physical Culture*, March 1925, 62.

134. Ibid., March 1922, 66.

135. Ibid., November 1918, 10.

136. In her study of twentieth-century courtship convention, Beth Bailey discusses in detail (ch. 3) the competitive nature of courtship between the two world wars.

137. There were several studies of "Ideal Husbands" in *True Story* magazine; see also Paul Popenoe, *Modern Marriage* (New York: Macmillan, 1925), 82.

THREE: *Styles of Masculinity*

1. Henry May, *The End of American Innocence* (New York: Knopf, 1959).

2. Floyd Dell, *Love in Greenwich Village* (New York: Doran, 1926).

3. On Mabel Dodge Luhan see Robert Crunden, *From Self to Society, 1919–41* (Englewood Cliffs, N.J.: Prentice Hall, 1971); Christopher Lasch, *The New Radicalism in America: The Intellectual as Social Type, 1890–1963* (New York: Knopf, 1965); Lois Rudnick, *Mabel Dodge Luhan: New Woman, New Worlds* (Albuquerque: University of New Mexico Press, 1984); Leslie Fishbein, *Rebels in Bohemia: The Radicals of the Masses, 1912–17* (Chapel Hill: University of North Carolina Press, 1982); Ellen Key, *Love and Marriage,* trans. Arthur G. Chater (New York: Putnam's, 1911); Edward Carpenter, *Love's Coming of Age* (London: Sonnenschein, 1906); Havelock Ellis, *Studies in the Psychology of Sex* (New York: Random House, 1936).

4. Randolph Bourne, *Youth and Life* (New York: Houghton Mifflin, 1913), 12. On Bourne see Edward Abraham, *The Lyrical Left: Randolph Bourne, Alfred Steiglitz, and the Origins of Cultural Radicalism in America* (Charlottesville: University of Virginia Press, 1984); Lasch, *New Radicalism in America,* 69–103.

5. Bourne, *Youth and Life,* 4.

6. Frederic Hoffman, *The Nineteen Twenties: American Writing in the Postwar Decade* (New York: Viking, 1955); Leslie Fiedler, *Love and Death in the American Novel,* rev. ed. (New York: Stein and Day, 1966).

7. Carl Van Doren, "Contemporary American Novelists," *Nation,* October 12, 1921, 407–12.

8. F. Scott Fitzgerald, *The Great Gatsby* (New York: Scribner's, 1925), 136.

9. Floyd Dell, *Moon-Calf* (New York: Knopf, 1920), 293.

10. Floyd Dell, *The Briary-Bush* (New York: Knopf, 1921), 240.

11. Floyd Dell, *Souvenir* (New York: Doubleday and Doran, 1929), 11.

12. Dedication to B. Marie Gage in Floyd Dell, *Moon-Calf* (New York: Sagamore, 1957); quoted in William Brevda, *Harry Kemp: The Last Bohemian* (Lewisburg, Pa.: Bucknell University Press, 1986), 121.

13. Dell, *Briary-Bush,* 34.

14. Dell, *Moon-Calf,* 165.

15. Ibid., 241.

16. Ibid., 210.

17. Ibid.

18. Carl Van Vechten, *Peter Whiffle: His Life and Works* (New York: Knopf, 1922), 98.

19. Stephen Benet, *Young People's Pride* (New York: Henry Holt, 1922).

20. Dell, *Moon-Calf,* 63.

21. Ibid., 334.

22. Floyd Dell, *Janet March* (New York: Knopf, 1923), 99.

23. Dell, *Briary-Bush,* 63.

24. Dell, *Moon-Calf,* 293.

25. Percy Marks, *The Plastic Age* (New York: Grosset and Dunlap, 1924), 85, 268, 269.

26. Stephen Benet, *The Beginning of Wisdom* (New York: Holt, 1921), 126.

27. Ibid., 145, 205.

28. Ludwig Lewisohn, *Stephen Escott* (New York: Harper's, 1930), 22.

29. Ibid., 25.

30. Ibid., 49.

31. F. Scott Fitzgerald, *This Side of Paradise* (New York: Knopf, 1920), 18, 58–59.

32. Dell, *Moon-Calf*, 293.

33. Ibid., 289.

34. Ibid., 314.

35. Floyd Dell, *Homecoming: An Autobiography* (New York: Farrar and Rinehart, 1933), 96.

36. Benet, *The Beginning of Wisdom*, 343.

37. Ibid., 106.

38. Katherine Brush, *Young Man of Manhattan* (New York: Farrar and Rinehart, 1930), 30.

39. Floyd Dell, *Janet March*, 309.

40. Lewisohn, *Stephen Escott*, 44.

41. Dell, *Janet March*, 121.

42. Ibid., 118.

43. Dell, *Moon-Calf*, 210.

44. Ibid., 203.

45. Ibid., 322.

46. Dell, *Briary-Bush*.

47. Ibid., 129.

48. Floyd Dell, *An Unmarried Father* (New York: Knopf, 1925), 30.

49. Fitzgerald, *This Side of Paradise*, 193.

50. Marks, *The Plastic Age*, 95.

51. Ibid.

52. Ibid., 318.

53. Ibid., 314.

54. Lewisohn, *Stephen Escott*, 162.

55. Benet, *The Beginning of Wisdom*, 36.

56. Dell, *Janet March*, 175.

57. F. Scott Fitzgerald, *The Beautiful and the Damned* (New York: Scribner's, 1922), 197.

58. Ibid., 200.

59. Floyd Dell, "Hallelujah, I'm a Bum," from *Love in Greenwich Village* (see note 2 above), 165; the importance of the tramp is explored in Kingsley Widmer, "Some Lifestyle Sources of the Literary Tough Guy and the Proletarian Hero," in David Madden, ed., *Tough Guy Writers of the 1930s* (Carbondale and Edwardsville: Southern Illinois University Press, 1968); Rupert Wilkinson, *The Tough Guy and American Character* (Westport, Conn.: Greenwood, 1984).

60. Dell, "Hallelujah," 160.

61. Ibid., 217.

62. William Brevda, *Harry Kemp* (see note 12 above), 120.

63. Ibid., 124.

64. Harry Kemp, *Tramping on Life: An Autobiographical Narrative* (New York: Boni and Liveright, 1922), 126.

65. Ibid.

66. Ibid., 17.

67. Ibid., 95.

68. Harry Kemp, *More Miles: An Autobiographical Novel* (New York: Boni and Liveright, 1926), 159.

69. Ibid., 27.

70. Ibid., 59, 60.

71. Ibid.

72. Ibid., 213.

73. Oscar Cargill, *Intellectual America: Ideas on the March* (New York: MacMillan, 1942), 323.

74. Sherwood Anderson, *Winesburg, Ohio* (New York: Buebsch, 1919), 224.

75. Ibid.

76. Sherwood Anderson, *Dark Laughter* (New York: Buebsch, 1925), 62.

77. Ibid., 43.

78. Ibid., 98–99.

79. Sherwood Anderson, *Many Marriages* (New York: Buebsch, 1923), 185; Anderson certainly had an agenda. He wrote to his brother, "Let the bourgeoisie worry about right and wrong, morality and respectability" (to Karl Anderson, May 31, 1923, in Howard Mumford Jones, ed., *The Letters of Sherwood Anderson* [Boston: Little, Brown, 1953]).

80. Greensboro North Carolina *Daily News*, May 13, 1923.

81. Ben Hecht, *Erik Dorn* (New York: Boni and Liveright, 1921), 166.

82. Ibid., 31.

83. Ibid., 223.

84. Ibid., 236.

85. Warner Fabian, *Flaming Youth* (New York: Macaulay, 1923), 288.

86. Carl Van Vechten, *Firecrackers* (New York: Knopf, 1925), 227.

87. Gladys Johnson, *Desire* (New York: Bunt, 1929), 34.

88. Marks, *The Plastic Age* (see note 25 above), 11.

89. However, O'Neill's characters, even when black, were more representative of the underworld than of their race (see Nathan Huggins, *The Harlem Rennaissance* [New York: Oxford University Press, 1971], 295).

90. Michael B. Stoff, "Claude McKay and the Cult of Primitivism," in Arno Bontemps, *The Harlem Rennaissance Remembered* (New York: Dodd, Mead, 1972), 126.

91. Anderson, *Dark Laughter*, 106.

92. Ibid.

93. Bruce Kellner, *Carl Van Vechten and the Irreverent Decades* (Norman: University of Oklahoma Press, 1968), 198; Emory Eliot, ed., *Columbia Literary History of the United States* (New York: Columbia University Press, 1988), 854. Van Vechten reminds us rather of a 1920s version of the Leonard Bernstein satirized by Tom Wolfe in *Radical Chic*. At his parties were "the kings and queens of the theatre . . . and . . . their darker opposite members. Here they rubbed shoulders, sipped cocktails, nibbled hors d'oevres, conversed, sang and danced . . . a novelty soon became commonplace, an institution" (Jervis Anderson, *This Was Harlem: A Cultural Portrait, 1900–1950* [New York: Farrar, Straus, Giroux, 1982], 215).

94. Van Vechten, *Nigger Heaven* (New York: Knopf, 1926), 25; the book was a sensation, selling one hundred thousand copies. It was not greeted with unanimous enthusiasm, however. W. E. B. DuBois wrote that it failed to see blacks as "individuals." They would do better to read the *Police Gazette* (Anderson, *This Was Harlem*, 219). D. H. Lawrence thought that it was a "false book by an author who lingers in nigger cabarets, hoping to heaven to pick up something to write about and, make sensational." See Chidi Konné, *From DuBois to Van Vechten: The Early New Negro Literature, 1903–1926* (Westport, Conn.: Greenwood, 1981), 24–35, which offers a measured consideration of Van Vechten's influence. Irvin Huggins, though, is harder on Van Vechten. He quotes Van Vechten as saying that his interest in blacks was "almost an addiction" [Huggins, *Harlem Rennaissance* (99), says that Van Vechten seemed to argue that the Negro civilizes himself at great cost (102), and describes the novel as representing a "deliberate dislocation of conventional morality" (93)].

95. DuBose Heyward, *Porgy* (London: Cape, 1928), 73. Irvin Huggins states that Heyward manipulated "stereotypes of Negro primitivism to great effect" (Huggins, *Harlem Rennaissance*, 295).

96. Waldo Frank, *Holiday* (Boston: Little, Brown, 1925), 40–41.

97. Anderson, *Dark Laughter*, 25. Anderson had an obsession with blacks. There are frequent references in his letters to the "dark, earthy laughter" of blacks that he contrasts with the "neuroticism, the hurry and self-consciousness of modern life" (to Horace Liveright, April 18, 1925, *Letters of Sherwood Anderson* [see note 79 above], 142). He asked his brother to come "look at the niggers" (to Karl Anderson, August 1924, *Letters of Sherwood Anderson*, 128).

98. Heyward, *Porgy*, 77.

99. Ibid.

100. Van Vechten, *Nigger Heaven*, 228.

101. Hoffman, *The 1920s* (see note 6 above), 118.

102. Cargill, *Intellectual America* (see note 73 above), 323–97; Hoffman, *The 1920s*, 320.

103. David Madden, ed., *The Tough Guy Writers of the 1930s* (see note 59 above).

104. Zane Grey, *Stairs of Sand* (New York: Black's, 1930), 84; see Carlton Jackson, *Zane Grey* (New York: Twayne, 1973), 49.

105. *Zane Grey*, passim.

106. Grey, *Stairs of Sand*, 294.

107. Zane Grey, *Lost Pueblo* (New York: Black's, 1928), 28.

108. Ibid., 154.

109. Zane Grey, *Under the Tonto Rim* (New York: Harper's, 1926), 19.

110. Ibid.; Hoffman, *The 1920s*, 269.

111. Ben Hecht, "The Wife-Beating Wave," *Collier's*, July 27, 1925; Nina Putnam, "Say It with Bricks," *Atlantic Monthly*, November 1922.

112. Katherine Gerould, *Harper's*, November 1922, 612.

113. "How Life's Lessons Came to Me," *True Story*, vol. II, no. 3, 23.

114. "Renee Finds a Link," *True Story*, vol. IV, no. 3, 79.

115. "A Secondhand Bride," *True Story*, vol. X, no. 1, 42.

116. "Confessions of a Chorus Girl," *True Story*, vol. VII, no. 1, 72.

206 • Four: Male Ideology

117. "So This Is Broadway," *True Story*, vol. VII, no. 5, 22.
118. Ibid.
119. Ibid.
120. "His Yesterdays," *True Story*, vol. IX, no. 5, 53–55.
121. Ibid.
122. "Can a Woman Come Back?" *True Story*, vol. X, no. 4, 73–74.
123. "The Lady Bug," *True Story*, vol. VII, no. 2, 64.
124. "Love's Turmoil," *True Story*, vol. XIII, no. 4.
125. "Suppose Your Husband Did This?" *True Story*, vol. IX, no. 5, 65.
126. Ibid.
127. "Through the Valley of Death," *True Story*, vol. IX, no. 5, 42.
128. "The Fickleness of Men," *True Story*, vol. XIII, no. 3, 135.
129. "The Girl Who Claimed My Husband," *True Story*, vol. VII, no. 4, 19.
130. "Her Caveman Wooing," *True Story*, vol. III, no. 2, 12.
131. Ibid.
132. "Out of the Shadow," *True Story*, vol. II, no. 6, 18.

F O U R : *Male Ideology*

1. James Thurber and E. B. White, *Is Sex Necessary? or, Why You Feel the Way You Do* (New York: Harper and Row, 1929).
2. "Sex O'Clock in America," *Current Opinion*, August 1913, 113–14. Phrase borrowed from William Marion Reedy, editor of the St. Louis *Mirror*; quoted in John C. Burnham, "The Progressive Era Revolution in American Attitudes towards Sex," *Journal of American History* 59 (March 1973): 885–903.
3. Floyd Dell, *Janet March* (New York: Knopf, 1923), 275.
4. Floyd Dell, *Love in the Machine Age: A Psychological Study of the Transition from Patriarchal Society* (New York: Farrar and Rinehart, 1930), 250; Warren Susman, "Uses of the Puritan Past," in *Culture as History* (New York: Pantheon, 1984), 39–49; this phenomenon is present in Bourne's work (especially *Youth and Life*) and, most influentially, in Van Wyck Brooks, especially in his *The Ordeal of Mark Twain* (see Anthony Hilter, *The Revolt from the Village, 1915–30* [Chapel Hill, N.C.: 1969], 117).
5. Christina Simmons, "Modern Sexuality and the Myth of Victorian Repression," in Kathy Peiss and Christina Simmons, eds., *Passion and Power* (Philadelphia: Temple University Press, 1989), 57–77.
6. Ben Hecht, *Erik Dorn* (New York: Boni and Liveright, 1924), 109.
7. Ibid., 245. Well-educated people such as Dell would not have subscribed to such a perversion of Freud.
8. Ludwig Lewisohn, *Stephen Escott* (New York: Harper's, 1930), 277.
9. Stephen Vincent Benet, *The Beginning of Wisdom* (New York: Holt, 1921), 132.
10. Percy Marks, *The Plastic Age* (New York: Grosset and Dunlap, 1924), 85.
11. Ben Hecht, *Erik Dorn*, 266.
12. *New York Times*, January 28, 1923, 24.

13. James Branch Cabell, *Jurgen: A Comedy of Justice* (New York: Crown, 1919).

14. George Henry Green, *Psychoanalysis in the Classroom* (London and New York: Putnam, 1922), 259. Helpful on the popular psychologists of the 1920s is John C. Burnham, "From Narcissism to Social Control," in *Paths into American Culture* (Philadelphia: Temple University Press, 1988), 69–95; originally published in 1968.

15. Andre Tridon, *Sex and Psychoanalysis* (New York: Knopf, 1920), 241.

16. *Physical Culture*, January 1922, 77.

17. Burnham, "From Narcissism to Social Control"; Fred Matthews, "The Americanization of Sigmund Freud," *Journal of American Studies* 1 (1967): 39–62; Henry Abelove, "Freud, Male Homosexuality, and the Americans," *Dissent* (1986): 59–69.

18. Samuel Schmalhausen, *Why We Misbehave* (New York: Macaulay, 1928), 14.

19. Ibid.

20. Oswald Garrisson Villard, "Sex, Art, Truth, and Magazines," *Atlantic Monthly*, March 1926, 393–405.

21. Frederick Lewis Allen, *Only Yesterday: An Informal History of the 1920s* (New York: Harper and Brothers, 1931), 83–84.

22. "A Midnight's Memories," *True Story*, vol. VII, no. 6, 112.

23. "Jungle's Shadow," *True Story*, vol. IX, no. 1, 40.

24. "Keeping Up with the Crowd," *True Story*, vol. VIII, no. 6, 46.

25. John D'Emilio and Estelle Freedman, *Intimate Matters: A History of Sexuality in America* (New York: Harper and Row, 1988), 277.

26. Frank Mallon, *Sauce for the Gander* (White Plains, N.Y.: Baldwin, 1954).

27. Oswald Garisson Villard, "Sex, Art, Truth, and Magazines," 395.

28. Ibid., 32.

29. Ibid., 34.

30. Frank Mott, *A History of American Magazines.* 5 vols. (Cambridge, Mass.: Harvard University Press, 1938–1968).

31. Mark Gabor, *An Illustrated History of Girlie Magazines* (New York: Harmony, 1984), 3.

32. Ibid.

33. Ibid.

34. Villard, "Sex, Art, Truth, and Magazines," 388.

35. Joseph Hershey, *Pulpwood Editor* (New York: Stokes, 1937), 232.

36. Will Irwin, *Propaganda and the News; or, What Makes You Think So* (New York and London: Whittlesey House, McGraw Hill, 1936), 93.

37. Gabor, *Illustrated History*, 367.

38. Villard, "Sex, Art, Truth, and Magazines," 392.

39. Ibid., 397.

40. Ibid., 392.

41. Ibid., 388.

42. Ibid.

43. Ibid.

44. Ibid.

45. Ibid. William Leuchtenberg also commented on Frank Kent's trip in *The Perils of Prosperity* (Chicago: University of Chicago Press, 1958), 168. Joseph Hershey confirmed this view in *Pulpwood Editor* (240).

46. Winfield Scott Hall, *Sexual Knowledge* (Philadelphia: Winston, 1918), 106.

47. Ibid.

48. E. B. Lowry, *Himself* (Chicago: Forbes, 1916), 65.

49. Frederic Gerrish, *Sex Hygiene: A Talk to College Boys* (Boston: Gorham, 1917), 30.

50. W. J. Robinson, *Sex Morality* (New York: Critic and Guide, 1919), 65.

51. W. F. Robie, *Sex and Life* (New York: Rational Life Publishing, 1924), 23.

52. Ibid.

53. Dell, *Love in the Machine Age*, 23.

54. Joseph Collins, *The Doctor Looks at Love and Life* (New York: Doran, 1926), passim.

55. Michel Foucault, *The History of Sexuality*. Vol. 1, *Introduction* (New York: Pantheon, 1978), 4.

56. Paul Robinson, *The Modernization of Sex: Havelock Ellis, Alfred Kinsey, William Masters, and Virginia Johnson* (New York: Harper and Row, 1978).

57. Foucault, *The History of Sexuality*, 42; quoted in D'Emilio and Freedman, *Intimate Matters* (see note 25 above), 26.

58. George Chauncey, Jr., "Christian Brotherhood or Sexual Perversion?" *Journal of Social History* 9 (Winter 1985): 189–211.

59. Gilman Ostrander, *American Civilization in the First Machine Age* (New York: Harper and Row, 1970); Alfred Kinsey, *Sexual Behavior in the Human Male* (Philadelphia: Saunders, 1948).

60. Floyd Dell, *Homecoming* (New York: Farrar and Rinehart, 1933), 295.

61. Floyd Dell, *The Briary-Bush* (New York: Knopf, 1920), 31.

62. Ibid.

63. Percy Marks, *The Plastic Age* (see note 10 above), 59.

64. Gore Vidal, *Pink Triangle and Yellow Star* (London: Granada, 1983), 71.

65. F. Scott Fitzgerald, *Tender Is the Night* (New York: Scribner's, 1934), 34. See Angus Collins, "F. Scott Fitzgerald: Homosexuality and the Genesis of *Tender Is the Night*," *Journal of Modern Literature* 13 (1986): 167–71.

66. Fitzgerald, *Tender Is the Night*, 149.

67. Ibid., 245.

68. Sinclair Lewis, *Dodsworth* (New York: Harcourt, Brace, Jovanovich, 1929), 223.

69. Robert MacAlmon, "Distinguished Air," in *Grim Fairy Tales* (Paris: Mountain Press, 1925). Only just over a hundred copies of this were made at the time but it was widely reviewed all the same. A copy is preserved in the Kinsey Institute for Research into Gender and Sexuality, Indiana University, Bloomington, Indiana. I found another at the University of Sussex in Brighton, England.

70. Ibid.

71. Ludwig Lewisohn, *Stephen Escott* (New York: Harper's, 1930).

72. Andre Tridon, *Psychoanalysis and Behavior* (New York: Knopf, 1923), 229.

73. Samuel Schmalhausen, "The War of the Sexes," in V. F. Calverton, *Women's Coming of Age: A Symposium* (New York: Liveright, 1931), 28.

74. James Oppenheim, *The Common Sense of Sex* (Girard, Kans.: Haldeman-Julius, 1924).

75. Clement Wood, *Manhood: The Facts of Life Presented to Men* (Girard, Kans.: Haldeman-Julius, 1924).

76. Collins, *The Doctor Looks at Love and Life* (see note 54 above).

77. Ibid., 73.

78. Ibid., 74.

79. Ibid., 65.

80. Ostrander, *American Civilization in the First Machine Age* (see note 59 above), 136.

81. McAlmon, "Distinguished Air," 36.

82. Oppenheim, *The Common Sense of Sex*, 53.

83. Robinson, *Sex Morality* (see note 50 above), 7.

84. Jonathan Katz, *Gay/Lesbian Almanac* (New York: Harper, 1983), 418.

85. Judge Ben B. Lindsey and Wainwright Evans, *The Revolt of Modern Youth* (Garden City, N.Y.: Garden City Publishing, 1925), 13.

86. Marks, *The Plastic Age* (see note 10 above), 165.

87. Warner Fabian, *Flaming Youth* (New York: Macauley, 1923), 205.

88. Schmalhausen, *Why We Misbehave* (see note 18 above), 139.

89. Burnham, "From Narcissism to Social Control" (see note 17 above), 87.

90. W. J. Fielding, *Man's Sexual Life* (Girard, Kans.: Haldeman-Julius, 1925), 5.

91. Robinson, *Sex Morality*, 26.

92. Oppenheim, *Common Sense of Sex*, 19.

93. Wood, *The Facts of Life Presented to Men*, 44.

94. Oppenheim, *Common Sense of Sex*.

95. Ibid.

96. Robinson, *Sex Morality*, 27.

97. Margaret Sanger, *Happiness in Marriage* (New York: Blue Ribbon, 1926), 47; this manual figures prominently in Peter Gardella's extraordinary *Innocent Ecstasy: How Christianity Gave America an Ethic of Sexual Pleasure* (New York: Oxford University Press, 1986).

98. Sanger, *Happiness in Marriage*.

99. Christina Simmons, "Marriage in the Modern Manner: Sexual Radicalism and Reform in America, 1914–41," Ph.D. diss., Brown University, 1982.

100. Thomas Galloway, *Sex and Social Health* (New York: American Social Hygiene Association, 1924), 155.

101. Ibid.

102. Irving Steinhardt, *Ten Talks to Boys* (Philadelphia and London: Lippincott, 1914), 77.

103. Max J. Exner, *Problems and Principles of Sex Education: A Study of 948 College Men* (New York: Association Press), 21; quoted in Simmons, "Marriage in the Modern Manner," 22.

104. Winfield Scott Hall, *Sexual Knowledge* (see note 46 above), 104.

105. Galloway, *Sex and Social Health*, 233.

106. Burnham, "Progressive Era Revolution" (see note 2 above), 895.

107. Allan Brandt, *No Magic Bullet: A Social History of Venereal Diseases* (Cambridge, Mass.: Harvard University Press, 1985), 52–122.

108. Ibid.

109. Ibid.

110. G. Stanley Hall, "Education and the Army," *Journal of Social Hygiene* 5 (June 1919): 44.

111. Karl B. Lashley and John B. Watson, "A Psychological Study of Motion Pictures in Relation to Venereal Disease Camps," *Journal of Social Hygiene* 7 (April 1921): 189.

112. Ibid.

113. Ibid.

114. Ibid.

115. David Pivar, "Cleansing the Nation," *Prologue* 12 (Spring 1980): 32.

116. Pivar, "Cleansing the Nation," 35.

117. ASHA, "Lecture to Troops," 23–24; quoted in Brandt, *No Magic Bullet*, 64.

118. ASHA, "Don't Take a Chance"; quoted in Brandt, *No Magic Bullet*, 63.

119. ASHA, *Fit to Fight* (Washington, 1918), 6–7; quoted in Brandt, *No Magic Bullet*, 63.

120. Simmons, "Marriage in the Modern Manner" (see note 99 above), 105–49.

121. Schmalhausen, *Why We Misbehave* (see note 18 above), 156.

122. Fielding, *Man's Sexual Life* (see note 90 above), 2.

123. For example, Ira Wile, *Marriage in the Modern Manner* (New York: Century, 1929), 57.

124. Sanger, *Happiness in Marriage* (see note 97 above), 27.

125. Paul Popenoe, *Modern Marriage: A Handbook* (New York: Macmillan, 1925), 157.

126. Charles Malchow, *The Sexual Life* (St. Louis, Mo.: C. V. Mosby, 1921), 132.

127. Van de Velde's *Ideal Marriage: Its Physiology and Technique* (New York: Random House, 1934) provides the revolutionary shift to vivid descriptions of technique; this was popular in the United States from the early 1930s.

128. This clearly reflects Ellis's influence. Ellis himself took the term from Ovid's "Ars Amatoria," but probably did not realize Ovid's work was satirical. (See Havelock Ellis, *Studies in the Psychology of Sex*, vol. 2 [New York: Random House, 1936], 514).

129. Wood, *Facts of Life* (see note 75 above).

130. Malchow, *The Sexual Life*, 47.

131. Sanger, *Happiness in Marriage*, 144.

132. Robert Binkley and Frances W. Binkley, *What Is Right with Marriage? An Outline of Domestic Theory* (New York and London: Appleton, 1929), 125. This manual is the best example in this period of what Dennis Brissuet and Lionel S. Lewis have called "sex as work" (*Social Problems* 15 [Summer 1967]: 8–18). The roots of this onerous trend were clearly set in the 1920s.

133. Sanger, *Happiness in Marriage*, 122.

134. Schmalhausen, *Why We Misbehave* (see note 18 above), 17.

135. Ibid., 146.

136. H. W. Long, *Sane Sex Life and Sane Sex Living* (New York: Eugenics, 1919), 118.

137. Sanger, *Happiness in Marriage*, 145.

138. Long, *Sane Sex Life and Sane Sex Living*, 118.

139. Long, *Sane Sex Life and Sane Sex Living*, 70.

140. Sanger, *Happiness in Marriage*, 122, 125.

141. Wile, *Marriage in the Modern Manner*, 56.

142. Long, *Sane Sex Life and Sane Sex Living*, 70.

143. Sanger, *Happiness in Marriage*, 126.

144. Popenoe, *Modern Marriage* (see note 125 above), 157.

145. Wood, *Facts of Life*, 3.

146. Sherwood Eddy, *Sex and Youth* (New York: Doubleday, Doran, 1928), 55.

147. Popenoe, *Modern Marriage*, 159.

148. Michael Gordon, "From an Unfortunate Necessity to a Cult of Mutual Orgasm," in James Henslin, ed., *The Sociology of Sex* (New York: Schocken, 1978), 59–83.

149. Long, *Sane Sex Life and Sane Sex Living*, 63.

150. Binkleys, *What Is Right with Marriage*, 242.

151. Wile, *Marriage in the Modern Manner* (see note 123 above), 54.

152. Sanger, *Happiness in Marriage* (see note 97 above), 183.

153. These words are used especially in the Haldeman-Julius manuals, e.g., Clement Wood, *Facts of Life* (see note 75 above), 9; Fielding, *Man's Sex Life* (see note 90 above), 2.

154. Sanger, *Happiness in Marriage*, 183.

155. Wile, *Marriage in the Modern Manner*, 178.

156. Sanger, *Happiness in Marriage*, 77.

157. Eddy, *Sex and Youth*, 129.

158. Heinrich Wolf, *The Male Approach* (New York: Covici Friede, 1929), 188.

159. Theodore Newcomb, "Recent Changes in Attitudes toward Sex and Marriage," *American Sociological Review* 2 (1937): 659–66.

160. Thurber and White, *Is Sex Necessary?* (see note 1 above), 53.

F I V E : *The Working-Class World of Leisure*

1. Lewis Erenberg, *Steppin' Out: New York Night-Life and the Transformation of American Culture, 1890–1930* (Westport, Conn.: Greenwood, 1980).

2. Kathy Peiss, *Cheap Amusements: Working Women and Leisure in Turn-of-the-Century New York* (Philadelphia: Temple University Press, 1986), 110–13; Joanne Meyerowitz, *Women Adrift: Independent Wage Earners in Chicago, 1880–1930* (Chicago: University of Chicago Press, 1988). There are some valuable references to the same phenomenon in Worcester, Mass., and Pittsburgh in Robert Rosensweig, *Eight Hours for What We Will: Workers and Leisure in an Industrial City* (New York: Cambridge University Press, 1983) and Francis Couvares, *The Remaking of Pittsburgh: Class and Culture in an Industrializing City, 1877–1919* (Albany: SUNY Press, 1984). See also Elizabeth Ewen, "City Lights: Immigrant Women and the Rise of the Movies," *Signs* 5 (Spring 1980): 45–65; and for a useful British comparison from the same time period see Ellen Ross, "Fierce Questions and Taunts: Working-Class Life in London, 1870–1914," *Feminist Studies* 8 (Fall 1982): 575–602.

3. Daniel Scott-Smith, "The Dating of the American Sexual Revolution: Evidence and Interpretations," in Michael Gordon, ed., *The American Family in Socio-Historical Perspective* (New York: St. Martin's, 1973), 321–35.

4. Working-class women, for example, were doing less sweated labor and were moving into the clerical professions and into retail while between 1880 and 1920 "the general trend was toward shorter working days for female wage-earners in factories and stores" (Peiss, *Cheap Amusements*, 38–39).

5. Christine Stansell, *City of Women: Sex and Class in New York: 1789–1860* (New York: Knopf, 1986), 83. Stansell argues unconvincingly for a class solidarity and hence relative equality—an at least "paternal" rather than "patriarchal" attitude on the part of men. I am not convinced by this, but have not found much evidence of cross-gender class solidarity in the heterosocial world of leisure in my period. On prostitution see John C. Burnham, "Medical Inspection of Prostitution in America in the Nineteenth Century: The St. Louis Experiment and Its Sequel," *Bulletin of the History of Medicine* 45 (May–June 1971): 203–18; David Pivar, *Purity Crusade* (Westport, Conn.: Greenwood, 1973); Ruth Rosen, *The Lost Sisterhood* (Baltimore: Johns Hopkins University Press, 1982); Robert E. Reigel, "Changing Attitudes toward Prostitution, 1800–1920," *Journal of the History of Ideas* 29 (1968): 457–62.

6. Christine Stansell, *City of Women*, 86, 89; Timothy Gilfoyle, "City of Eros: New York City, Prostitution, and the Commercialization of Sex, 1790–1920" (Ph.D diss., Columbia, 1987), notes how the new leisure world grew up in close proximity to prostitution (426–27).

7. George Kneeland, *Commercialized Prostitution in New York City* (New York, 1917), xi. Rev. ed., Montclair, N.J.: Patterson Smith, 1969.

8. Walter Reckless, *Vice in Chicago* (Chicago: University of Chicago Press, 1933), 137.

9. Lewis Erenberg, *Steppin' Out*, passim. See also John Kasson, *Amusing the Million: Coney Island at the Turn of the Century* (New York: Hill and Wang, 1978).

10. On the impact of the movies on the working class see John Cumbler, *Working-Class Community in Industrial America: Work, Leisure, and Struggle in Two Industrial Cities, 1880–1930* (Westport, Conn.: Greenwood, 1979). See also Lary May, *Screening Out the Past: The Birth of Mass Culture and the Motion Picture Industry* (New York: Oxford University Press, 1980). Although I have used the term "working class," I am hardly talking about a group with a fully fledged class consciousness: ethnicity was probably more important to these men and women. I am not talking about families or older, more settled groups, but about the young in a particular area: participants in the heterosocial dance culture in the cities. A more accurate term in Marxist terminology might be "lumpenproletariat." But, nevertheless, it is this group that has had most influence on mainstream American culture in the twentieth century—unfortunately. And, despite these caveats, there are important generalizations here about the American working class.

11. On immigration and "Americanization" see Peiss, *Cheap Amusements*, 31.

12. John D'Emilio and Estelle Freedman, *Intimate Matters: A History of Sexuality in America* (New York: Harper and Row, 1988), 195.

13. Harvey Zorbaugh, "The Dweller in Furnished Rooms: An Urban Type," in Ernest W. Burgess, ed., *The Urban Community: Selected Papers from the Proceedings*

of the American Sociological Society (Chicago: University of Chicago Press, 1926), 3.

14. Reckless, *Vice in Chicago*, 123.

15. Zorbaugh, "The Dweller in Furnished Rooms," 117.

16. John Modell, *Into One's Own: From Youth to Adulthood in the United States, 1920–1975* (Los Angeles and Berkeley: University of California Press, 1989), 72.

17. On dance palaces see Russel B. Nye, "Saturday Night at the Dance Palais," *Journal of Popular Culture* 5 (1973): 1–15.

18. Peiss, *Cheap Amusements*, 8, suggests she is not arguing for "trickle-up." Her evidence suggests otherwise.

19. New York and Chicago were well-documented centers of ferment in the sexual revolution, and a rich and largely untapped record of life in these cities has survived. My discussion of Chicago draws on the 1920s studies of the Chicago sociologists, largely completed by the students of the distinguished pioneer of qualitative sociology, Ernest Burgess. Paul Cressey, for example, who published the classic *Taxi-Dance Hall*—an examination of Chicago's seamier dance-hall world—left a rich record of related investigations that were not quoted in the book. I have also used earlier Vice Commission reports from the first decade of the century, as well as the stories of George Ade, who documented working-class life in Chicago around 1900. For New York, I have used the 1910s reports of the Committee of Fourteen, a group of vice investigators set up in order to free the city from vice. In addition, I have used the Rockefeller Foundation's Bureau of Social Hygiene reports from the 1920s.

There are, of course, certain dangers in using these kinds of sources, especially those of organizations designed to investigate vice with the intent of stamping it out. Whatever one thinks of their moralistic purposes—and the importance of disease should not be underestimated in a society where 10 percent of Americans, mainly working class, were infected with some sort of venereal disease—they had a tendency to read more into situations than actually existed as well as to exaggerate incidents. After all, the investigators' credibility with the organizations for which they worked depended on the uncovering of vice. Yet these investigators have provided us with fascinating material precisely because they themselves endeavored to participate in the underworld. They have not, however, provided us with many life histories and follow-up studies. This is a pity because we are left with an incomplete picture of each case. There can be no certainty as to the context of individual situations, a limitation that cannot be avoided. What can be attained, though, is a general picture of the dilemmas and power relations that existed in this social world, perhaps because what has survived is what was most shocking to the investigators. In addition, the validity of the vice investigators' work is underlined by the similar conclusions of the Chicago sociologists, who lacked the ideological zeal or shockability of the vice reporters. While we cannot, of course, be sure that in doing so they were free of biases, they were more likely to get closer to an objective analysis of what was really going on in the dance halls. Further, while this study is strictly qualitative, the Alfred Kinsey sex survey contains material on the working class that does provide a useful quantitative backdrop, especially as his findings in fact complement those of eyewitness investigators.

20. Alfred Kinsey, et al., *Sexual Behavior in the Human Male* (Philadelphia: Saunders, 1948), 396. Theodore Newcomb noted that "working-class boys are more apt to move suddenly from relative indifference to girls to overt sex relations, with little or no intermediate stages of petting" (in "Recent Changes in Attitudes towards Sex and Marriage," *American Sociological Review* 2 [1937]: 663).

21. Kinsey, *Human Male*, 364.

22. Ibid.

23. Jane Addams, *The Spirit of Youth and the City Streets* (Chicago: University of Chicago Press, 1911), 69.

24. Richard Henry Edwards, *Popular Amusements* (New York, 1915), 142.

25. Eleanor Rowland Wembridge, "Social Backgrounds in Sex Education," *Journal of Social Hygiene* 9 (February 1923): 71.

26. D'Emilio and Freedman, *Intimate Matters*, 195.

27. Paul Cressey Notes, "Gang," Section 9, Box 129, Folder 5, Ernest Burgess papers, Special Collections, Joseph Regenstein Library, University of Chicago, Chicago. (hereinafter referred to as the Burgess Papers).

28. Ibid., Section 8.

29. Ibid., Section 10.

30. No author, "Saturday Night at the Movies," Reel 6, Folder 229, p. 10 (University Microfilms, 1979), originals in Bureau of Social Hygiene Archives, Rockefeller Archive Center, North Tarrytown, N.Y. (hereinafter referred to as BSH).

31. Frederic Thrasher, *The Gang* (Chicago: University of Chicago Press, 1923), 234; On gangs in New York in the late nineteenth century see Benedict Giamo, *On the Bowery: Confronting Homelessness in American Society* (Iowa City: University of Iowa Press, 1989).

32. Paul Cressey Notes, "Gang," Section 13, Box 129, Folder 5, Burgess Papers.

33. Saul Alinsky and Constance Weinberger, "Vernon Athletic Club," in "The Public Dance Hall," term paper in Social Pathology, Fall 1928, under Professor Burgess, Section 3, Box 126, Folder 10, Burgess Papers.

34. Investigator's Report, Strand Roof Cafeteria, New York, May 16, 1915, Box 28, Records of the Committee of Fourteen, Rare Books and Manuscripts Division, The New York Public Library, Astor, Lenox, and Tilden Foundations (hereinafter referred to as COF).

35. Alinsky and Weinberger, "The Public Dance Hall," Section 3, Burgess Papers.

36. NYU Boy's Club study, under the direction of Paul Cressey and Frederic Thrasher, p. 11, Folder 229, Reel 6, BSH.

37. Louise de Koven Bowen, "A Study of Public Dance Halls," *Survey*, June 3, 1911, 385.

38. Paul Cressey Notes, "Sex Attitudes and History," August 7, 1919, Box 186, Folder 6, Burgess Papers.

39. Hutchins Hapgood, *Types from City Streets* (New York: Funk and Wagnall's, 1911), 28.

40. Investigator's Report, Clare Hotel, 2150 8th. Avenue, Tuesday, March 5, 1918, p. 2, Box 28, COF.

41. Investigator's Report, July 29, 1912, Box 28, COF; Investigator's Report, July 8, 1913, Box 28, COF.

42. No author, no title, Box 129, Folder 6, Burgess Papers.

43. Paul Cressey Notes, New American, n.p., April 3, 1926, Box 129, Folder 6, Burgess Papers.

44. Investigator's Report, 1935, "Joe Pete," p. 276, Reel 7, Box 12, Folder 234, BSH.

45. Ibid., p. 275.

46. NYU Boy's Club Study, "Sex Practices and Stimuli," 1929, p. 14, Reel 6, Folder 229, BSH. Originals in the Rockefeller Center Archive.

47. Thrasher, *The Gang*, 29.

48. NYU Boy's Club Study, By Italian Boy of Eighteen, "The Neighborhood Credo: the Boys Conflicts and Wishes," Reel 6, Folder 229, BSH.

49. Investigator's Report, 364 E. 149th. Street, January 30, 1914, Box 28, COF; for similar patterns of male violence in the nineteenth century see Pamela Haag, "The 'Ill-Use of a Wife': Patterns of Working-Class Violence in Domestic and Public New York City, 1860–1880," *Journal of Social History* 25 (Spring 1992): 447–77.

50. Paul Cressey Notes, "Primary and Secondary Group Contacts at Gaelic Park," p. 34, Box 129, Folder 7, Burgess Papers.

51. Ibid.

52. Investigator's Report, Terrace Garden, September 25, 1919, Box 28, COF.

53. Paul Cressey, *The Taxi-Dance Hall: A Sociological Study in Commercialized Recreation and City Life* (Chicago: University of Chicago Press, 1932), 69.

54. Investigator Report, Terrace Garden, September 16, 1911, Box 28, COF.

55. NYU Boy's Club Study, "Sex Practices and Stimuli," p. 13, Reel 7, Folder 234, BSH.

56. Louise de Koven Bowen, "A Study of Public Dance Halls," 386.

57. Investigator's Report, Lafayette Casino, June 12, 1912, Box 28, COF.

58. William Foote Whyte, "A Slum Sex Code," *American Journal* of Sociology 49 (July 1943): 25.

59. Syracuse Morals Commission, *The Social Evil in Syracuse* (Syracuse, N.Y., 1911), 44.

60. Thrasher, *The Gang* (see note 31 above), 238.

61. Investigator's Report, Lafayette Casino, June 12, 1912, Box 28, COF.

62. Investigator's Report, August 4, 1913, Box 28, COF.

63. Ibid.

64. Investigator's Report, July 8, 1913, Box 28, COF.

65. Ibid.

66. Paul Cressey Notes, "Sex Attitudes and History," Young Man, New Orleans, 19 years old, p. 1, Box 186, Folder 6, Burgess Papers.

67. Investigator's Report, July 29, 1912, Box 28, COF.

68. Investigator's Report, 1910–1912, Box 28, COF.

69. Alinsky and Weinberger, "The Public Dance Hall" (see note 33 above), 4.

70. Cressey, *Taxi-Dance Hall*, 123–24.

71. Ibid., 124.

72. Investigator's Report, 1910–1912, Box 28, COF.

73. Paul Cressey Notes, Sam C——g, 59 years old, n.p., Box 129, Folder 6, Burgess Papers.

74. George Chauncey, Jr., "Christian Brotherhood or Sexual Perversion: Homosexual Identities and the Construction of Sexual Boundaries in the World War One Era," *Journal of Social History* 19 (Winter 1985): 189–211.

75. John C. Burnham, "Early References to Homosexual Communities in American Medical Writings," *Medical Aspects of Human Sexuality* 7 (1973): 40–49.

76. Research Report, no author (Earl Bruce?) n.p., Homosexual Materials, Box 98, Folder 11, Burgess Papers.

77. NYU Boy's Club Study, By Italian Boy of Eighteen (see note 48 above).

78. Edwin A. Teeter, Research Report, p. 4, Box 186, Folder 6, Burgess Papers.

79. Ibid.

80. Ibid.

81. Research Report, n.p., Homosexual Materials, Box 98, Folder 3, Burgess Papers.

82. Research Report, "Jack, aged 26," p. 8, Homosexual Materials, Box 98, Folder 3, Burgess Papers.

83. Investigator's Report, 18th. and 125th. Streets, April–May 1913, Box 28, COF.

84. Kinsey, *Human Male* (see note 20 above), 383; Timothy Gilfoyle in "City of Eros" (see note 6 above), notes this same tolerance (252).

85. Research Report, "Case History, Walt Lewis," p. 1, Homosexual Materials, Box 98, Folder 3, Burgess Papers.

86. Ibid., 5.

87. Armin Minske, "My Experiences with a Homosexual Person," Social Pathology Class, Box 126, Folder 19, Burgess Papers.

88. Research Report, p. 1, Homosexual Materials, Box 98, Folder 3, Burgess Papers.

89. Ibid., 4; and no author, "Motion Picture Theater Study," ca. 1930, p. 237, Folder 234, Box 12, BSH.

90. Ibid.

91. Nels Anderson, "The Hobo: The Sociology of the Homeless Man" (M.A. thesis, University of Chicago, 1935; repr. University of Chicago Press, 1975), 147. Anderson reported this same phenomenon was noted by the 1911 Vice Commission of Chicago.

92. Research Report, September 1929, n.p., Homosexual Materials, Box 98, Folder 3, Burgess Papers.

93. Ibid.

94. Ibid.

95. Ibid.

96. Research Report, September 1927, n.p., Homosexual Materials, Box 98, Folder 5, Burgess Papers.

97. No author, "Motion Picture Theater Study," ca. 1930, p. 236, Folder 234, Box 12, BSH.

98. Ibid., September 1927.

99. Kinsey, *Human Male*, 383.

100. Research Report, "Chicago Coast Guard Station," n.p., Box 186, Folder 6, Burgess Papers.

101. Thrasher, *The Gang* (see note 31 above), 239.

102. Ibid., 223.

103. Alinsky and Weinberger, "The Public Dance-Hall" (see note 33 above), 4.

104. Research Report, p. 21, Homosexual Notebooks, Box 144, Folder 8, Burgess Papers.

105. Whyte, "A Slum Sex Code" (see note 58 above), 25–44. Whyte's study is of Boston but, at least in Buffalo, Italian-Americans had "extraordinarily low illegitimacy rates" (D'Emilio and Freedman, *Intimate Matters* [see note 12 above], 185), which indicates the "extraordinary" strength of the double standard in this group. The men waited to marry their "good" Italian women, but had fun with women of other races and ethnicities in the meantime.

106. Whyte, "A Slum Sex Code" (see note 58 above), 26.

107. Ibid.

108. Kinsey, *Human Male* (see note 20 above), 364.

109. Research Report, p. 21, Homosexual Notebooks, 1933, Box 144, Folder 8, Burgess Papers.

110. Addams, *The Spirit of Youth and the City Streets* (see note 23 above), 11.

111. Paul Cressey Notes, "Sex Attitudes and History," Box 186, Folder 6, Burgess Papers.

112. NYU Boy's Club Study, By a Boy of Eighteen, "Neighbourhood Credo: the Boys Wishes and Conflicts," p. 114, Reel 6, Folder 229, BSH.

113. Daniel Russell, "The Roadhouse: A Study of Commercialized Amusements in the Environs of Chicago" (Ph.D diss., University of Chicago, 1931), 116.

114. Paul Cressey Notes, n.p., Box 129, Folder 6, Burgess Papers.

115. Russell, "The Roadhouse," 115.

116. Russell, "The Roadhouse," 116.

117. Paul Cressey Notes, "Case of William Kr——r," p. 1, Box 129, Folder 6, Burgess Papers.

118. Ibid., 2.

119. Ibid., 4.

120. Alinsky and Weinberger, "The Public Dance Hall," Section 2, Box 126, Folder 10, Burgess Papers.

121. Ibid.

122. NYU Boy's Club Study, "Saturday Night at the Movies," 1930, p. 3, Folder 229, Reel 7, BSH.

123. Hutchins Hapgood, *Types from City Streets* (see note 39 above), 28.

124. The reference to "it" in the 1920s suggested "sex appeal" as in the use of the expression "it" girl. See Mary Ryan, "The Projection of a New Womanhood: The Movie Moderns in the 1920s," in Friedman and Shade, *Our American Sisters* (Boston: Heath, 1982), 500–518.

125. NYU Boy's Club study, "Saturday Night at the Movies," p. 11, Folder 229, Box 6, Reel 6, BSH.

126. Russell, "The Roadhouse," 115.

127. George Ade, *Artie* (Chicago: University of Chicago Press, 1963; originally published 1896), 20.

128. George Ade, *Artie*, 20, 29.

129. Investigator's Report, Strand Cafeteria, Box 28, COF.

130. Ibid.

131. Cumbler, *Working-Class Community* (see note 10 above), 97.

132. Paul Cressey Notes, Madison Dancing School, Box 129, Folder 6, Burgess Papers.

133. Paul Cressey, "Thirty years old," n.p., Box 129, Folder 6, Burgess Papers.

134. Ibid.

135. No author, no title, p. 224, Folder 229, Reel 6, BSH.

136. Hapgood, *Types from City Streets*, 36.

137. Paul Cressey Notes, "Case of William K——r," Box 129, Folder 6, Burgess Papers.

138. Research Report, Case Study of X, p. 3, Box 186, Folder 6, Burgess Papers.

139. NYU Boy's Club Study, "Description by Superior Boy of Dance Hall," 1930, p. 7, Folder 229, Reel 6, BSH.

140. Research Report, Alana N——n Z——r, p. 4, Box 129, Folder 6, Burgess Papers.

141. Whyte, "The Slum Sex Code" (see note 58 above), 25.

142. Cressey, *The Taxi-Dance Hall* (see note 53 above), 121–23.

143. Investigator's Report, Clare Hotel, 2150 8th. Avenue, Tuesday, March 5, 1918, p. 2, Box 28, COF.

144. Cressey, *Taxi-Dance Hall*, 121–23.

145. Paul Cressey Notes, Old Man Newell at Plaza Dancing School, n.p., Box 129, Folder 6, Burgess Papers.

146. Cressey, *Taxi-Dance Hall*, 126.

147. Ibid., 147.

148. Ibid., 149.

149. Paul Cressey Notes, Box 129, Folder 8, Burgess Papers.

150. Paul Cressey Notes, "Autobiography of a Filipino," n.p., Box 129, Folder 8, Burgess Papers.

151. Researcher's Report, New American, Ed G——s, alias Dale, Box 129, Folder 6, Burgess Papers.

152. Ibid.

153. Ibid.

S I X : *The Failure of the Feminist Option*

1. Estelle Freedman, "The New Woman: Changing Views of Women in the 1920s," *Journal of American History* 61 (March 1974): 389.

2. Elaine Showalter, *These Modern Women: Autobiographical Essays from the Twenties* (Old Westbury, N.Y.: Feminist Press, 1978), 5.

3. Havelock Ellis, *Studies in the Psychology of Sex* (New York: Random House, 1936): Edward Carpenter, *Love's Coming of Age* (London: Sonnenschein, 1906); Ellen Key, *Love and Marriage* (New York: Source Book Press, 1970).

4. Kay Trimberger, "Feminism, Men, and Modern Love: Greenwich Village, 1900–1930," in Ann Snitow, Christine Stansell, and Sharon Thompson, eds., *Powers of Desire: The Politics of Sexuality* (New York: Monthly Review Press, 1983), 131–

52; Leslie Fishbein, *Rebels in Bohemia: The Radicals of the Masses, 1912–17* (Chapel Hill: University of North Carolina Press, 1982).

5. I first looked for marriages on the basis of availability of sources as well as the participants' self-conscious attempt to practice equalitarianism in gender relations. I found that material in nine appropriate marriages had survived.

6. See Leila J. Rupp, "Feminism and the Sexual Revolution of the Early Twentieth Century: The Case of Doris Stevens," *Feminist Studies* 15 (Summer 1989): 289–309; Kevin White, "Men Supporting Women: Male Women's Suffragists in Britain and America, 1909–1920," *Maryland Historian* 17 (Spring/Summer 1987): 47–59.

7. Richard O'Connor, *Heywood Broun: A Biography* (New York: Putnam's, 1975), 48.

8. Marcet Haldeman-Julius to Geliebe Grosmuter, March 21, 1916; quoted in A. N. Cothran, "The Little Blue Book Man and the Big American Parade" (Ph.D. diss., University of Maryland, 1966), 56.

9. Jane Grant, *Ross, the New Yorker, and Me* (New York: Reynal, 1968), 124.

10. Dudley Field Malone (DFM) to Doris Stevens (DS), August 2, 1918, Carton 2, File 27, (76-246) Doris Stevens Papers, Arthur and Elizabeth Schlesinger Library of the History of Women in America, Radcliffe College, Cambridge, Mass. (hereinafter referred to as SL).

11. Jane Grant, "Confessions of a Feminist," *American Mercury* (December 1943): 687.

12. O'Connor, *Heywood Broun*, 75.

13. Heywood Broun, "Ruth Hale," in *The Collected Heywood Broun* (New York: Harcourt, Brace, 1941), 323–25.

14. Heywood Broun, "Holding a Baby," in *The Collected Heywood Broun*, 80.

15. Ibid.

16. Heywood Broun, "The Boy Grew Older" in *The Collected Heywood Broun*, 129.

17. Ibid.

18. Dale Kramer, *Heywood Broun: A Biographical Portrait* (New York: Current Books, 1949), 143.

19. Mildred Evans Gilman, "The Reminiscences of Mildred Gilman," transcripts of Interviews conducted by P. Madow for the Oral History Office of Columbia University, part 2, p. 4.

20. Haldeman-Julius's writings are littered with this term.

21. Heywood Hale Broun, *Whose Little Boy Are You?: A Memoir of the Broun Family* (New York: St. Martin's Press, 1983), 45.

22. Harold Ross to Jane Grant, ca. 1928, Box 1, Folder 4, Jane Grant Collection, Special Collections, Knight Library, University of Oregon, Eugene, Oregon.

23. Jane Grant, *Ross, the New Yorker, and Me* (see note 9 above), 252, 261.

24. DS to DFM, December 1925, Carton 2, Box 39, Doris Stevens papers, SL.

25. DS to DFM, Valentine's Day, 1917, Carton 2, File 37, Doris Stevens papers, SL.

26. Ibid.

27. Ibid.

28. Doris Stevens, "Mental Cruelty," Mss. p. 4, n.d. (1927?) Carton 2, File 43, Doris Stevens papers, SL.

29. DS to DFM 4:00 Tuesday, June 21, 1927, Carton 2, File 40, Doris Stevens papers, SL.

30. Stevens, "Mental Cruelty," Mss. p. 4 n.d. (1927?), Carton 2, File 43, Doris Stevens papers, SL.

31. Mildred Gilman, Press clipping, n.d., Carton 2, File 45, Doris Stevens papers, SL.

32. For example, the percentage of women lawyers went up from 1.4 to 2.1 percent between 1920 and 1930 and of physicians dropped from 5.0 to 4.4 in those years (see Nancy F. Cott, *The Grounding of Modern Feminism* [New Haven, Conn.: Yale University Press, 1987], 219).

33. Susan Van Ness, *Jane Grant, Co-Founder of the New Yorker*, M.A. thesis, University of Kansas, 1983.

34. James Thurber to Mr. Churchill, September 6, 1947, in Helen Thurber and E. Weeks, eds., *Letters of James Thurber* (Boston: Little, Brown, 1981), 198.

35. James Thurber, *The Years with Ross* (New York: Ballantine, 1960), 180.

36. Cothran, "The Little Blue Book Man," 32, states that Marcet did the actual writing of their "joint" novel *Dust*; quote is from Marcet Haldeman-Julius to Emmanuel Haldeman-Julius, June 30, 1925, Haldeman-Julius family papers, Special Collections, The University Library, University of Illinois at Chicago, Chicago, Illinois.

37. E. Haldeman-Julius, "Thoughts on My Thirty-Sixth Birthday," *Haldeman-Julius Weekly* (1925): 21–32.

38. MHJ to EHJ, June 30, 1925, p. 2, Haldeman-Julius family papers, Special Collections, The University Library, University of Illinois at Chicago, Chicago, Illinois.

39. Broun, "Ruth Hale" (see note 13 above), 325.

40. O'Connor, *Heywood Broun* (see note 7 above), 193.

41. Hale Broun, *Whose Little Boy Are You?* (see note 21 above), 70.

42. Mildred Evans Gilman transcripts (see note 19 above), 4.

43. Broun, "Wife of Lot," in *The Collected Heywood Broun* (see note 13 above), 176.

44. Broun, "Ruth Hale," 324.

45. Westbrook Pegler, "Fair Enough," n.d., Syndicated Column, Press clipping, Carton 2, File 45, Doris Stevens papers, SL.

46. Mildred Gilman transcripts, 42.

47. Ibid., 29.

48. Ibid., 61.

49. Doris Stevens to Mr. Connor, June 23, 1927, Carton 2, File 43, Doris Stevens papers, SL.

50. Nancy Cott, *The Grounding of Modern Feminism* (New Haven, Conn.: Yale University Press, 1987).

51. DFM to DS, March 16, 1920, Carton 2, File 38, Doris Stevens papers, SL.

52. DS to Jonathan Mitchell, Monday, November 12, 1923, Carton 3, File 47, Doris Stevens papers, SL.

53. Jonathan Mitchell, "taped reminiscences of Doris Stevens," Mss. p. 10, (86-M29), Doris Stevens papers, SL.

54. DFM to DS, September 7, 1916, Carton 2, File 37, Doris Stevens papers, SL.

55. DFM to DS, August 28, 1916, Carton 2, File 37, Doris Stevens papers, SL.

56. Doris Stevens, "Mental Cruelty" (see note 30 above), 4.

57. O'Connor, *Heywood Broun* (see note 13 above), 47.

58. Broun, "The Boy Grew Older" (see note 16 above), 23

59. Hale Broun, *Whose Little Boy Are You?*, 162.

60. Dale Kramer, *Heywood Broun* (see note 18 above), 152.

61. Jane Grant, *Ross, the New Yorker, and Me* (see note 9 above), 7.

62. James Thurber, *The Years with Ross* (see note 35 above), 10.

63. Ibid., 178.

64. Brendan Gill, Harold Ross, *Dictionary of American Biography*, Supplement 5 (1951-1955): 513-14. E. B. White even stopped talking to Thurber.

65. James Thurber to Mr. Churchill September 6, 1947, *The Letters of James Thurber* (see note 34 above), 57.

66. Grant, *Ross, the New Yorker, and Me*, 257.

67. Dale Kramer, *Ross and the New Yorker* (London: Gollancz, 1952), 42, 201.

68. Haldeman-Julius, "The Conquest of Prudery," *Western Comrade* (May 1913): 44-45.

69. Ibid.

70. Joe Dubbert, "Progressivism and the Masculinity Crisis," in Pleck and Pleck, *The American Man* (Englewood Cliffs, N.J.: Prentice Hall, 1980), 303-20; James McGovern, "David Graham Phillips and the Virility Impulse of the Progressive Era," *New England Quarterly* (July 1966): 340-65.

71. DFM to DS, September 8, 1916, Carton 2, File 37, Doris Stevens papers, SL.

72. DFM to DS, September 4, 1916, Carton 2, File 37, Doris Stevens papers, SL.

73. DFM to DS, September 2, 1916, Carton 2, File 37, Doris Stevens papers, SL.

74. DS. Diary, June 12, 1927, Carton 7, Doris Stevens papers, SL.

75. Doris Stevens, "Mental Cruelty" (see note 30 above), 3.

76. DS. Diary, May 13, 1924, Carton 7, Doris Stevens papers, SL.

77. Kramer, *Ross and the New Yorker*.

78. Grant, *Ross, the New Yorker, and Me*, 255.

79. James Thurber, *The Years with Ross* (see note 35 above), 97.

80. Grant, *Ross, the New Yorker, and Me*, 43.

81. Thurber, *The Years with Ross*, 133.

82. Brendan Gill, *Here at the New Yorker* (New York: Random House, 1975), 29.

83. Ibid., 30.

84. Ibid.

85. Ibid., 29, 30.

86. DS Primus, n.d., Carton 7, File 210, Doris Stevens papers, SL.

87. Thurber, *The Years with Ross*, 182.

88. Kramer, *Ross and the New Yorker*, 219.

89. Thurber, *The Years with Ross*, 183.

90. Ibid.

91. Marcet Haldeman-Julius, "What the Editor's Wife Is Thinking About," *Haldeman-Julius Weekly* (1925): 19.

92. Sue Haldeman-Julius, "Emmanuel Haldeman-Julius: The Little Blue Book Man," *Little Balkan Review* 16 (Winter 1982): 1–145.

93. Kramer, *Heywood Broun* (see note 18 above), 148.

94. Mildred Gilman transcripts (see note 19 above), 27.

95. "Dudley Field Malone to Wed Dancer," Press clipping, n.d., Carton 2, File 45, Doris Stevens papers, SL.

96. Marcet Haldeman-Julius to Alice Haldeman-Julius, April 1, 1935, p. 2, Emmanuel Haldeman-Julius Collection, Special Collections, Leonard H. Axe Library, Pittsburg State University, Pittsburg, Kansas.

97. Hale Broun, *Whose Little Boy Are You?* (see note 21 above), 173.

98. Ibid.

99. O'Connor, *Heywood Broun* (see note 13 above), 176.

100. Hale Broun, *Whose Little Boy Are You?*, 173.

101. O'Connor, *Heywood Broun*, 176, 205.

102. Judge Ben B. Lindsey and Wainwright Evans, *The Companionate Marriage* (New York: Boni and Liveright, 1927).

103. As reported by Sue Haldeman-Julius, "Emmanuel Haldeman-Julius," 3.

S E V E N : *The Success of the Feminist Option*

1. See especially June Sochen, *The New Woman: Feminism in Greenwich Village* (New York: Schocken, 1970); Ellen Kay Trimberger, "Feminism, Men, and Modern Love: Greenwich Village, 1900–1925," in Ann Snitow, Christine Stansell, and Sharon Thompson, eds., *Powers of Desire: The Politics of Sexuality* (New York: Monthly Review Press, 1983), 131–52.

2. Newspaper clipping, *Sunday Evening Telegram*, n.d. (1916?), Folder 384, Freda Kirchwey papers (MC 280), Arthur and Elizabeth Schlesinger Library of the History of Women in America, Radcliffe College, Cambridge, Mass. (hereinafter referred to as SL).

3. Inez Haynes Irwin, *The Adventure of Will Irwin*, Box 3, Folder 16, Inez Haynes Irwin papers (A-25), SL.

4. George Middleton, "What Feminism Means to Me," Mss. p. 10, Box 67, George Middleton papers, Manuscript Collections, Library of Congress, Washington, D.C. (hereinafter referred to as LC).

5. Ibid.

6. Maynard Shipley to Miriam Allen DeFord Shipley, n.d., p. 6, Manuscript Collections, California Historical Society, San Francisco, California (hereinafter referred to as CHS).

7. Miriam DeFord Shipley, *Uphill All the Way: The Biography of Maynard Shipley* (Yellow Springs, Ohio: Antioch University Press, 1956), 233.

8. Sarah Alpern, *Freda Kirchwey: A Woman of the Nation* (Cambridge, Mass.: Harvard University Press, 1987), 115.

9. Jonathan Mitchell (JM), "For D.C.S. Journal," Mss. p. 12, Carton 3, File 67, (86-M29) Doris Stevens papers, SL.

10. Ibid., 25.

11. JM to DCS, Friday, March 4, 1927, Carton 3, File 57, Doris Stevens papers, SL.

12. JM to DCS, Tuesday, August 28, Carton 3, File 62, Doris Stevens papers, SL.

13. JM to DCS, Carton 3, File 62, September 11, 1928, Doris Stevens papers, SL.

14. JM to DCS, Thursday, March 31, 1927, Carton 3, File 57, Doris Stevens papers, SL.

15. JM to DCS, Saturday, March 5, 1927, p. 3, Carton 3, File 57, Doris Stevens papers, SL.

16. Ibid., 3

17. Ibid., 3.

18. Inez Haynes Irwin, "The Adventure of Will Irwin," Mss. p. 573, Box 4, Folder 16, Inez Haynes Irwin papers, SL.

19. "Will Irwin Interviews His Wife," Biographical Catalog, SL.

20. Ibid.

21. George Middleton, "What Feminism Means to Me," Mss. pp. 1–2, Box 67, George Middleton papers, LC.

22. Ibid., 10

23. Ibid., 17

24. George Middleton, "A Play Extract," Box 67, George Middleton papers, LC.

25. Evans Clark to Freda Kirchwey, Monday before Lunch (1915), Box 23, Folder 388, Freda Kirchwey papers, SL.

26. Ibid.

27. EC to FK, September 9, 1915, Box 23, Folder 388, Freda Kirchwey papers, SL.

28. EC to FK, 1915, Box 23, Folder 388, Freda Kirchwey papers, SL.

29. Alpern, *A Woman of the Nation*, 103.

30. GM to FL, Thursday night, February 1924, Box 39, George Middleton papers, SL.

31. GM to FL, December 16, 1938, Box 37, George Middleton papers, SL.

32. Inez Haynes Irwin, "The Adventure of Will Irwin," Mss. p. 573, Box 3, Folder 16, Inez Haynes Irwin papers, SL.

33. Ibid., 574.

34. Jonathan Mitchell, "taped reminiscences of Doris Stevens," n.d., p. 19, Stevens papers, SL.

35. GM to FL, March 4, 1922, Box 37, George Middleton papers, LC.

36. EC to FK, "1915, Wednesday after Supper," Box 23, Folder 388, Freda Kirchwey papers, SL.

37. FK to EC, Saturday, February 1, 1930, Box 1, Folder 19, Freda Kirchwey papers, SL.

38. Ibid.

39. Alpern, *A Woman of the Nation* (see note 8 above), 66.

40. Freda Kirchwey, Memorandum, August 5, 1943, p. 161, Box 1, Folder 22, Freda Kirchwey papers, SL.

41. FK to EC, February 1, 1930, Box 1, Folder 19, Freda Kirchwey papers, SL.

42. Maynard Shipley to Miriam DeFord Collier, p. 3, n.d., Miriam DeFord Collier Shipley papers, SL.

43. Jonathan Mitchell, "For D.C.S. Journal," Mss. p. 31, Carton 3, Folder 67, Doris Stevens papers, SL.

44. JM to DS, Thursday, March 3, 1927, Carton 3, Folder 67, Doris Stevens papers, SL.

45. GM to FL, June 9, 1924, Box 37, George Middleton papers, LC.

46. Shipley, *Uphill All the Way* (see note 7 above), 80.

47. GM to FL, Paris, 1922, Box 1, George Middleton papers, LC.

48. Shipley, *Uphill All the Way*, 168.

49. Ibid.

50. Maynard Shipley, *Alone*, Dec. 1, Miriam Shipley papers, CHS.

51. Maynard Shipley to MDS, Saturday A.M., n.d., Miriam Shipley papers, CHS.

52. MS to MDS, Monday evening, n.d., Miriam Shipley papers, CHS.

53. Ibid.

54. MS to MDS, Wednesday evening, n.d., Miriam Shipley papers, CHS.

55. Ibid.

56. Ibid.

57. Ibid.

58. Jonathan Mitchell, "taped reminiscences of Doris Stevens," n.d., 7, Doris Stevens papers, SL.

59. Ibid., 11.

60. Ibid., 31.

61. Jonathan Mitchell, "For D.C.S. Journal," Mss. p. 29, Carton 3, File 67, Doris Stevens papers, SL.

62. Ibid., 29.

63. Jonathan Mitchell, "taped reminiscences of Doris Stevens," Mss. p. 31, Doris Stevens papers, SL.

64. Sarah Alpern, "Freda Kirchwey: A Woman of the Nation" (Ph.D. diss., University of Maryland, 1978), 31.

65. FK to EC, Feb. 1, 1930, Box 1, Folder 19, Freda Kirchwey papers, SL.

66. Ibid.

67. Jonathan Mitchell, "For D.C.S. Journal," Mss. p. 18, Carton 3, File 67, Doris Stevens papers, SL.

68. Jonathan Mitchell, "taped reminiscences of Doris Stevens," Mss. p. 24, Doris Stevens papers, SL.

69. JM to DCS, Friday, May 9, 1924, p. 3, Carton 3, File 51, Doris Stevens papers, SL.

70. JM to DCS, July 21, 1923, Carton 3, File 48, Doris Stevens, SL.

71. Ibid.

72. Will Irwin, *The Making of a Reporter* (New York: Doubleday, 1942), 8.

73. Ibid., 198.

74. Ibid.

75. Trimberger, "Feminism, Men, and Modern Love" (see note 1 above), 135.

76. MS to MDS, n.d., p. 13, Miriam Shipley papers, CHS.

77. FK to EC, Saturday, February 8, 1930, Box 1, Folder 19, Freda Kirchwey papers, SL.

78. Jonathan Mitchell, "For D.C.S. Journal," Mss. p. 4, Carton 3, File 67, Doris Stevens papers, SL.

79. Ibid., 8

80. Ibid., 9.

81. Ibid., 20.

82. JM to DCS, Friday, May 9, p. 3, Carton 3, File 51, Doris Stevens papers, SL.

83. "For DCS Journal," p. 19.

84. GM to FL, June 24, 1942, Box 67, George Middleton papers, LC.

85. Irwin, *Making of a Reporter*, 389.

86. Shipley, *Uphill All the Way* (see note 7 above), 153.

87. Ibid., 196.

88. George Middleton, *These Things Are Mine* (New York: Macmillan, 1947), 123.

89. Jonathan Mitchell, "For DCS Journal," p. 10, Carton 3, File 67, Doris Stevens papers, SL.

90. Ibid., 11

91. Ibid., 15.

92. Jonathan Mitchell, "taped reminiscences of Doris Stevens," Mss. p. 11, Doris Stevens papers, SL.

93. New York Wednesday evening, JM to DCS, July 21, 1923, Carton 3, File 48, Doris Stevens papers, SL.

E I G H T : *Modern American Male Heterosexuality*

1. Paula Fass, *The Damned and the Beautiful: American Youth in the 1920s* (New York: Oxford University Press, 1977).

2. Beth Bailey, *From Front Porch to Back Seat: Courtship in Twentieth-Century America* (Baltimore, Md.: Johns Hopkins University Press, 1988), 80; Ellen Rothman, *Hands and Hearts: A History of Courtship in America* (New York: Basic, 1985); John Modell, *Into One's Own: From Youth to Adulthood in the United States, 1920–1975* (Los Angeles and Berkeley: University of California Press, 1989).

3. Sherwood Eddy, *The Sex Life of Youth* (New York: Doubleday, 1933), 53.

4. To explore the changes and confusions, I have examined a variety of sources that go beyond the college youth who have so far been the major focus of attention. First of all, I have made extensive use of twentieth-century sex surveys. Kinsey of course, because of the sheer size of his sample, must remain the most valuable, but his bias towards the college-educated group and towards Indiana limit his worth significantly. He did, however, provide an invaluable generational comparison between those who matured between 1910 and 1925 and those who matured after that date. While this cannot make up for the inevitable lack of a survey from the Victorian period, it does reveal important trends. I have also used the 1938 study, *Psychological Factors in Marital Happiness* by Lewis Terman, whose findings in some ways complement those of Kinsey. These studies provide the quantitative

framework for my analysis and give the best guides possible to changing sexual behavior.

Second, I have looked at a variety of sources that provide qualitative information on people's attitudes and behaviors. These include the personal advice columns from the *New York Daily News* (written by Doris Blake) and the first year of the Martha Carr columns from the *St. Louis Post-Dispatch* (1930–1931); men's confessional stories, published in the periodical literature of the time; the in-house publications of the YMCA, which are a valuable calibrator of male attitudes towards women because these publications were written by independent young men living in the YMCA dorms, who were especially free to date young women; studies of the impact of the movies on youth carried out under the editorship of Ohio State psychologist W. W. Charters; and a series of about a hundred letters, asking advice, addressed to Judge Lindsey in 1925 to 1927, at the height of his influence (these are preserved in the Library of Congress and are mainly from readers of *Physical Culture*, to which Lindsey was a contributor). Taken together, these sources contain material about men's experiences across a broad spectrum of the middle class, from the lower-middle to the upper-middle class.

The class of the voices I have used from the qualitative sources is important. There may be some working-class elements in the *New York Daily News* readership, as the *New York Daily News* had a working-class to middle-class readership, but the concern about etiquette revealed here suggests that these young men and women were not of the working-class subculture. Further, Blake's answers were aimed at a middle-class audience. The *St. Louis Post-Dispatch* material is definitely middle-class in tenor. The YMCAs have a distinct lower-middle-class mood. The tone of the periodical literature is distinctly middle to upper-middle class. The letters to Lindsey were from solidly middle-class men on account of the readership of *Physical Culture*. The Charters material suggests a similar group, though his authors were not specific about the makeup of the groups they examined. Taken together, these items give a wide cross-section of 1920s middle-class youth.

5. Alfred Kinsey, et al., *Sexual Behavior in the Human Female* (Philadelphia: Saunders, 1954), 299.

6. Alfred Kinsey, et al., *Sexual Behavior in the Human Male* (Philadelphia: Saunders, 1948), 603; for critiques of Kinsey see Donald Porter Geddes, *An Analysis of the Kinsey Reports on Sexual Behavior in the Human Male and Female* (London: Muller, 1954); Regina Morantz, "The Scientist as Sex Crusader: Alfred C. Kinsey and American Culture," *American Quarterly* 28 (1977): 563–89.

Kinsey specifically identified the younger group with the men I am studying. Incredibly, he concluded that the samples indicated that "the sexual patterns of the younger generation are so nearly identical with the sexual patterns of the older generation." Kinsey seems to have missed entirely the qualitative implications of his sample. The Kinsey study was a study of fifty-three hundred males, conducted between 1940 and 1948. The study is of men from all over the United States (not the world as the title suggests). It is heavily biased towards Indiana, not perhaps an atypical state. But it is more seriously biased towards college-educated people. Further, Kinsey has been criticized for focusing so exclusively on quantitative material that concerns behavior. But, for my purposes, none of these problems is so significant as the possibility that those who volunteered to give their sex histories were probably more active than the rest of the population. However, Kinsey was very careful about this. He emphasized that he examined a broad cross-section of the population, from lawyers, professors, and clergymen to pimps and prostitutes. He insisted, further, that he refused to take histories from "recognizable psychotics." He insisted too on the "altruistic motives" that guided most of his subjects in agreeing to interview for the survey (Kinsey, *Human Male*, 3–34).

7. Winifred Vanderbilt Richmond, *The Adolescent Boy: A Book for Parents and Teachers* (New York: Farrar and Rinehart, 1933), 190.

8. Lewis Terman, *Psychological Factors in Marital Happiness* (New York: McGraw Hill, 1938), 321; his subjects were largely professional or semiprofessional. The major problem with Terman is his bias to California, surely not a very representative state. But he at least drew from the northern part of the state, which is more typical than the southern part.

9. Ibid., 321.

10. Ibid., 323.

11. Modell, *Into One's Own*, 41.

12. Kinsey, *Human Female*, 243.

13. Kinsey, *Human Female*, 281.

14. Ibid.

15. Lorine Pruette, "Conditions Today," in Ira Wile, *Sex Life in the Unmarried Adult* (New York: Vanguard, 1934), 289; Theodore Newcomb, "Recent Changes in Attitudes towards Sex and Marriage," *American Sociological Review* 2 (1937): 659.

16. Phyllis Blanchard and Carolyn Mannasses, *New Girls for Old* (New York: Macaulay, 1930), 59.

17. Letter to Lindsey, April 14, 1925, Box 351, Judge B. Lindsey papers, Library of Congress, Washington, D.C. Many, though not all, of the names of the correspondents were removed from the letters by Lindsey's wife in order to protect their anonymity.

18. Letter to Lindsey, January 8, 1925, Lindsey papers.

19. Letter to Lindsey, December 20, 1926, from Phoenix, Arizona, Lindsey papers.

20. Cyrus H. E——n to Judge Lindsey, December 12, 1926, Lindsey papers.

21. Paul Strong Achilles, *The Social Effects of Social Hygiene Literature* [New York: American Social Hygiene Association (ASHA), 1923]. Achilles studied 1,449. These were primarily high school and college students from the New York City area.

22. M. W. Peck and F. L. Wells, "On the Psycho-Sexuality of College Graduate Men," *Mental Hygiene* 7 (1923): 697–714; and "Further Studies in the Psycho-Sexuality of College Graduate Men," *Mental Hygiene* 9 (1925): 502–20. This was a questionnaire study of fifty-five men who had been to college by the National Research Council's Committee for Research on Sex Problems, which Kinsey noted attained results that were "close to those obtained in our study."

23. W. L. Hughes, "Sex Experiences of Boyhood," *Journal of Social Hygiene* 12 (1924): 262–73. This was a group-administered questionnaire of unmarried 15- to 20-year-olds, from rural and urban South Carolina, which Kinsey described as "a fair cross-section."

24. Gilbert Hamilton, *A Research in Marriage* (New York: Boni, 1929), 436–37. This study was of a hundred couples who had been through his psychiatric practice, and who consisted of a number of New York theater people.

25. Dorothy Bromley and F. L. Britten, *Youth and Sex: A Study of Thirteen Hundred College Students* (New York: Harper and Brothers, 1938), 143. Kinsey specifically states that these figures are unreliable for homosexuality and masturbation, but he is referring to behaviors for which "incidence was lower than for any other investigation." This only serves to confirm my observation of the strong homophobia.

26. Ibid.

27. Gilbert Hamilton, *A Research in Marriage*, 478.

28. Ibid.

29. Bromley and Britten, *Youth and Sex*, 210–12.

30. "Gay" historians have mostly not fallen into this trap. But there is a popular misconception.

31. Warren Susman, "Personality and the Development of Twentieth-Century Culture," in *Culture as History* (New York: Pantheon, 1984), 273–84.

32. Willard Waller, "The Rating and Dating Complex," *American Sociological Review* 2 (1937): 727–34.

33. Ibid., 730.

34. Michael Gordon, "Was Waller Ever Right?" *Journal of Marriage and the Family* 43 (February 1981): 67–75.

35. Waller, "Rating and Dating Complex," 733.

36. Ibid.

37. Ibid.

38. John L. Coughey, "Artificial Social Relations," *American Quarterly* 30 (Spring 1978): 70–89.

39. Charles Peterson, *Motion Pictures and Standards of Morality* (New York: Macmillan, 1933), 229.

40. Ibid., 254–55.

41. Herbert Blumer, *Movies and Conduct* (New York: Macmillan, 1933), 53.

42. *St. Louis Post-Dispatch*, July 30, 1931.

43. *New York Daily News*, April 2, 1928.

44. *New York Daily News*, December 20, 1928.

45. *New York Daily News*, June 9, 1921.

46. *New York Daily News*, May 19, 1926.

47. *New York Daily News*, January 25, 1926.

48. *New York Daily News*, February 11, 1925.

49. *New York Daily News*, February 22, 1926.

50. *New York Daily News*, September 26, 1929.

51. By John Modell in *Into One's Own* (see note 2 above), 366.

52. Blumer, *Movies and Conduct*, 55.

53. Ibid.

54. Ibid., 154.

55. Ibid.

56. Ibid., 113.

57. Richmond, *The Adolescent Boy* (see note 7 above), 88.

58. Floyd Dell, "Why They Pet," *Parent's Magazine*, October 1931, 63.

59. Charles Rosenberg, "Sexuality, Class, and Social Role," *American Quarterly* 25 (May 1973): 131–53.

60. From Central YMCA, Binghamton, New York, to Lindsey, March 2, 1925, Lindsey papers (see note 17 above).

61. F. E. U——l to Judge Lindsey, October 20, 1926, Lindsey papers.

62. To Marie Stopes, December 28, 1928, PP/MCS/A. 169, Contemporary Medical Archives Centre, Wellcome Institute for the History of Medicine, 183 Euston Road, London, NW1 2BN.

63. *New York Daily News*, January 4, 1929.

64. *New York Daily News*, August 2, 1923.

65. *New York Daily News*, January 7, 1929.

66. Letter to Judge Lindsey, May 8, 1925, Lindsey papers.

67. To Judge Lindsey from Chicago, May 10, 1925, Lindsey papers.

68. Letter to Lindsey, December 1, 1926, Lindsey papers.

69. Ibid.

70. Read Bain, "Changed Beliefs of College Students," *Journal of Abnormal and Social Psychology* 31 (1936): 11–19.

71. Kinsey, *Human Male* (see note 5 above), 364.

72. Ibid.

73. Donald J. N——son to Judge Lindsey, November 7, 1926, Lindsey papers.

74. Ernest W. Burgess, "Sociological Aspects of the Sex Life of the Unmarried Adult," Ira Wile, ed., *Sex Life of the Unmarried Adult* (see note 15 above), 125.

75. Theodore Newcomb, "Recent Changes" (see note 15 above), 663.

76. Ibid., 663.

77. Robert and Helen Lynd, *Middletown: A Study in American Culture* (New York: Harcourt, Brace, Jovanovich, 1929).

78. Robert and Helen Lynd, *Middletown in Transition* (New York: Harcourt, Brace, Jovanovich, 1937).

79. Newcomb, "Recent Changes," 663; Ira Reiss, writing in 1960, described the twentieth-century sexual system as one of "permissiveness with affection" (*Premarital Sexual Standards in America* [Glencoe, Ill.: Free Press, 1960], passim). The historical dimension is missing from this valuable analysis. But its precariousness should be self-evident.

80. Clarence Robinson, *A Boy and His Girlfriends* (New York: YMCA, 1924), 9.

81. Ibid.

82. Ira Wile, *Sex Life of the Unmarried Adult*, 247.

83. *New York Daily News*, February 11, 1926.

84. William K——e to Lindsey, November 17, 1925, Lindsey papers (see note 17 above).

85. H——e L. H——s to Lindsey, March 31, 1925, Lindsey papers.

86. Donald J. N——n to Lindsey, May 16, 1928, Lindsey papers.

87. ? to Judge Lindsey, November 6, 1926, Lindsey papers.

88. 24-year-old orphan to Judge Lindsey, from Rochester, Minn., April 7, 1922, Lindsey papers.

89. *St. Louis Post-Dispatch*, June 22, 1931.

90. Kinsey, *Human Male*, 364.

91. 11 W. 115th Street to Judge Lindsey, January 7, 1926, Lindsey papers.

92. Daniel Katz and Floyd Allport, *Student Attitudes: A Report of the Syracuse University Reaction Study* (Syracuse, N.Y.: Craftsman, 1931), 253.

93. Ibid.

94. *Fortune*, January 1937, 5.

95. Katz and Allport, *Student Attitudes*, 253.

96. Ibid., 254.

97. *New York Daily News*, September 6, 1926.

98. *New York Daily News*, January 8, 1925.

99. *New York Daily News*, January 9, 1925.

100. *St. Louis Post-Dispatch*, June 8 and June 25, 1931.

101. *New York Daily News*, October 21, 1926.

102. *New York Daily News*, August 25, 1926.

103. Anthony Rotundo, "Romantic Friendship and Male Intimacy Among Middle-Class Youth in the Northern United States, 1800–1900," *Journal of Social History* 23 (Fall 1989): 1–25.

104. "West Side Men," New York West Side YMCA, April 5, 1929, 1.

105. Ibid.

106. Ibid.

107. Ibid., May 3, 1929.

108. *New York Daily News*, December 24, 1925.

109. Percy Marks, *The Plastic Age* (New York: Grosset and Dunlap, 1924), 155.

110. Beatrice Hinkle, "Women and the New Morality," *Nation*, November 29, 1924, 541–43.

111. Lorine Pruette, "Conditions Today," in Ira Wile, *Sex Life of the Unmarried Adult* (see note 15 above), 283.

112. Ernest Burgess, "Sociological Aspects of the Sex Life of the Unmarried Adult," in ibid., 133.

113. S. M. Stoke and E. D. West, "The Conventional Interests of College Students," *School and Society* 32 (1930): 567–70.

114. Walter Buck, "A Measurement of the Changes in Attitudes and Interests over a Ten-Year Period," *Journal of Abnormal and Social Psychology* 31 (1936): 11–19.

115. *New York Daily News*, December 20, 1929.

116. *New York Daily News*, September 7, 1926.

117. Blanchard and Mannasses, *New Girls for Old* (see note 16 above), 64.

118. *New York Daily News*, January 24, 1925.

119. *New York Daily News*, February 1, 1924.

120. G. W. L——y to Judge Lindsey, n.d., Lindsey papers (see note 17 above).

121. Eleanor Rowland Wembridge, "Petting and the Campus," *Survey* 34 (1925): 394.

122. *New York Daily News*, January 16, 1929.

123. *St. Louis Post-Dispatch*, May 22, 1931.

124. *St. Louis Post-Dispatch*, June 19, 1931.

125. "West Side Men" (see note 104 above), April 5, 1929. This, as the colloquialism "nappers" ("mad") suggests, was originally published by the YMCA in

Liverpool, England; hence the "2m" reference to the number of women who were thought to be in surplus because of World War I. But it was published in New York, presumably as an indication of Anglo-American male solidarity.

126. "The Too High Cost Of Courting," *American*, September 1924. Beth Bailey makes much of this article in *Courtship in Twentieth-Century America* (see note 2 above).

127. Ibid.

128. Ibid.

129. *New York Daily News*, July 4, 1929.

130. Ibid.

131. *New York Daily News*, November 16, 1926.

132. *St. Louis Post-Dispatch*, November 16, 1931.

133. *New York Daily News*, January 3, 1925.

134. Robert Wiebe, *The Search for Order* (New York: Hill and Wang, 1967); T. J. Jackson Lears and Richard Wightman Fox, *The Culture of Consumption* (New York: Pantheon, 1983).

135. Grace Elliott and Harry Bone, "The Sex Life of Youth," *YMCA Intercollegian*, January 1922, 8. This was later published as a separate manual.

136. *New York Daily News*, March 28, 1923.

137. *New York Daily News*, May 10, 1923.

138. Doris Blake, personal advice columns, *New York Daily* News, passim.

139. "Why Men Won't Marry the New Woman," *Collier's*, March 14, 1925, 22–23.

140. *New York Daily News*, May 10, 1923.

141. *St. Louis Post-Dispatch*, March 30, 1931.

142. "Why Men Won't Marry the Modern Girl," *Delineator*, December 1921, 82.

143. James Oppenheimer, *How to Be Happy Though Married*, (Girard, Kans.: Haldeman-Julius, 1924).

144. "Under Sentence of Marriage," *True Story*, vol. III, no. 2, 38–39.

145. "Why Men Won't Marry the Modern Girl," *Delineator*, 82.

146. "Why Men Won't Marry the New Woman," *Collier's*, 22–23.

147. Ibid.

148. *St. Louis Post-Dispatch*, August 31, 1931.

149. George Ade, "Joys of Single Blessedness," *Atlantic Monthly*, June 1921, 11–13.

150. *Life*, January 1920, 903.

151. Theodore Pratt, "If You Have a Bachelor Complex, Get Yourself a Female Jumping Jellybean," *New Yorker*, October 8, 1927, 20.

152. Beatrice Hinkle, "Chaos of Marriage," *Harper's*, December 1925, 7.

153. Ira Wile, *Sex Life of the Unmarried Adult* (see note 15 above), 246.

154. Ben B. Lindsey and Wainwright Evans, *The Companionate Marriage* (New York: Boni and Liveright, 1927).

155. Ibid., 7.

156. Figure from Paul H. Jacobson, *American Marriage and Divorce* (New York: Rinehart, 1959), 21.

157. Lynd and Lynd, *Middletown in Transition* (see note 78 above), 52.

158. Kinsey, *Human Male* (see note 6 above), 368.

159. Ibid.

160. Hamilton, *A Research in Marriage* (see note 24 above), 178; Robert Latou Dickinson, however, found that only ten of the thousand married couples he examined practiced "fellatio, cunnilingus or soixante neuf" (*A Thousand Marriages*, [Baltimore, Md.: Williams and Wilkins, 1931], 366). These were of a decidedly older group, being drawn from visitors to his gynecological practice from the 1880s to the 1930s.

161. Lewis Terman, *Psychological Factors in Marital Happiness* (see note 8 above), 310.

162. Ibid., 296.

163. Ibid.

164. To Marie Stopes from University Club of Chicago, August 10, 1931, CMAC: PP/MCS/A. 63, Wellcome Institute for the History of Medicine, London.

165. Elaine Tyler May, *Great Expectations: Marriage and Divorce in Post-Victorian America* (Chicago: University of Chicago Press, 1980), 62.

166. Ernest Burgess, "The Family as a Unity of Interacting Personalities," *Family* 1 (1926): 9.

167. Ernest Mowrer, *The Family* (Chicago: University of Chicago Press, 1933), 275.

168. Ibid.

169. Ernest Groves, "Marriage," *American Youth*, January 1920, 24.

170. Margaret Marsh, "Suburban Men and Masculine Domesticity," *American Quarterly* 40 (June 1988): 165–88.

171. Ibid.

172. Ernest Groves, *Marriage* (New York: Holt, 1933), 443.

173. "The Fifty/Fifty Marriage," *Women's Home Companion*, April 1928, 130.

174. Ibid.

175. "We Both Had Jobs," *Women's Home Companion*, August 1925, 34.

176. "Should Husbands Do Housework?" *Good Housekeeping*, January 1926, 18–19. Nancy Cott has also examined these articles in her *The Grounding of Modern Feminism* (New Haven, Conn.: Yale University Press, 1987).

177. Virginia McMakin Collier, *Marriage and Careers: A Study of One Hundred Women Who Are Wives, Mothers, Homemakers, and Professional Workers for the Bureau of Vocational Information* (New York: Channel Bookshop, 1926), 85, 86.

178. Lorine Pruette, *Women and Leisure: A Study of Social Waste* (New York: Dutton, 1924), 99.

179. Nancy Cott, *The Grounding of Modern Feminism* (New Haven, Conn.: Yale University Press, 1987), 183.

180. Alexander Black, "American Husbands," *Harper's*, September 1923, 50.

181. "The Decline and Fall of the American Husband," *Life*, February 15, 1917, 258.

182. Abraham Myerson, "Nervous Husband," *Ladies' Home Journal*, September 1, 1921, 1.

183. Ibid.

184. Florence Woolston, "Delicatessen Husband," *New Republic*, April 25, 1923, 236.

185. Smiley Blanton and Woodbridge Riley, "Shell Shocks of Family Life," *Forum*, November 1929, 287.

186. "End of the Trail," *Sunset*, April 1923, 40.

187. "Shall I Divorce My Wife?" *Atlantic*, August 1924, 157–59.

188. Hamilton, *A Research in Marriage* (see note 24 above), 60.

189. Marcus Ravage, "My Wife Won't Let Me Be a Gypsy," *American Monthly*, June 1927, 47; Joseph Hergesheimer, "Can You Be Married and Free?" *Pictorial Review*, June 1927, 203–4.

190. Hergesheimer, "Can You Be Married and Free?", 203–4.

191. Suzanne LaFollette, *Concerning Women* (New York: Boni and Liveright, 1926), 35.

192. *St. Louis Post-Dispatch*, April 1, 1931.

193. "These Modern Husbands," letter in the *Nation*, January 12, 1927, 39.

194. Hamilton, *A Thousand Marriages* (see note 160 above), 65.

CONCLUSION: *New Moralities, New Masculinities*

1. Warren Susman, "Personality and the Development of Twentieth-Century Culture," in *Culture as History* (New York: Pantheon, 1984), 271–84.

2. Christina Simmons, "The Myth of Victorian Repression," in Simmons and Peiss, *Passion and Power* (Philadelphia: Temple University Press, 1989), 157–77.

3. Joseph Wood Krutch, "Love or the Life and Death of a Value," *Atlantic Monthly*, September 1928, 199–210. Argument is reminiscent too of Aldous Huxley, *Brave New World* (London: Chatto and Windus, 1932).

4. Walter Lippmann, *A Preface to Morals* (London: Allen and Unwin, 1931).

5. Barbara Ehrenreich, *The Hearts of Men: American Dreams and the Flight from Commitment* (New York: Doubleday, 1983).

6. Susan Brownmiller, *Against Our Will: Men, Women, and Rape* (New York: Simon and Schuster, 1975).

7. Andrea Dworkin, *Pornography: Men Possessing Women* (London: Women's Press, 1981).

8. The feminist position was expounded by Warren Farrell, *The Liberated Male* (New York: Bantam, 1974); the masculinist position by Herb Goldberg, *The Hazards of Being Male* (New York: New American Library, 1976).

9. Clyde Franklin, *The Changing Definition of Masculinity* (New York and London: Plenum, 1984); Joseph H. Pleck, *The Myth of Masculinity* (Cambridge, Mass.: MIT Press, 1981).

10. Harry Brod, ed., *The Making of Masculinities* (London: Unwin and Hyman, 1987).

11. Robert Bly, *Iron John: A Book about Men* (New York: Addison, Wesley, 1990).

12. Lynne Segal, *Slow Motion: Changing Masculinities, Changing Men* (London: Virago, 1990).

13. David Potter, *People of Plenty* (Chicago: University of Chicago Press, 1954).

Bibliography

PRIMARY SOURCES

Manuscript Collections

California Historical Society, San Francisco, California.
    Miriam Allen DeFord papers.
Columbia University Oral History Collection Interviews.
    Mildred Gilman.
The Kinsey Institute for the Study of Sex and Gender, Indiana University, Bloomington, Indiana.
    Rare Books.
Library of Congress, Washington, D.C.
    Judge Ben B. Lindsey papers.
    George Middleton papers.
New York Public Library, Rare Books and Manuscripts Division, New York, New York.
    Committee of Fourteen papers.
Ohio State University, Thurber Manuscript Collection, Columbus, Ohio.
    William Charters papers.
Arthur and Elizabeth Schlesinger Library on the History of Women in America, Radcliffe College, Cambridge, Massachusetts.

Inez Haynes Irwin papers.
Freda Kirchwey papers.
Doris Stevens papers.
University of Chicago, Joseph Regenstein Library, Chicago, Illinois.
Ernest Burgess papers.
University of Illinois at Chicago, Chicago, Illinois.
Haldeman-Julius Family papers.
University of Minnesota, YMCA of the USA Archives, St. Paul, Minnesota.
Early twentieth-century YMCA papers.
University of Oregon, Manuscript Collection, Eugene, Oregon.
Jane Grant papers.
University of Pittsburg, Pittsburg, Kansas.
Haldeman-Julius papers.
Wellcome Institute for the History of Medicine, Wellcome Institute, London, England.
Marie Stopes papers.

Popular Periodicals and Newspapers

American, 1926.
American Youth, 1920.
Association Men, 1920–1926.
Collier's, 1925–1926.
Delineator, 1920–1925.
Life, 1919–1926.
New York Daily News, 1920–1930.
Physical Culture, 1919–1926.
St. Louis Post-Dispatch, 1930–1931.
Saturday Evening Post, 1919, 1920, 1925.
True Story, 1919–1926.
Vanity Fair, 1925.
West Side Men, 1927–1929.

Periodical Articles

Ade, George. "Joys of Single Blessedness." *Atlantic Monthly*, June 1921, 11–13.
Anon. "End of the Trail by a Bewildered Husband." *Sunset*, April 1923, 40–43.
Anon. "Letter from a Husband." *Nation*, January 12, 1927, 39.
Anon. "Should Husbands Do Housework?" *Good Housekeeping*, January 1926, 18–19.
Anon. "Solomon's Sartorial Glory Rivalled by the Modern He-Man." *Literary Digest*, March 3, 1923, 56–57.
Anon. "The Too High Cost of Courting," *American*, September 1924, 27.
Anon. "We Both Had Jobs." *Women's Home Companion*, August 1924, 4.
Anon. "Why Men Won't Marry the New Woman." *Delineator*, December 1921, 3.

Black, Alexander, "Is the Young Person Coming Back?" *Harper's*, January 1924, 510.

Blanton, Smiley, M.D., and Riley Woodbridge. "Shell Shocks of Family Life." *Forum*, November 1929, 282–87.

Burgess, Ernest. "The Family as a Unity of Interacting Personalities." *Family* 1 (1926): 9–16.

By Himself. "The Fifty-Fifty Husband." *Women's Home Companion*, April 1928, 130.

De Coven Bowen, Louise. "Dance Halls." *Survey*, June 3, 1911, 23–41.

Editorial. "Who Reads the Tabloids?" *New Republic*, May 25, 1927, 6–7.

Grant, Jane. "Confessions of a Feminist." *American Mercury*, March 1941, 687–93.

Groves, Ernest. "Marriage." *American Youth*, January 1920, 24.

Hale, Charles B., and Wesley B. Caroll. "What Freshmen Read." *Educational Review* 70 (December 1925): 260–63.

Hall, Burnham. "Shall I Divorce My Wife?" *Atlantic Monthly*, July 1924, 155–62.

Hartt, R. L. "Some Thoughts on the Usual Subject." *Century*, January 1927, 304–7.

Hergesheimer, Joseph. "Can You Be Married and Free?" *Pictorial Review*, January 10, 1926.

Hinkle, Beatrice. "Chaos of Marriage." *Harper's*, December 1925, 62–70.

Johnston, William. "Why Men Won't Marry." *Collier's*, March 14, 1925.

Kennedy, John B. "The Devil's Dance Dens." *Collier's*, March 14, 1925.

Kimball, Reginald Stevens. "What Magazines Do High School Students Read?" *School and Society* 24 (October 1920): 486–588.

Krutch, Joseph Wood. "Love, or the Life and Death of a Value." *Atlantic Monthly*, September 1928, 199–210.

Mason, Gregory. "Satan in the Dance-Hall." *American Mercury*, 1924, 175–82.

Myerson, Abraham. "Nervous Husbands." *Ladies Home Journal*, September 1, 1921, 27.

Newcomb, Theodore. "Recent Changes in Attitudes towards Sex and Marriage." *American Sociological Review* 2 (1937): 659–67.

Pratt, Theodore. "If You Have a Bachelor Complex, Get Yourself a Female Jumping Jelly Bean." *New Yorker*, October 8, 1927, 3.

Ravage, Marcus. "My Wife Won't Let Me Be a Gypsy." *American Monthly*, June 1927, 47.

Seabury, David. "Bogy of Sex." *Century*, September 1927, 528–36.

Stoke, S. M., and E. D. West. "The Conversational Interests of College Students." *School and Society* 32 (1930): 567–70.

Van Doren, Carl. "Contemporary American Novelists." *Nation*, October 1921, 407–12.

Villard, Oswald Garrison. "Sex, Art, Truth, and Magazines." *Atlantic Monthly*, March 1926, 396–405.

Waller, Willard. "The Rating and Dating Complex." *American Sociological Review* 2 (1937): 727–34.

Watson, John B., and Karl B. Lashley. "A Psychological Study of Motion Pictures in Relation to Venereal Disease Campaigns." *Journal of Social Hygiene* 7 (April 1921): 189.

Wembridge, Eleanor Rowland. "Petting and the Campus." *Survey* 34 (1925): 394.
———. "Social Background in Sex Education." *Journal of Social Hygiene* 9 (February 1923).
Whyte, William Foote. "A Slum Sex Code." *American Journal of Sociology* 49 (1943): 24–31.
Woolston, Florence. "Delicatessen Husband." *New Republic*, April 25, 1923, 235–38.

Sex Surveys

Achilles, Paul Strong. *The Effectiveness of Certain Social Hygiene Literature*. New York: American Social Hygiene Association, 1923.
Buck, Walter. "A Measurement of Changes in Attitudes and Interests of College Students over a Ten-Year Period." *Journal of Abnormal and Social Psychology* 31 (1936): 12–19.
Davis, Katherine Bement. *Factors in the Sex Life of Twenty-two Hundred Women*. New York: Harper and Brothers, 1929.
Dickinson, Robert L. *A Thousand Marriages: A Study of Sex Adjustment*. Baltimore, Md.: Williams and Wilkins, 1931.
Exner, Max J. *Problems and Principles of Sex Education: A Study of 948 College Men*. New York: Association Press, 1914.
Hamilton, G. V. *A Research in Marriage*. New York: Boni, 1929.
Hughes, W. L. "Sex Experiences of Boyhood." *Journal of Social Hygiene* 12 (1926): 262–73.
Katz, Daniel, and Floyd Henry Allport. *Student Attitudes: A Report of the Syracuse University Reaction Study*. Syracuse, N.Y.: Craftsman, 1931.
Kinsey, Alfred, et al. *Sexual Behavior in the Human Female*. Philadelphia: Saunders, 1954.
———. *Sexual Behavior in the Human Male*. Philadelphia: Saunders, 1948.
Kirkpatrick, Clifford. "Student Attitudes toward Marriage and Sex." *Journal of Education Sociology* 9 (1936): 556.
Lundberg, George A. "Sex Differences on Social Questions." *School and Society* 23 (1926): 595–600.
Merrill, L. "A Summary of Findings in a Study of Sexualism among a Group of Five Hundred Delinquent Boys." *Journal of Juvenile Research* 3 (November 1918): 255–67.
Mosher, Clelia Duel. *The Mosher Survey: Sexual Attitudes of Forty-Five Victorian Women*. James Mahood and Kristine Wenberg, eds. New York: Arno, 1980.
Peck, M. W., and F. L. Wells. "Further Studies in the Psycho-Sexuality of College Men." *Mental Hygiene* 9 (1925): 502–20.
———. "On the Psycho-Sexuality of College Men." *Mental Hygiene* 7 (1923): 697–714.
Taylor, W. S. "A Critique of Sublimation in Men: A Study of Forty Superior Men." *Genetic Psychology Monogram* 13 (1932): 1–15.
Terman, Lewis. *Psychological Factors in Marital Happiness*. New York: MacGraw Hill, 1938.

Sex and Marriage Manuals

Binkley, Robert C., and Frances W. Binkley. *What Is Right with Marriage?* New York and London: Appleton, 1929.

Collins, Joseph. *The Doctor Looks at Love and Life.* New York: Doran, 1926.

David, F. A. *Plain Talks on Avoided Subjects.* Philadelphia, 1899.

Eddy, Sherwood. *The Sex Life of Youth.* New York: Doubleday, Doran, 1928.

Fielding, William J. *Man's Sexual Life.* Girard, Kans.: Haldeman-Julius, 1924.

———. *Psychoanalysis and Human Behavior.* Girard, Kans.: Haldeman-Julius, 1921.

Gallichan, Walter. *Sex Education.* Boston: Small, Maynard, 1921.

Galloway, Thomas W. *Sex and Life.* New York: YMCA, 1919.

———. *Sex and Social Health.* New York: ASHA, 1924.

Gerrish, Frederic. *Sex Hygiene: A Talk to College Boys.* Boston: Gorham, 1917.

Hall, Winfield Scott. *Sexual Knowledge.* Philadelphia: Winston, 1918.

Long, H. W. *Sane Sex Life and Sane Sex Living.* New York: Eugenics, 1919.

Lowry, E. B. *Himself.* Chicago: Forbes, 1916.

Macfadden, Bernarr. *Manhood and Marriage.* New York: Macfadden, 1915.

Malchow, Charles. *The Sexual Life.* St. Louis: Mosby, 1921.

Oppenheim, James. *The Common Sense of Sex.* Girard, Kans.: Haldeman-Julius, 1926.

———. *How to Be Happy Though Married.* Girard, Kans.: Haldeman-Julius, 1927.

Popenoe, Paul. *Modern Marriage.* New York: Macmillan, 1925.

Robie, W. F. *Rational Sex Ethics.* Boston: Badger, 1918.

———. *Sex and Life.* New York: Rational Life Publishing, 1924.

Robinson, William. *Sex Morality.* New York: Critic and Guide, 1919.

Sanger, Margaret. *Happiness in Marriage.* New York: Blue Ribbon, 1926.

Steinhardt, Irving. *Ten Sex Talks to Boys.* Philadelphia and London: Lippincott, 1914.

Thurber, James, and E. B. White. *Is Sex Necessary? or, Why You Feel the Way You Do.* New York: Harper and Brothers, 1929.

Van de Velde, Theodore H. *Ideal Marriage: Its Physiology and Technique.* New York: Random House, 1934.

Wile, Ira S., and Mary Winn. *Marriage in the Modern Manner.* New York: Century, 1929.

Wolf, Heinrich. *The Male Approach.* New York: Friede, 1929.

Wood, Clement. *The Facts of Life Presented to Men.* Girard, Kans.: Haldeman-Julius, 1924.

Novels

Anderson, Sherwood. *Dark Laughter.* New York: Buebsch, 1925.

———. *Winesburg, Ohio.* New York: Buebsch, 1919.

Benet, Stephen. *The Beginning of Wisdom.* New York: Holt, 1921.

———. *Young People's Pride.* New York: Holt, 1922.

Brush, Katherine. *Young Man of Manhattan.* New York: Farrar and Rinehart, 1930.

Cabell, James Branch. *Jurgen: A Comedy of Justice.* New York: Crown, 1919.

Dell, Floyd. *The Briary-Bush.* New York: Knopf, 1921.

———. *Janet March.* New York: Knopf, 1923.

——. *Moon-Calf.* New York: Knopf, 1920.

——. *Souvenir.* New York: Doubleday, Doran, 1929.

——. *An Unmarried Father.* New York: Knopf, 1925.

Fabian, Warner. *Flaming Youth.* New York: Macaulay, 1923.

Fitzgerald, F. Scott. *The Beautiful and the Damned.* New York: Scribner's, 1922.

——. *The Great Gatsby.* New York: Scribner's, 1925.

——. *Tender Is the Night.* New York: Scribner's, 1934.

——. *This Side of Paradise.* New York: Scribner's, 1920.

Frank, Waldo. *Holiday.* Boston: Little, Brown, 1925.

Grey, Zane. *Lost Pueblo.* New York: Black's, 1928.

——. *Stairs of Sand.* New York: Black's, 1930.

——. *Under the Tonto Rim.* New York: Black's, 1930.

Hecht, Ben. *Erik Dorn.* New York: Boni and Liveright, 1921.

Heyward, DuBose. *Porgy.* London: Cape, 1928.

Johnson, Gladys. *Desire.* New York: Burt, 1929.

Kelley, Edith Summers. *Weeds.* New York: Harcourt, Brace, 1926.

Kemp, Harry. *More Miles.* New York: Boni and Liveright, 1926.

——. *Tramping on Life.* New York: Boni and Liveright, 1922.

Lewis, Sinclair. *Dodsworth.* New York: Harcourt, Brace, Jovanovich, 1929.

Lewisohn, Ludwig. *Stephen Escott.* New York: Harper's, 1930.

London, Jack. *The Call of the Wild.* New York: Macmillan, 1903.

Marks, Percy. *The Plastic Age.* New York: Grosset and Dunlap, 1924.

Norris, Frank. *McTeague: A Story of San Francisco.* New York: Norton, 1977.

Van Vechten, Carl. *Firecrackers.* New York: Knopf, 1925.

——. *Nigger Heaven.* New York: Knopf, 1926.

——. *Peter Whiffle: His Life and Works.* New York: Knopf, 1922.

Books and Monographs

Addams, Jane. *The Spirit of Youth and the City Streets.* Chicago: University of Chicago Press, 1911.

Ade, George. *Artie.* Chicago: University of Chicago Press, 1963. Originally published 1894.

Blanchard, Phyllis, and Carolyn Manasses. *New Girls for Old.* New York: Macaulay, 1930.

Blumer, Herbert. *Movies and Conduct.* New York: Macmillan, 1933.

Bourne, Randolph. *Youth and Life.* New York: Houghton, Mifflin, 1913.

Bromley, Dorothy and F. L. Britten. *Youth and Sex: A Study of Thirteen Hundred College Students.* New York: Harper and Row, 1938.

Calverton, V. F. *The New Generation.* New York: Macaulay, 1930.

Calverton, V. F., and Samuel Schmalhausen. *Women's Coming of Age.* New York: Macaulay, 1930.

Carpenter, Edward. *Love's Coming of Age.* London: Sonnenschein, 1906.

Chicago Vice Commission. *The Social Evil in Chicago: A Study of Existing Conditions with Recommendations by the Chicago Vice Commission.* Chicago, 1911.

Cressey, Paul. *The Taxi-Dance Hall.* Chicago: University of Chicago Press, 1932.

Dell, Floyd. *Homecoming*. New York: Farrar and Rinehart, 1933.

———. *Love in Greenwich Village*. New York: Doran, 1926.

———. *Love in the Machine Age*. New York: Farrar and Rinehart, 1930.

Edwards, Richard Henry. *Popular Amusements*. New York, 1915.

Ellis, Havelock. *Studies in the Psychology of Sex*. New York: Random House, 1936.

Gray, William S., and Ruth Monroe. *The Reading Interests and Reading Habits of Adults*. New York: Macmillan, 1930.

Green, George Henry. *Psychoanalysis in the Classroom*. London and New York: Putnam, 1922.

Groves, Ernest. *The Marriage Crisis*. New York: Longman's, Green, 1928.

Hall, G. Stanley. *Adolescence*. New York: Appleton, 1904.

———. *Senescence: The Last Stage of Life*. New York: Appleton, 1922.

Hapgood, Hutchins. *Types from City Streets*. New York: Funk and Wagnall's, 1910.

Harland, Robert O. *The Vice Bondage of a Great City*. Chicago: Busch, 1922.

Hershey, Joseph. *Pulpwood Editor*. New York: Stokes, 1937.

Irwin, Will. *The Making of a Reporter*. New York: Doubleday, 1942.

———. *Propaganda and the News, or, What Makes You Think So?* New York: MacGraw Hill, 1936.

Key, Ellen. *Love and Marriage*. New York: Source Book Press, 1970. Originally published 1911.

Kneeland, George. *Commercialized Vice in New York City*. New York: Century, 1917.

LaFollette, Susan. *Concerning Women*. New York: Boni and Liveright, 1927.

Lindsey, Ben B., and Wainwright Evans. *The Companionate Marriage*. New York: Boni and Liveright, 1927.

———. *The Revolt of Modern Youth*. Garden City, N.Y.: Garden City Publishing, 1925.

Lippmann, Walter. *A Preface to Morals*. London: Allen and Unwin, 1931.

Louisville Vice Commission. *Report of the Louisville Vice Commission*. Louisville, Ky., 1911.

Lynd, Robert S., and Helen Merrill Lynd. *Middletown: A Study in American Culture*. New York: Harcourt, Brace, and World, 1929.

———. *Middletown in Transition*. New York: Harcourt, Brace, Jovanovich, 1937.

Mallen, Frank. *Sauce for the Gander*. White Plains, N.Y.: Baldwin, 1954.

Marryat, Captain Frederick. *A Diary in America*. London: Orme, Brown, Greene, and Longman's, 1839.

Middleton, George. *These Things Are Mine*. New York: Macmillan, 1947.

Mowrer, Ernest. *The Family*. Chicago: University of Chicago Press, 1932.

Moxon, Reverend Phillip. *The White Cross: For Men Only—A Statement of the Movement*. New York: YMCA, 1888.

Nystrom, Paul H. *The Economics of Fashion*. New York: Ronald, 1928.

Peters, Charles C. *Motion Pictures and Standards of Morality*. New York: Macmillan, 1933.

Pruette, Lorine. *Women and Leisure*. New York: Dutton, 1924.

Reckless, Walter. *Vice in Chicago*. Chicago: University of Chicago Press, 1932.

Richmond, Winifred. *The Adolescent Boy*. New York: Farrar and Rinehart, 1933.

Robinson, Clarence. *A Boy and His Girlfriends*. New York: YMCA, 1924.

Roosevelt, Theodore. *The Strenuous Life: Essays and Addresses*. New York, 1900.

Schmalhausen, Samuel. *Why We Misbehave*. New York: Macaulay, 1928.

Syracuse Moral Survey Commission. *The Social Evil in Syracuse*. Syracuse, N.Y., 1911.

Thrasher, Frederic. *The Gang: A Study of 1,313 Gangs in Chicago*. Chicago: University of Chicago Press, 1927.

Tridon, Andre. *Psychoanalysis and Behavior*. New York: Knopf, 1923.

———. *Sex and Psychoanalysis*. New York: Knopf, 1920.

Wile, Ira. *The Sex Life of the Unmarried Adult*. New York: Garden City Publishing, 1934.

SECONDARY SOURCES

Ph.D. Dissertations and Master's Theses

Cothran, Andrew N. "The Little Blue-Book and the Big American Parade." Ph.D diss., University of Maryland, 1966.

Ellis, Leonard. "Men among Men: An Exploration of All-Male Relationships in Victorian America." Ph.D diss., Columbia University, 1984.

Gilfoyle, Timothy. "City of Eros: New York City, Prostitution, and the Commercialization of Sex, 1790–1920." Ph.D diss., Columbia University, 1987.

Herder, Dale. "Education for the Masses: The Haldeman-Julius Little Blue Books as Popular Culture in the 1920s." Ph.D diss., Michigan State University, 1975.

Paoletti, Jo. "Changes in the Masculine Image: A Content Analysis of Popular Humor about Dress, 1880–1910." Ph.D diss., University of Maryland, 1981.

Simmons, Christina. "Marriage in the Modern Manner: Sexual Radicalism and Reform, 1914–1941." Ph.D diss., Brown University, 1982.

Van Ness, Susan. "Jane Grant: Co-Founder of the *New Yorker*," M.A. thesis, University of Kansas, 1983.

Waugh, Clifford J. "Bernarr Macfadden, the Muscular Prophet." Ph.D diss., SUNY Buffalo, 1979.

Wilder, Robin. "The Mind of Heywood Broun." Ph.D. diss., University of Wisconsin, Madison, 1984.

Monographs, Articles, and Books

Abelove, Henry. "Freud, Male Homosexuality, and the Americans." *Dissent* (1986): 59–69.

Abraham, Edward. *The Lyrical Left: Randolph Bourne, Alfred Stieglitz, and the Origins of Cultural Radicalism in America*. Charlottesville: University of Virginia Press, 1984.

Allen, Frederic Lewis. *Only Yesterday: An Informal History of the 1920s*. New York: Harper and Brothers, 1931.

Alpern, Sara. *Freda Kirchwey: A Woman of the Nation*. Cambridge, Mass.: Harvard University Press, 1987.

Anderson, Jervis. *This Was Harlem: A Cultural Portrait, 1900–1950*. New York: Farrar, Straus, Giroux, 1982.

Banner, Lois W. *American Beauty*. New York: Knopf, 1983.

Barker-Benfield, Graham J. *The Horrors of the Half-Known Life: Male Attitudes towards Women and Sexuality in Nineteenth-Century America*. New York: Harper and Row, 1976.

Blumin, Stuart. *The Emergence of the Middle Class: Social Experience in the American City, 1770–1920*. New York: Cambridge University Press, 1989.

Bly, Robert. *Iron John: A Book about Men*. London: Addison, Wesley, 1991.

Bontemps, Arno. *The Harlem Rennaissance Remembered*. New York: Dodd, Mead, 1977.

Brandt, Allan. *No Magic Bullet: A Social History of Venereal Diseases in the United States since 1880*. New York: Oxford University Press, 1985.

Brisset, Dennis, and Lionel S. Lewis. "Sex as Work." *Social Problems* 15 (Summer 1967): 8–18.

Brod, Harry, ed. *The Making of Masculinities: The New Men's Studies*. Boston: Allen and Unwin, 1987.

Broun, Heywood. *The Collected Heywood Broun: A Memoir of the Broun Family*. New York: Harcourt, Brace, 1941.

———. *Whose Little Boy Are You?* New York: St. Martin's, 1983.

Brownmiller, Susan. *Against Our Will: Men, Women, and Rape*. New York: Simon and Schuster, 1975.

Burnham, John C. "Early References to Homosexual Communities in American Medical Writings." *Medical Aspects of Sexuality* 7 (1973): 40–49.

———. *Paths into American Culture: Psychology, Medicine, and Morals*. Philadelphia: Temple University Press, 1988.

———. "The Progressive Era Revolution in American Attitudes towards Sex." *Journal of American History* 59 (March 1973): 885–903.

Cargill, Oscar. *Intellectual America: Ideas on the March*. New York: Macmillan, 1942.

Chauncey, George, Jr. "Christian Brotherhood or Sexual Perversion? Homosexual Identities and the Construction of Sexual Boundaries in the World War One Era." *Journal of Social History* 9 (Winter 1985): 189–211.

———. "From Sexual Inversion to Homosexuality: Medicine and the Changing Conception of Female Deviance." *Salmagundi* 58–59 (Fall 1982–Winter 1983): 114–46.

Chesney, Kellow. *The Anti-Society: An Account of the Victorian Underworld*. Boston: Gambit, 1970.

Coben, Stanley. *Rebellion against Victorianism: The Impetus for Cultural Change in 1920s America*. New York: Oxford University Press, 1991.

Collier, Virginia MacMakin. *Marriage and Careers*. New York: Bureau of Vocational Information, 1926.

Cominos, Peter. "Late Victorian Sexual Respectability and the Social System." *International Review of Social History* 8 (1963): 18–48, 216–50.

Cott, Nancy. *The Grounding of Modern Feminism*. New Haven, Conn.: Yale University Press, 1987.

———. "Passionlessness: An Interpretation of Victorian Sexual Ideology." *Signs* 4 (1978): 219–36.

Coughey, John L. "Artificial Social Relations." *American Quarterly* 30 (Spring 1978): 70–89.

Couvares, Francis. *The Remaking of Pittsburgh: Class and Culture in an Industrializing City, 1877–1919*. Albany, N.Y.: State University of New York Press, 1984.

Crunden, Robert. *From Self to Society, 1919–1941*. Englewood Cliffs, N.J.: Prentice Hall, 1972.

Cumbler, John T. *Working-Class Community in Industrializing America*. Westport, Conn.: Greenwood, 1979.

Davis, David Brion. *From Homicide to Slavery: Studies in American Culture*. New York: Oxford University Press, 1986.

Degler, Carl N. "What Ought to Be and What Was: Women's Sexuality in Nineteenth-Century America." *American Historical Review* 79 (December 1974): 1467–90.

D'Emilio, John, and Estelle Freedman. *Intimate Matters: A History of Sexuality in America*. New York: Harper and Row, 1988.

Dubbert, Joe L. *A Man's Place: Masculinity in Transition*. Englewood Cliffs, N.J.: Prentice Hall, 1980.

———. "Progressivism and the Masculinity Crisis." In Pleck and Pleck, *The American Man*. Englewood Cliffs, N.J.: Prentice Hall, 1980. 303–20.

Dworkin, Andrea. *Pornography: Men Possessing Women*. London: Women's Press, 1981.

Ehrenreich, Barbara. *The Hearts of Men: American Dreams and the Flight from Commitment*. Garden City, N.Y.: Anchor/Doubleday, 1983.

Erenberg, Lewis A. *Steppin' Out: New York Nightlife and the Transformation of American Culture, 1890–1930*. Westport, Conn.: Greenwood, 1980.

Ewen, Elizabeth. "City Lights: Immigrant Women and the Rise of the Movies." *Signs* 5 (1980): 545–65.

Ewen, Stuart. *Captains of Consciousness: Advertising and the Roots of the Consumer Culture*. New York: MacGraw Hill, 1976.

Farrell, Warren. *The Liberated Male*. New York: Bantam, 1974.

Fass, Paula S. *The Damned and the Beautiful: American Youth in the 1920s*. New York: Oxford University Press, 1977.

Fiedler, Leslie. *Love and Death in the American Novel*. New York: Stein and Day, 1966.

Filene, Peter. *Him/Her/Self: Sex Roles in Modern America*. 2d ed. Englewood Cliffs, N.J.: Prentice Hall, 1986.

Fishbein, Leslie. *Rebels in Bohemia: the Radicals of the Masses, 1911–1917*. Chapel Hill: University of North Carolina Press, 1982.

Foucault, Michel. *The History of Sexuality*. Vol. 1, *An Introduction*. New York: Pantheon, 1978.

Fox, Richard Wightman, and T. J. Jackson Lears. *The Culture of Consumption*. New York: Pantheon, 1983.

Franklin, Clyde. *The Changing Definition of Masculinity.* New York: Plenum, 1984.

Fraser, John. *America and the Patterns of Chivalry.* New York: Cambridge University Press, 1982.

Freedman, Estelle. "The New Woman: Changing Views of Women in the 1920s." *Journal of American History* 64 (1974): 389–411.

Freud, Sigmund. *Civilisation and Its Discontents.* London: Hogarth, 1929.

Gabor, Mark. *An Illustrated History of Girlie Magazines.* New York: Harmony, 1984.

Geddes, Donald Porter, ed. *An Analysis of the Kinsey Reports on Sexual Behavior in the Human Male and Female.* London: Muller, 1954.

Gill, Brendan. *Here at the New Yorker.* New York: Random House, 1975.

Goldberg, Harvey. *The Hazards of Being Male.* New York: New American Library, 1976.

Gordon, Linda. *Heroes of Their Own Lives: The Politics and History of Family Violence, Boston, 1880–1960.* New York: Viking, 1988.

Gordon, Michael. "From an Unfortunate Necessity to a Cult of Mutual Orgasm: Sex in Marital Education Literature, 1830–1940." In James Henslin, ed., *The Sociology of Sex.* New York: Schocken, 1978. 53–67.

———. "Was Waller Ever Right? The Rating and Dating Complex Reconsidered." *Journal of Marriage and the Family* 43 (1981): 67–76.

Gorn, Eliot. *The Manly Art: Bare-Knuckle Prize Fighting in Victorian America.* Ithaca, N.Y.: Cornell University Press, 1986.

Gramsci, Antonio. *Selections from Prison Notebooks.* Trans. Q. Hoare and G. N. Smith. New York: Basic, 1983.

Grant, Jane. *Ross, the New Yorker, and Me.* New York: Raynal, 1968.

Green, Harvey. *Fit for America: Health, Fitness, Sport, and American Society.* Baltimore, Md.: Johns Hopkins University Press, 1988.

Griswold, Robert L. *Family and Divorce in California, 1850–1890: Victorian Illusions and Everyday Realities. Albany: State University of New York Press,* 1982.

Haag, Pamela. "The 'Ill Use of a Wife': Patterns of Working-Class Violence in Domestic and Public New York City, 1860–1880." *Journal of Social History* 25 (Spring 1992): 447–77.

Haldeman-Julius, Sue. "Emmanuel Haldeman-Julius, the Little Blue Book Man." *Little Balkan Review* 16 (Winter 1982): 1–15.

Hale, Nathan. *Freud and the Americans: The Beginnings of Psychoanalysis in the United States, 1876–1917.* New York: Oxford University Press, 1971.

Hare, Peter. *A Woman's Quest for Science: A Portrait of Anthropologist Elsie Clews Parsons.* Buffalo, N.Y.: Prometheus, 1985.

Higham, John. "The Reorientation of American Culture in the 1890s." In *Writing American History: Essays in Modern Scholarship.* Bloomington: Indiana University Press, 1970.

Hilter, Anthony. *The Revolt from the Village, 1915–1930.* Chapel Hill: University of North Carolina Press, 1979.

Hoffmann, Frederic. *The 1920s: American Writing in the Post-War Decade.* New York: Viking, 1955.

Huggins, Irvin. *The Harlem Rennaissance.* New York: Oxford University Press, 1971.

Jackson, Carlton. *Zane Grey*. New York: Twayne, 1973.

Jacobson, Paul. *American Marriage and Divorce*. New York: Rinehart, 1959.

Jones, Howard Mumford, ed. *Letters of Sherwood Anderson*. Boston: Little, Brown, 1954.

Kasson, John F. *Amusing the Million: Coney Island at the Turn of the Century*. New York: Hill and Wang, 1978.

———. *Rudeness and Civility: Manners in Nineteenth-Century America*. New York: Hill and Wang, 1991.

Katz, Jonathan, ed. *Gay/Lesbian Almanac: A New Documentary*. New York: Harper and Row, 1983.

Kellner, Bruce. *Carl Van Vechten and the Irreverent Decades*. Norman: University of Oklahoma Press, 1968.

Kett, Joseph F. *Rites of Passage: Adolescence in America, 1790 to the Present*. New York: Basic, 1977.

Kimmel, Michael S. "Pro-Feminist Men in Turn-of-the-Century America." *Gender and Society* 1 (September 1987): 261–83.

Konné, Chidi. *From DuBois to Van Vechten: The Early New Negro Literature, 1903–1926*. Westport, Conn.: Greenwood, 1981.

Kramer, Dale. *Heywood Broun: A Biographical Portrait*. New York: Current Books, 1949.

———. *Ross and the New Yorker*. Garden City, N.Y.: Doubleday, 1951.

Lasch, Christopher. *The Culture of Narcissism: American Life in an Age of Diminishing Expectations*. New York: Knopf, 1979.

———. *The New Radicalism in America: The Intellectual as Social Type*. New York: Knopf, 1965.

Lears, T. J. Jackson. *No Place of Grace: Antimodernism and the Transformation of American Culture*. New York: Pantheon, 1981.

———. "Some Versions of Fantasy: Towards a Cultural History of American Advertising, 1880–1930." *Prospects* 9 (1984): 349–405.

Leuchtenberg, William. *The Perils of Prosperity, 1914–1932*. Chicago: University of Chicago Press, 1958.

Lystra, Karen. *Searching the Heart: Women, Men, and Romantic Love in Nineteenth-Century America*. New York: Oxford University Press, 1989.

Macfadden, Mary, with Emile Gavreau. *Dumbbells and Carrot-Strips: The Story of Bernarr Macfadden*. New York: Holt, 1953.

Madden, David, ed. *The Tough Guy Writers of the 1930s*. Carbondale and Edwardsville: Southern Illinois University Press, 1968.

Marchand, Roland. *Advertising the American Dream: Making Way for Modernity, 1920–1940*. Berkeley and Los Angeles: University of California Press, 1985.

Marcus, Steven. *The Other Victorians: A Study of Sexuality and Pornography in Nineteenth-Century England*. New York: Basic, 1966.

Marsh, Margaret. "Suburban Men and Masculine Domesticity." *American Quarterly* 40 (June 1988): 165–88.

Matthews, Fred H. "The Americanisation of Sigmund Freud." *Journal of American Studies* 1 (1967): 39–62.

May, Elaine Tyler. *Great Expectations: Marriage and Divorce in Post-Victorian America*. Chicago: University of Chicago Press, 1980.

May, Henry. *The End of American Innocence: A Study of the First Years of Our Own Time, 1912–1917.* New York: Knopf, 1959.

May, Lary. *Screening Out the Past: The Birth of Mass Culture and the Motion Picture Industry.* New York: Oxford University Press, 1980.

McGovern, James. "The American Woman's Pre–World War One Freedom in Manners and Morals." *Journal of American History* 58 (September 1968): 315–31.

———. "David Graham Phillips and the Virility Impulse of the Progressive Era." *New England Quarterly* 39 (September 1966): 340–49.

Meyer, Donald. *Sex and Power: The Rise of Women in America, Russia, Sweden, and Italy.* Middletown, Conn.: Wesleyan University Press, 1988.

Meyerowitz, Joanne. *Women Adrift: Independent Wage Earners in Chicago, 1880–1930.* Chicago: University of Chicago Press, 1988.

Modell, John. "Dating Becomes the Way of American Youth." In David Levine, et al., eds., *Essays on the Family and Historical Change.* Arlington: University of Texas Press, 1983. 91–126.

———. *Into One's Own: From Youth to Adulthood in the United States, 1920–1975.* Berkeley and Los Angeles: University of California Press, 1989.

Morantz, Regina Markell. "The Scientist as Sex Crusader: Alfred C. Kinsey and American Culture." *American Quarterly* 29 (1979): 563–89.

Mott, Frank. *A History of American Magazines.* New York: Cambridge University Press, 1938. 5 vols., to 1968.

Mowry, George. *The Urban Nation, 1920–1965.* New York: Hill and Wang, 1965.

Nash, Roderick. *The Call of the Wild.* New York: Braziller, 1970.

Nissenbaum, Stephen. *Sex, Diet, and Debility in Jacksonian America.* Westport, Conn.: Greenwood, 1980.

Nye, Russel. "Saturday Night at the Paradise Ballroom; or, Dance-Halls in the 1920s." *Journal of Popular Culture* 7 (1973): 1–15.

O'Connor, Richard. *Heywood Broun: A Biography.* New York: Putnam's, 1975.

O'Neill, William. *Divorce in the Progressive Era.* New Haven, Conn.: Yale University Press, 1967.

———. *Everyone Was Brave: The Rise and Fall of Feminism in America.* Chicago: Quadrangle, 1969.

Ostrander, Gilman. *American Civilization in the First Machine Age.* New York: Harper and Row, 1970.

Peiss, Kathy. *Cheap Amusements: Working Women and Leisure in Turn-of-the-Century New York.* Philadelphia: Temple University Press, 1986.

———. *Passion and Power: Sexuality in History.* Philadelphia: Temple University Press, 1989.

Peterson, Theodore. *American Magazines in the Twentieth Century.* Urbana: University of Illinois Press, 1956.

Pivar, David J. "Cleansing the Nation: The War on Prostitution, 1917–1921." *Prologue* 9 (Spring 1980): 29–40.

———. *Purity Crusade.* Westport, Conn.: Greenwood, 1980.

Pleck, Elizabeth H. *Domestic Tyranny: The Making of American Social Policy against Family Violence from Colonial Times to the Present.* New York: Oxford University Press, 1987.

Pleck, Elizabeth H., and Joseph H. Pleck. *The American Man*. Englewood Cliffs, N.J.: Prentice Hall, 1980.

Pleck, Joseph H. *The Myth of Masculinity*. Cambridge, Mass.: Massachusetts Institute of Technology Press, 1981.

Pope, Daniel. *The Making of Modern Advertising*. New York: Basic, 1983.

Potter, David. *People of Plenty*. Chicago: University of Chicago Press, 1954.

Rader, Benjamin. *American Sports: From the Age of Folk Games to the Age of Spectators*. Englewood Cliffs, N.J.: Prentice Hall, 1980.

Reisman, David. *The Lonely Crowd*. New York: Oxford University Press, 1950.

Reiss, Ira. *Pre-Marital Sexual Standards in America*. Glencoe, Ill.: Free Press, 1960.

Robinson, Paul. *The Modernization of Sex: Havelock Ellis, Alfred Kinsey, William Masters, and Virginia Johnson*. New York: Harper and Row, 1976.

Rose, David W. "Prostitution and the Sporting Life: Aspects of Working-Class Culture and Sexuality in Nineteenth-Century Wheeling." *Upper Ohio Valley Historical Review* 16 (1987): 1–27.

Rosen, Ruth. *The Lost Sisterhood*. Baltimore, Md.: Johns Hopkins University Press, 1982.

———, ed. *The Maimie Papers*. Old Westbury, N.Y.: Feminist Press, 1977.

Rosenberg, Caroll Smith. "The New Woman as Androgyne: Social Disorder and Gender Crisis, 1870–1936." In *Disorderly Conduct: Visions of Gender in Victorian America*. New York: Knopf, 1985.

Rosenberg, Charles E. "Sexuality, Class, and Role in Nineteenth-Century America." *American Quarterly* 25 (May 1973): 131–53.

Rosenzweig, Roy. *Eight Hours for What You Will: Workers and Leisure in an Industrial City, 1870–1936*. New York: Cambridge University Press, 1983.

Ross, Ellen. "Fierce Questions and Taunts: Working-Class Life in London, 1870–1914." *Feminist Studies* 8 (Fall 1982): 23–40.

Rothman, Ellen K. *Hands and Hearts: A History of Courtship in America*. New York: Basic, 1984.

Rotundo, E. Anthony. "Learning about Manhood: Gender Ideals and the Middle-Class Family in Nineteenth-Century America." In Walvin and Mangan, eds. *Manliness and Morality*. London and Manchester: Manchester University Press, 1987. 35–48.

———. "Romantic Friendship: Male Intimacy and Middle-Class Youth in the Northern United States, 1800–1900." *Journal of Social History* 23 (Fall 1989): 1–25.

Rudnick, Lois. *New Woman, New Worlds*. Albuquerque: University of New Mexico Press, 1984.

Rupp, Leila J. "Feminism and the Sexual Revolution in the Early Twentieth Century: The Case of Doris Stevens." *Feminist Studies* 15 (Summer 1989): 289–309.

Ryan, Mary. "The Projection of a New Womanhood: The Movie Moderns in the 1920s." In Jean E. Friedman and William G. Shade, *Our American Sisters: Women in American Life and Thought*. Lexington, Mass.: Heath, 1982. 500–518.

Segal, Lynne. *Slow Motion: Changing Masculinities, Changing Men*. London: Virago, 1990.

Shipley, Miriam DeFord. *Uphill All the Way: The Life of Maynard Shipley*. Antioch, Ohio: Antioch University Press, 1956.

Showalter, Elaine. *These Modern Women: Autobiographical Essays from the Twenties.* Old Westbury, N.Y.: Feminist Press, 1977.

Shumsky, Neil Larry. "Tacit Acceptance: Respectable Americans and Segregated Prostitution, 1870–1910." *Journal of Social History* 19 (Fall 1986): 664–79.

Smith, Daniel Scott. "The Dating of the American Sexual Revolution: Evidence and Interpretation." In Michael Gordon, ed., *The American Family in Socio-Historical Perspective.* New York: St. Martin's, 1973. 321–35.

Smith, Henry Nash. *Virgin Land: The West as Myth and Symbol.* New York: Oxford University Press, 1953.

Stansell, Christine. *City of Women: Sex and Class in New York, 1789–1860.* New York: Knopf, 1986.

Susman, Warren. "Personality and the Development of Twentieth-Century Culture." In *Culture as History.* New York: Pantheon, 1984. 271–84.

———. "Uses of the Puritan Past." In *Culture as History.* New York: Pantheon, 1984. 39–49.

Thurber, Helen, and E. Weeks, eds. *Letters of James Thurber.* Boston: Little, Brown, 1981.

Thurber, James. *Alarms and Diversions.* New York: Harper and Brothers, 1957.

———. *The Years with Ross.* New York: Ballantine, 1960.

Trimberger, Ellen Kay. "Feminism, Men, and Modern Love: Greenwich Village, 1900–1925." In Ann Snitow, Christine Stansell, and Sharon Thompson, eds. *Powers of Desire: The Politics of Sexuality.* New York: Monthly Review Press, 1983. 131–52.

Ueda, Reed. *Avenues to Adulthood: The Origins of the High School and Social Mobility in an American Suburb.* New York: Cambridge University Press, 1987.

Vidal, Gore. *Pink Triangle and Yellow Star and Other Essays.* London: Granada, 1983.

Welter, Barbara. "The Cult of True Womanhood." *American Quarterly* 18 (1966): 151–74.

Whorton, James. *Crusaders for Fitness: the History of American Health Reformers.* Princeton, N.J.: Princeton University Press, 1982.

Wiebe, Robert. *The Search for Order.* New York: Hill and Wang, 1967.

Williams, Raymond. "Advertising the Magic System." In *Problems in Materialism and Culture.* London: Verso, 1980. 170–95.

Williamson, Judith. *Decoding Advertisements: Ideology and Meaning in Advertising.* London: Boyar, 1977.

Wolfenstein, Martha. "Fun Morality: An Analysis of Recent American Child-Training Literature." Reprinted in Margaret Mead and Martha Wolfenstein, eds., *Childhood in Contemporary Cultures.* Chicago: University of Chicago Press, 1954.

Wyatt-Brown, Bertram. *Southern Honor: Ethics and Behavior in the Old South.* New York: Oxford University Press, 1982.

Wyllie, Irvin. *The Self-Made Man in America: The Myth of Rags to Riches.* New York: Free Press, 1954.

Yellis, Kenneth. "Prosperity's Child: Some Thoughts on the Flapper." *American Quarterly* 21 (1969): 44–64.

Index

Abbott, Lyman, 9
Absorbine, Jr., 23
Achilles, Paul Strong, 151, 227n
Addams, Jane, 98
Ade, George, 14, 100
Advertisements: Arrow Man, 26; for clothing, 24–27; cult of youth, 20, 21 23, 180; for hair, 23; for perfumes, 21; for shaving, 20; for shirts, 24; for skin, 22; for soap, 21–22; for sportswear, 26; for swimming, 23–24; for tanning, 23; theories of, 19–20, 197n 198n; and therapeutic ethos, 19–20; for underwear, 25
Alger, Horatio, 3
Alinsky, Saul, and Constance Weinberger, 88, 92. *See also* Chicago sociologists
Allen, Frederic Lewis, 60. *See also* Revolution in morals
Allport, Floyd, 103, 163–64
American Expeditionary Force, and social hygienists, 73–75
American Magazine, 168
"American Manners" (Twain), 4–5

American Monthly, 52, 178
American Social Hygiene Association, 14. *See also* Social hygienists
Amusements, 14. *See also* New amusements
Anderson, Sherwood: and black culture, 50, 250n; cult of the body, 46, 48; *Dark Laughter*, 50; as "epitome of primitivism," 47; *Many Marriages*, 48; retreat from commitment, 48; violence against women, 48; *Winesburg, Ohio*, 47
Angels and Amazons (Irwin), 128
Antifeminism, 115
Aqua Velva, 20
Arrow Man, 26
"Ars Amatoria" (Ovid), 210n.
Art Albums, 62
"Artificial Social Relations" (Coughlin), 156
Art Models, 62
Art Poses, 62
Art Studies, 62
Aspen, Colorado, 119
Association Men, 23. *See also* YMCA
Athletic underwear, 25

Atlantic Monthly, 61
Atlas, Charles, 32
Automobiles, 91
"Awful Discourses of the Hotel Dieu
Nunnery of Montreal" (Monk), 8

Bachelors, 171, 184. *See also* Retreat from
commitment
Bad breath, 22
"Bad" women, 80, 82, 84, 91, 92, 96, 98,
102, 104, 183. *See also* "Good" women
Bain, Read, 161
Baker, Colonel Valentine, 5
Baldness, 23
Baseball, 8
Beautiful and Damned, The (Fitzgerald), 44
Beecher, Henry, 9. *See also* Protestantism;
Religion
Beginning of Wisdom, The (Benet), 41, 42,
43
Benet, Stephen, 38; *The Beginning of
Wisdom*, 41, 42, 43
Berstein, Leonard, 204n
Binkley, Robert L., 76, 77
Birth control, 172
Bisexuality, 64
Black, Alexander, 176
Black Americans, 82, 95, 138. *See also*
Black culture
Black culture, 8, 181; as epitome of
primitivism, 49, 50; Harlem Renaissance
and, 49–50; homosexuality in, 95;
middle-class interest in, 49–50, 204n;
and tramp Bohemian ideal, 49–50;
violence of, 49–50; and working class,
82. *See also* Black Americans
Blake, Doris, 157, 159, 160, 162, 164, 166,
167, 168, 169, 226n
Blanchard, Phyllis, 150
Bly, Robert, 187
Body builders, 17, 28, 30, 31, 32, 33, 34,
99. *See also* Physical Culture
Bohemians, 39, 53, 171. *See also*
Greenwich Village Bohemians
Boston, Massachusetts, 97
Bounders, 164
Bourne, Randolph: and cult of youth, 37;
Youth and Life, 37
Boxing, 8, 11, 12
"Boy Grew Older, The" (Broun), 110
Breadwinner, 3, 34, 39, 107

Breezy Stories, 61
Briary-Bush, The (Dell), 43, 65
Britten, F. L., 152–54, 228n
Bromley, Dorothy, 152–54, 228n
Broun, Connie, 124
Broun, Heywood, 108, 113, 123, 126;
affair with Lydia Lopokova, 118, 124;
break-up with Ruth Hale, 115; Connie
Broun, 124; fatherhood, 110; greater
career success than wife, 113, 114–15;
Lucy Stone League, 109; marriage
contract, 108; on polygamy, 118;
encounters with sexual subculture, 123;
support for feminism, 109–10;
Victorianism of, 118
Broun, Heywood Hale, 115
Bruce, Earl, 95
Buck, Walter, 166
Buckingham tobacco, 21
Buckley, William F., Jr., 128
Burdick Body Culturor, 23
Bureau of Social Hygiene (Rockefeller
Foundation), 87, 89, 93, 95, 100, 102
Burgess, Ernest, 95, 213n
Burke, Billie, 21
Burroughs, Edgar Rice, 11
BVDs, 25

Cads, 164
California, 148
Call of the Wild (London), 12
Calls, 6, 14, 147
Calverton, Vernon F., 129
Canby, Henry Seidl, 6
Canvas shoes, 26
Capitalism, 59, 181. *See also* Culture of
consumption
Career marriages, 175–76. *See also* Male
attitudes to women
Cargill, Oscar, 47
Carpenter, Edward, 37, 107
Carr, Martha, 157, 159, 163, 165, 167,
168, 169, 170, 171, 178, 226n
Catcher in the Rye, 38
"Cavemen," 52
Celibacy, 3, 9, 47, 160. *See also* Chastity;
Purity
Champknit athletic underwear, 25–26
Changing men, 187
Chaperonage, 6, 147